Gender and Climate Finance in Africa

MULTIDISCIPLINARY PERSPECTIVES ON GLOBAL AFRICA

Published in partnership with the African Studies and Research Forum

Series Editor: Abdul Karim Bangura

Breaking fresh ground, *Multidisciplinary Perspectives on Global Africa* transcends the boundaries of understanding Africa and its Diaspora. A series comprising of monographs and edited volumes, this endeavour brings together an esteemed group of social science scholars from across the globe to showcase a multifaceted exploration of Africa's past, present, and future, with topics delving into the intricate tapestry of its culture, history, and diasporic connections. The contributors, hailing from both the *African Studies and Research Forum* and beyond, present a comprehensive and global vista of Africa.

Embracing the richness and complexities of African issues through multidisciplinary social scientific analyses, this series has a global readership that thrives on intellectual diversity, across the Global North and Global South. Through this unique lens that navigates the dynamic interplay between disciplinary boundaries, the series explores cutting-edge topics such as Africa and globalisation, democracy, good governance, and law, corruption, and poverty, economic development and the environment, foreign aid, international trade, and foreign direct investments, regional integration and organisations and continental organisations, peace and conflict resolution, gender studies, education and health, decolonisation, and more.

Editorial Advisory Board

Gender and Climate Finance in Africa: Addressing Inequalities and Bridging Gaps

EDITED BY

TINUADE ADEKUNBI OJO

University of Johannesburg, South Africa

AND

OMOSEFE OYEKANMI

University of Johannesburg, South Africa

emerald PUBLISHING

United Kingdom – North America – Japan – India – Malaysia – China

Emerald Publishing Limited
Emerald Publishing, Floor 5, Northspring, 21-23 Wellington Street, Leeds LS1 4DL.

First edition 2026

British Library Cataloguing in Publication Data
A catalogue record for this book is available from the British Library

ISBN: 978-1-83742-086-5 (Print)
ISBN: 978-1-83742-085-8 (Online)
ISBN: 978-1-83742-087-2 (Epub)

Printed and bound by CPI Group (UK) Ltd, Croydon, CR0 4YY

Contents

List of Abbreviations

ADP	Agricultural Development Programme
AF	Adaptation Fund
AfDB/AFDB	African Development Bank
AFOLU	Agriculture, Forestry and Land Use
AFS/AFSs	Agrifood Systems
AICCRA	Accelerating Impacts of CGIAR Climate Research for Africa
AU	African Union
AWDF	African Women's Development Fund
BARMM	Bangsamoro Autonomous Region in Muslim Mindanao
BCG	Boston Consulting Group
CA$	Canadian Dollar
CBDR	Common but Differentiated Responsibilities
CGIAR	Consultative Group on International Agricultural Research
CIF	Climate Investment Funds
CILSS	Comité Permanent Inter-États de Luttecontre la Sécheressedans le Sahel (Permanent Interstate Committee for Drought Control in the Sahel)
CPI	Climate Policy Initiative
CRGE	Climate-Resilient Green Economy
DBSA	Development Bank of Southern Africa
DCF	Decentralised Climate Fund/Decentralising Climate Funds
DEEC	Direction de l'Environnement et des Établissements Classés (Senegal)
EAC	East African Community
ECOWAS	Economic Community of West African States
EDA	Enhanced Direct Access
FAO	Food and Agriculture Organization (of the United Nations)
FAOSTAT	Food and Agriculture Organization Statistical Database
FINDEV	Financial Development
GAP/GAPs	Gender Action Plan(s)
GCF	Green Climate Fund
GDP	Gross Domestic Product

GEF	Global Environment Facility
GGCA	Global Gender and Climate Alliance
GHG	Greenhouse Gas
GLI	Gender-Lens Investing
GRB	Gender-Responsive Budgeting
GRCF	Gender-Responsive Climate Finance
GSMA	Global System for Mobile Communications Association
HAC	Heteroskedasticity- and Autocorrelation-Consistent
HDI	Human Development Index
ICF	International Climate Finance
ICT	Information and Communication Technology
IDP/IDPs	Internally Displaced Person(s)
IFC	International Finance Corporation
IGAD	Intergovernmental Authority on Development
IIED	International Institute for Environment and Development
IITA	International Institute of Tropical Agriculture (Alliance of Bioversity International and IITA)
IPCC	Intergovernmental Panel on Climate Change
IUCN	International Union for Conservation of Nature
JETP	Just Energy Transition Partnership
KMD	Kenya Meteorological Department
km^2	Square Kilometres
LDC/LDCs	Least Developed Country (or Countries)
LEAP	Livelihood Empowerment Against Poverty
LGA/LGAs	Local Government Area(s)
M&E	Monitoring and Evaluation
MEDA	Mennonite Economic Development Associates
MFIs	Microfinance Institutions
MSME/MSMEs	Micro, Small, and Medium-sized Enterprise(s)
NAP/NAPs	National Adaptation Plan(s)
NAPA	National Adaptation Programmes of Action
NAPGCC	National Action Plan on Gender and Climate Change
NDA	National Designated Authority
NDC/NDCs	Nationally Determined Contribution(s)
NEPAD	New Partnership for Africa's Development
NGO/NGOs	Non-Governmental Organisation(s)
NiMet	Nigerian Meteorological Agency
OECD	Organisation for Economic Co-operation and Development
OLS	Ordinary Least Squares
PPP	Polluter Pays Principle
PSI	Population Services International
REC/RECs	Regional Economic Community (or Communities)
REIPPPP	Renewable Energy Independent Power Producer Procurement Programme

SADC	Southern African Development Community
SDGs	Sustainable Development Goals
SE/SEs	Standard Error(s)
SIDS	Small Island Developing States
SNEEG	Stratégie Nationale pour l'Équité et l'Égalité de Genre (National Gender Equity and Equality Strategy, Senegal)
SSA	Sub-Saharan Africa
UNCDF	United Nations Capital Development Fund
UNDP	United Nations Development Programme
UNECA	United Nations Economic Commission for Africa
UNEP	United Nations Environment Programme
UNFCCC	United Nations Framework Convention on Climate Change
UN Women	United Nations Entity for Gender Equality and the Empowerment of Women
USD	United States Dollar
WAEMU	West African Economic and Monetary Union
WASCAL	West African Science Service Centre on Climate Change and Adapted Land Use
WDI	World Development Indicators
WEDO	Women's Environment and Development Organisation
ZimStat	Zimbabwe National Statistics Agency

List of Contributors

Modinat Mosunmola Adekunle
Nigerian Institute of Social and Economic Research (NISER), Nigeria

Yetunde A. Aluko
Nigerian Institute of Social and Economic Research (NISER), Nigeria

Adebukola Yewande Daramola
Nigerian Institute of Social and Economic Research (NISER), Nigeria

Prince Dzingirayi
Women's University in Africa, Zimbabwe

Joy Oluwatomi Folorunso
Nigerian Institute of Social and Economic Research (NISER), Nigeria

Akeju Kemi Funlayo
Ekiti State University, Nigeria

Kafilah Lola Gold
University of Johannesburg, South Africa

Anthonia Folasade Ibitoye
University of Johannesburg, South Africa

Samson Sambian Konlan
University of Johannesburg, South Africa

Tinuade Adekunbi Ojo
University of Johannesburg, South Africa

Tope I. Omirin
Nigerian Institute of Social and Economic Research (NISER), Nigeria

Omosefe Oyekanmi
University of Johannesburg, South Africa

Tanusha Raniga
University of Johannesburg, South Africa

Olalere Sunday Shina
Ekiti State University, Nigeria

Alison Nyaradzo Zuva
University of Johannesburg, South Africa

Foreword

Antonia T. Simbine
Nigerian Institute of Social and Economic Research, Ibadan, Nigeria

It is an honour to introduce this edited volume, *Gender and Climate Finance in Africa*, a timely and incisive contribution to one of the most urgent scholarly and policy debates of our time. Comprising 10 expertly crafted chapters, the book advances a central argument that is as compelling as it is necessary: that climate finance in Africa cannot be understood, let alone transformed, without examining the gendered power structures that shape access, vulnerability, and decision-making across the continent.

As a scholar who has worked extensively at the intersection of gender, development, and environmental governance, I am convinced that this collection breaks new ground. While many texts cover the broad terrain of climate finance and adaptation, the editors' work distinguishes itself by focusing specifically on the gendered political economy of climate finance in Africa. Their innovative methodology and wide-ranging evidence offer a fresh, multidimensional perspective that will undoubtedly become essential reading for anyone engaging with climate justice, feminist development studies, or African policy reform.

The strength of this volume lies not only in its conceptual clarity but also in its remarkable methodological diversity. The 10 chapters, spanning feminist political economy, intersectionality, ecological justice, econometric modelling, comparative case studies, participatory mapping, and policy analysis, come together to form an interdisciplinary tapestry. This plurality of approaches ensures that the book speaks simultaneously to academic researchers, policymakers, practitioners, and civil society actors. It situates climate finance within a broader intellectual lineage while also carving out a distinct niche: the interrogation of how gendered hierarchies govern the flow, distribution, and impact of climate resources.

In the wider scholarly discourse, this volume responds to a noticeable gap: despite global commitments such as the Paris Agreement emphasising gender equality, practical implementation across African contexts remains inconsistent and often symbolic. What this book offers is not just critique but clarity, showing how institutional inertia, patriarchal norms, and unequal financial architectures limit women's participation, even as they bear the brunt of climate impacts. In doing so, it reframes climate finance not as a neutral or technocratic exercise but as a profoundly political arena where questions of power, representation, and justice must be confronted.

The chapters bring to light a series of cross-cutting insights: the structures that impede women's equitable access to adaptation and mitigation funds; the intersecting vulnerabilities that shape differentiated climate risks across regions and livelihoods; the gaps between national gender policies and their implementation; and the remarkable resilience and ingenuity of women who are forging alternative pathways through cooperatives, digital finance, cooperative and savings groups, and community-driven adaptation models. The regional breadth, spanning West, East, Central, North, and Southern Africa, adds depth and nuance, demonstrating that gender-responsive climate finance requires both continental vision and local sensitivity.

On a personal note, my engagement with the manuscript has been both intellectually rewarding and profoundly affirming. Knowing the editors' longstanding commitment to feminist scholarship and to grounded, community-based research in Africa, I expected a rigorous text. What I encountered, however, exceeded those expectations. Each chapter not only contributes original evidence but also reflects a deep ethical commitment to justice, amplifying women's voices, challenging extractive models of research, and envisioning climate futures where equity is not an afterthought but a guiding principle.

I endorse this work wholeheartedly. It is a scholarly achievement of the highest order on the part of the duo of editors and their contributors and a policy intervention of considerable importance. At a moment when Africa faces escalating climate pressures and widening inequality, this book offers both diagnosis and direction. It invites us to reimagine climate finance as a transformative tool, one capable of redistributing power, reshaping institutions, and centring those who have long been marginalised in climate discourse.

Gender and Climate Finance in Africa is thus essential reading for academics, policymakers, development practitioners, and all who care about building a more just and sustainable continent. I commend the editors and contributors for producing a volume that will influence debates, inform policy, and inspire future research for years to come.

Preface

Omosefe Oyekanmi and Tinuade Adekunbi Ojo

In Africa, the realities of climate change are inseparable from questions of inequality. Vulnerability, access, and survival are deeply gendered, shaped by systems of power that govern both the environment and finance. Even though women, who form the backbone of Africa's agricultural and informal economies, bear the brunt of erratic rainfall, soil degradation, droughts, and floods, they however remain marginal in climate finance structures that determine access to adaptation and mitigation resources. This imbalance reflects a wider global paradox, while gender equality is central to international commitments like the Paris Agreement, its practical realisation within African contexts remains fragmented and often symbolic.

This book intervenes in this critical discourse by interrogating how financial systems, policy architectures, and local innovations can be reconfigured to achieve transformative equity. The volume situates climate finance not simply as an environmental or economic issue, but as a profoundly political arena, one in which gendered hierarchies shape who receives, manages, and benefits from financial flows. It highlights that without addressing structural discrimination, the continent's climate responses risk reproducing the very inequalities they seek to dismantle.

Distinctive in both regional breadth and methodological diversity, the book draws evidence from across Africa's subregions, West, East, North, Central, and Southern Africa, through a range of case studies spanning agriculture, migration, renewable energy, and governance. Its methodological palette is equally wide, combining econometric analyses, comparative case studies, participatory qualitative research, survey data, and policy reviews. The theoretical scaffolding is drawn from feminist political economy, intersectionality, ecological justice, and development finance, enabling a holistic exploration of how power operates through institutions, policies, and social norms.

Method and Theoretical Approach

The volume is underpinned by an interdisciplinary framework that brings feminist theory into direct conversation with climate finance and development economics. Feminist political economy illuminates the power asymmetries that structure global and national financial systems. Intersectionality unpacks how gender interacts with class, geography, and livelihood to produce differentiated vulnerabilities; and ecological justice redefines sustainability through the lenses of equity and care. Together, these frameworks reveal that climate finance cannot be gender-neutral. It either reinforces or challenges existing hierarchies.

Methodologically, the book demonstrates a balance between empirical rigour and contextual sensitivity. Quantitative chapters provide data-driven insights into financial flows, vulnerability indices, and comparative access across regions, while qualitative contributions reveal the lived experiences of women negotiating climate challenges. Comparative approaches, between countries, institutions, and financing models, allow for continental generalisations without losing local nuance. This blend of breadth and depth strengthens the volume's claim that inclusive climate finance requires both structural reform and community agency.

Thematic Overview

Theme One: Structures of Inequality and Access

The first theme interrogates the material and institutional barriers that prevent women from equitably accessing climate finance. Through case studies from Nigeria, Senegal, Kenya, and Zimbabwe, these chapters show how financial systems remain dominated by male gatekeepers, with women constrained by limited land ownership, weak property rights, and exclusion from credit and technology. The evidence demonstrates that while funding mechanisms exist, their governance and eligibility criteria often mirror existing social hierarchies. Quantitative analyses reveal that less than 5% of global climate finance explicitly targets gender equality, while qualitative fieldwork exposes how patriarchal norms within local cooperatives and ministries further restrict women's participation. These chapters collectively argue that climate finance must move beyond token inclusion towards redistributive justice, restructuring access itself as a question of rights and representation.

Theme Two: Intersectionality and Vulnerability

The second theme deepens the discussion by exploring how gendered vulnerability is compounded by intersecting factors such as age, income, geography, and livelihood. Drawing on data from Northern Nigeria, Kenya's arid lands, and Zimbabwe's fragile economy, these chapters depict how women's climate risks are differentiated not only by gender but also by socio-economic and spatial location. The 'vulnerability gradient' identified across contexts shows that the poorest, least-educated rural women face the greatest exposure to climate shocks yet receive the smallest share of adaptive finance. Methodologically, these studies combine surveys, regression models, and participatory mapping, providing both statistical precision and grounded insight. The findings underscore the need for localised adaptation models and gender-responsive finance mechanisms tailored to specific vulnerabilities rather than one-size-fits-all solutions.

Theme Three: Institutions and Policy Frameworks

The third theme turns to the institutional and governance dimensions of climate finance, analysing how national governments, regional bodies, and international agencies shape the distribution of funds. Comparative studies of ECOWAS, East African states, and North African countries reveal persistent gaps between policy commitments and implementation. Despite the proliferation of gender action plans and quota frameworks, institutional inertia and weak accountability mechanisms undermine inclusion. A policy analysis of East and North Africa exposes the paradox of strong frameworks but poor execution, while regional reviews of ECOWAS highlight the gendered consequences of displacement and migration linked to climate change. Collectively, these chapters argue that inclusive governance requires more than policy rhetoric, it demands institutional transformation, transparency, and the embedding of gender expertise within decision-making structures.

Theme Four: Resilience and Transformation

The final theme focuses on possibilities for change, and how women and communities are creating alternative financial pathways that challenge the mainstream. Empirical studies from Northern Ghana, Kenya, and South Africa reveal how women's cooperatives, savings groups, and digital finance initiatives are building adaptive capacity and reshaping local economies. These contributions demonstrate that women are not merely recipients of aid but agents of resilience, experimenting with gender-responsive budgeting, green entrepreneurship, and locally governed adaptation funds. By integrating feminist perspectives on care, collaboration, and collective action, the chapters envision a climate finance model rooted in transformation rather than mitigation alone.

Synthesis and Contribution

Across its chapters, *Gender and Climate Finance in Africa* advances a unified argument that financial flows alone cannot resolve the continent's climate crisis without structural, institutional, and cultural change. True resilience requires reimagining climate finance as a tool for justice, redistributing power, resources, and decision-making authority. By integrating feminist theory, empirical research, and regional diversity, the book bridges disciplinary and policy divides, reframing climate finance from a technocratic exercise into a site of gendered negotiation and transformation.

This volume stands as both a scholarly contribution and a policy intervention, offering grounded evidence and theoretical innovation. It moves the debate beyond the quantitative question of how much finance reaches Africa to the qualitative one of who controls access, under what conditions, and towards what ends. In doing so, it re-centres African women not as peripheral beneficiaries but as critical architects of the continent's climate future.

Chapter 1

Climate Finance Distribution and Gender Mainstreaming in Africa

Omosefe Oyekanmi[a] *and Tinuade Adekunbi Ojo*[b]

[a]*Institute for Pan African Thoughts and Conversation, University of Johannesburg, South Africa*
[b]*Centre for the Study of Race, Gender and Class, University of Johannesburg, South Africa*

Abstract

This chapter examines the intersection of climate finance distribution and gender mainstreaming in Africa, focusing on the ways financial flows for climate adaptation and mitigation are unevenly allocated across regions, sectors, and social groups. It adopts a qualitative, conceptual, and theoretical approach based on desk-based analysis of existing scholarly literature, policy documents, and institutional reports on climate finance and gender mainstreaming in Africa. Despite Africa's minimal contribution to global emissions, it bears a disproportionate burden of climate impacts and thus depends heavily on international finance to strengthen adaptive capacity. Current distribution patterns remain skewed towards mitigation projects and urban areas, even though rural populations, especially women, are the most exposed and vulnerable. Structural barriers such as gender discrimination, unequal access to resources, and exclusion from decision-making in climate-sensitive sectors like land, water, and forests further limit the effectiveness of climate investments. Globally, less than 4% of climate finance directly targets gender equality, revealing persistent gaps in funding mechanisms. This chapter's original contribution lies in its integrated intersectional analysis of climate finance distribution and gender mainstreaming in Africa, linking structural inequalities, institutional design, and gendered vulnerability within a single analytical framework. It identifies critical gaps that could be addressed through stronger gender analysis, institutional capacity-building, gender-responsive budgeting, and inclusive policy reforms. The chapter concludes by recommending a rebalancing of

Gender and Climate Finance in Africa: Addressing Inequalities and Bridging Gaps, 1–19

Published under exclusive licence by Emerald Publishing Limited
doi:10.1108/978-1-83742-085-820261001

financial flows towards adaptation and prioritising gender-responsive approaches that empower women and vulnerable groups as central actors in Africa's climate response.

Keywords: Climate finance distribution; gender mainstreaming; Africa; climate resilience; equality

Introduction

The complexity of climate change impact in its varying degree across much of the world demands urgent attention towards effective distribution of finance to all groups, particularly those related to gender mainstreaming. Climate finance is an essential strategy aimed at supporting the development of sustainable development patterns as well as adaptation and reduction of vulnerability to climate change in developing countries.

From the prism of the United Nations Framework Convention on Climate Change (UNFCCC), climate finance essentially involves the flow of funds from developed countries to developing countries on the basis of the Common but Differentiated Responsibilities (CBDR) and Polluter Pays Principles (PPP). These principles are hinged on environmental laws and policies supporting the action that the cost of managing climate impact should be borne by States who produce the pollution. Such funds accrued from environmental polluters are expected to decrease greenhouse gas emissions and strengthen climate change vulnerability by investing in mitigation and adaptation (Kabaseke, 2023). Despite these legal frameworks, the distribution of climate finance has been fraught with gender insensitivity, particularly among developing countries.

The effect of climate change on women is adverse compared to any other group, due to their vulnerability to climate-sensitive resources such as water, forest, and land especially in rural and low-end societies. This is further complicated knowing that even though women participate actively in mitigation and adaptation processes, they are excluded from fundamental decision-making mechanisms, inadequately informed, and hampered by numerous processes (UNFCCC, 2021).

The strategic approach of gender mainstreaming, which seeks to integrate the concerns and experiences of both men and women into the policy design and entire process of climate finance has not been fully actualised. Currently, some of the fund mechanisms of climate finance, including the Green Climate Fund (GCF) and the Global Environment Facility (GEF), though have officially been endorsed, the effect of these policies has not translated into the desired result in Africa. The institutionalisation of gender-responsive approaches within these frameworks remains weak, resulting in limited integration of gender considerations in the design, allocation, and execution of climate finance initiatives (UNFCCC, 2021).

Consequently, *gender mainstreaming* has been adopted as a key strategy to redress structural gender inequalities within climate finance frameworks and to promote the equitable distribution of both risks and rewards across sexes. Gender mainstreaming as a concept is informed by international policies like Beijing Platform for Action and UN-SWAP, which refers to processes of promoting gender perspectives throughout policy and programme formulations, implementations, and assessments. While there has been some success in integrating gender factors into different sectors, gender mainstreaming in climate finance is still poor and challenged by poor representation, lack of funding, and persistent structural barriers (UNFCCC, 1992, 2019).

In this chapter, climate finance distribution and gender mainstreaming are examined in relation to each other in Africa. It seeks to understand how climate finance is distributed and skewed in the favour of certain region and sectors, what challenges limit women access to climate finance, and how gender-sensitive climate finance instruments are assigned. Climate change and climate variability have profound impacts across Africa, manifesting through rising temperatures, extreme weather events, shifts in vegetation cover, and increased disease prevalence, all of which pose serious threats to livelihoods and national economies. Despite contributing minimally to global greenhouse gas emissions, the continent faces escalating adaptation and mitigation costs, making climate finance a critical mechanism for addressing these challenges (Kabaseke, 2023). However, the distribution of climate finance across Africa remains uneven, with certain regions and sectors receiving disproportionately higher funding than others. In particular, adaptation projects, which are essential for strengthening the resilience of disadvantaged populations, tend to receive less financial support compared to mitigation initiatives such as renewable energy investments (Lam et al., 2024).

The structure of climate finance delivery, whether through grants, loans, or equity, also significantly influences its accessibility and effectiveness. Grants are typically preferred for adaptation initiatives targeting vulnerable groups but remain far less available than loans, which risk increasing the debt burdens of recipient nations. Furthermore, issues of timeliness, transparency, and accountability in fund disbursement have repeatedly been identified as key bottlenecks undermining the efficient use of climate finance in Africa (Kabaseke, 2023).

In essence, this chapter seeks to answer the following questions: How is climate finance currently distributed across Africa, and what disparities exist? To what extent are gender considerations mainstreamed in climate finance policies and projects? What are the barriers to accessing climate finance for women in Africa? How effective are gender-responsive climate finance (GRCF) projects in addressing gender inequalities? What policy changes are needed to enhance gender mainstreaming in climate finance?

It is worthy to note that the gender mainstream process has not been coherent. Across Africa, efforts to integrate gender considerations into climate finance remain uneven. In countries such as Kenya, Ethiopia, and Uganda, national and international climate initiatives have begun incorporating gender components; however, women's participation and access to adaptation resources often remain limited. Evaluations show that gender measures are frequently added late in project design, reducing their impact on local women's resilience and decision-making.

This chapter therefore adopts a conceptual and theoretical approach, incorporating a review of existing literature, an analysis of emerging challenges in climate finance distribution and gender mainstreaming, an examination of the impact of gender mainstreaming on climate finance, and concludes with a summary of key findings and policy recommendations.

Conceptual and Theoretical Framework

Climate Finance and Climate Finance Distribution

There is no universally agreed definition of climate finance, and the term is often used interchangeably to describe a range of financial flows and instruments directed towards climate-related objectives. Within the context of this chapter, climate finance is conceptualised as any form of financial support that enables credible climate action. This encompasses investments in renewable energy such as wind and solar power, energy efficiency, afforestation and reforestation, climate resilient infrastructure, and initiatives aimed at either reducing greenhouse gas emissions or adapting to the impacts of a changing climate. Fundamentally, climate finance seeks to mobilise resources that facilitate green growth and climate resilient development. It also includes financial flows that advance climate goals indirectly, commonly referred to as *climate-aligned finance*. Climate finance can take various forms, including grants, concessional loans, equity investments, guarantees, lines of credit, carbon market instruments, and green bonds. These mechanisms are provided by a diverse range of actors across the financial system, including governments, institutional investors, asset owners, individuals, and philanthropic or non-governmental organisations (UK Nigeria Infrastructure Advisory Facility (UKNIAF), 2024).

According to the Climate Finance Playbook (2021), climate finance refers to financial resources mobilised from local, national, or transnational sources, whether public, private, or innovative, to support mitigation and adaptation actions that address the impacts of climate change. These resources encompass a broad spectrum of financial instruments, including public expenditure, development bank loans, private equity, and government funding. Within the framework of the UNFCCC, climate finance assumes a more specific definition, referring to the transfer of funds from developed to developing countries in accordance with the principles of *CBDR* and the *PPP* doctrine (UNFCCC, 1992). This framing underscores the global finance gap between the Global North and the Global South. However, climate finance remains conceptually diffuse, lacking a universally accepted definition and standardised reporting mechanisms. As a result, the monitoring of climate finance flows is often inconsistent and largely qualitative. For instance, grants constitute only about 2.3% of total climate finance commitments, highlighting the dominance of loans and the growing tendency among financial institutions to prioritise investment returns before committing resources (Climate Finance Playbook, 2021).

In essence, climate finance distribution involves the allocation of funds to manage and mitigate the effects of climate change. Kabaseke (2023) defines it as the mobilisation of financial resources by public and private actors at domestic and international levels to support emission reduction and adaptation initiatives. Similarly, Schalatek and Nakhooda (2016) emphasise that equitable climate finance should aim to reduce inequalities, particularly by ensuring that resources reach vulnerable populations, including women and girls, whose livelihoods are most affected by climate risks. In Africa, climate finance distribution reflects an urgent need to address the continent's disproportionate vulnerability to climate change impacts through targeted investments in renewable energy, sustainable agriculture, and resilience building. Yet, the pattern of financial flows remains uneven, with a strong bias towards urban and mitigation projects, while rural and adaptation-focused initiatives receive comparatively less support (Lam et al., 2024). Moreover, women, who play a central role in community-level climate action, continue to face systemic barriers in accessing these funds due to structural gender discrimination, limited institutional diversity, and weak policy frameworks for gender-responsive financing (Schalatek & Nakhooda, 2016).

Gender Mainstreaming

Gender mainstreaming represents a strategic approach aimed at embedding gender considerations within the structures, processes, and outcomes of policy and institutional practice. Rather than functioning as a discrete intervention, it operates as a transformative framework that seeks to reorient governance systems, organisational cultures, and development agendas towards gender equality and inclusivity. This approach encompasses a range of interrelated processes such as gender inclusion, gender mapping, and gender auditing, all of which are designed to ensure that women and men have equitable access to opportunities, resources, and decision-making spaces (Renee, 2018). Conceptually, gender mainstreaming evolved as a response to the limitations of earlier women-specific policies, which often operated in isolation from mainstream planning and budgeting. By contrast, it emphasises the systematic integration of gender perspectives across all sectors and levels of policymaking, thereby transforming the very logic of institutional action.

Within international policy frameworks, particularly those shaped by the Council of Europe and the United Nations, gender mainstreaming is positioned as both a process and a strategy for structural change. It requires continuous assessment of how proposed policies, legislation, or programmes affect women and men differently, ensuring that gender considerations are integral to their design, implementation, monitoring, and evaluation (Neimanis, 2000). In this sense, gender mainstreaming transcends token representation, seeking to embed gender equity within the operational fabric of governance and development practice. It not only promotes balanced participation but also challenges the entrenched norms and institutional biases that perpetuate inequality. Thus, gender mainstreaming serves as a dynamic mechanism for transforming policy into an instrument of social justice and sustainable development.

Theoretical Framework

This chapter is anchored in intersectionality theory, which provides a robust analytical foundation for examining how multiple and overlapping forms of inequality shape access to, and outcomes of, climate finance and gender mainstreaming in Africa. Originally developed by Kimberlé Crenshaw, intersectionality explains how interconnected systems of power, such as gender, class, race, geography, and age, interact to produce complex and differentiated forms of marginalisation (Cho et al., 2013; Ngum & Bastiaensen, 2020). Rather than treating gender as an isolated category, the framework recognises that climate vulnerability and financial exclusion are produced through the interaction of social, economic, spatial, and institutional forces. In the context of climate finance, intersectionality illuminates how institutional hierarchies, geographic location, livelihood status, and access to assets converge to privilege certain populations while deepening the vulnerability of others, particularly rural women and low-income groups.

Thus, intersectionality is applied as an analytical lens to examine how overlapping systems of power and structural inequalities, primarily gender, but also geographic location (rural/urban disparities, national-level imbalances), differential access to resources and finance, and exclusion from institutional decision-making, converge to create and reinforce disparities in access to, and benefits from, climate finance in Africa. These variables are applied in examining who accesses climate finance, which sectors attract gender-responsive investments, and whose vulnerabilities are prioritised or neglected in adaptation and mitigation funding. Through this application, disparities in climate finance distribution are interpreted not as mere administrative inefficiencies but as outcomes of deeper structural and institutional inequalities embedded within governance systems and development financing architectures. This framework thus enables a critical assessment of how climate finance mechanisms may either reproduce or challenge existing patterns of gendered and socioeconomic exclusion.

Methodology

Methodologically, the chapter adopts a qualitative, desk-based research design, which is well suited for analysing the institutional, political, and socioeconomic dimensions of climate finance distribution and gender mainstreaming in Africa. Data for the study were drawn from a systematic review of peer-reviewed journal articles, policy documents, institutional reports, and empirical studies accessed primarily through academic databases. In addition, grey literature from multilateral climate finance institutions, development agencies, and international policy bodies was incorporated to complement the academic sources. The review focused predominantly on materials published during the period when global climate finance architecture expanded significantly and formal gender policies became more prominent within major climate funding mechanisms.

Quantitative claims referenced in the chapter, such as the relative proportions of adaptation and mitigation finance, the share of gender-tagged funding, and the dominance of loans over grants, were derived from global climate finance tracking reports, development finance monitoring datasets, and official institutional financial disclosures. Each numerical figure is explicitly linked to its original source to ensure transparency and analytical reliability.

Literature and Analytical Review

According to a growing body of literature, scholars and policymakers have vigorously debated the most effective mechanisms for ensuring climate finance achieves both its environmental and social justice objectives. This discourse increasingly centres on the critical role of gender but however diverges on the pathways from recognition to implementation.

Gerasimenko (2024) underscores the centrality of gender in climate finance and the critical role of adopting a gender lens in achieving sustainable climate solutions. The analysis emphasises that integrating gender considerations into climate finance mechanisms is essential to meeting the objectives of the Paris Agreement. Although many countries reference gender within their national adaptation plans and nationally determined contributions (NDCs), these commitments often lack the necessary compliance frameworks, rendering them largely symbolic. Gerasimenko further explores gender lens investing as a viable approach to reducing climate-related risks while advancing gender equality. The CA$250 million Canada–IFC Blended Climate Finance Program, for instance, illustrates how embedding gender-responsive strategies in climate initiatives can simultaneously enhance social inclusion and investment value. This approach links gender mainstreaming with improved climate outcomes, particularly by strengthening the resilience of vulnerable households. Gerasimenko argues that such models are replicable across other national contexts, demonstrating that gender equality can serve as both a moral and practical pathway to advancing climate justice. The work concludes by advocating for greater use of gender-responsive financial instruments as a means of fostering structural transformation and sustainable poverty reduction.

Building on this perspective, GRCF represents not only an ethical necessity but also a strategic mechanism for enhancing climate resilience and effectiveness. By positioning women at the centre of climate action, the research work underscores how systemic gender inequalities, manifested through restricted access to land, income, and political participation, intensify vulnerability to climate change, particularly in developing regions. Women's dual roles as food producers and community caretakers position them as critical agents in adaptation and mitigation processes, yet their contributions often remain overlooked within conventional, technocratic approaches to climate finance.

Schalatek and Nakhooda highlight that meaningful progress has been made in integrating gender considerations into global finance instruments, notably within the GCF and the Kyoto Protocol Adaptation Fund. These mechanisms have institutionalised gender mandates through accreditation standards and results-based frameworks that require gender analysis and sex-disaggregated data. However, they caution that such inclusion frequently occurs retrospectively and lacks consistent implementation due to limited institutional capacity and expertise. The authors argue convincingly that gender mainstreaming should not be viewed as a peripheral fairness issue but as an essential factor in improving the quality and impact of climate finance. Evidence from gender-sensitive agricultural and disaster management projects supports this position, showing that empowering women leads to stronger and more sustainable outcomes. In this sense, Schalatek and Nakhooda provide a foundational argument that links gender equity with both climate effectiveness and social transformation.

Edidah et al. (2020) also examine the gender dimension of agricultural and climate change policies in Uganda and Tanzania, revealing both strengths and persistent gaps within governance systems. Using a mixed-methods approach that combines qualitative and quantitative data, the authors analyse policy and budgetary documents across multiple governance levels. Their findings indicate that while gender considerations are formally integrated into national policies, subnational implementation remains weak and underfunded. For example, only a small proportion of district-level documents explicitly address financing for gender-related activities, and many policies frame gender issues narrowly as women's problems without addressing the underlying structural factors. In rural contexts, sociocultural norms continue to limit women's decision-making power and access to resources, compounding their vulnerability to climate change.

Edidah et al. (2020) emphasise the importance of gender-sensitive budgeting, capacity development, and coordinated policy implementation across governance levels. They argue that allocating financial and institutional resources to gender-responsive approaches enables policymakers to address root causes of inequality that impede effective mitigation and adaptation. Importantly, the authors call for a reconceptualisation of how gender is discursively constructed in climate policies, advocating for its integration as a central component of climate resilience strategies. This approach not only enhances the effectiveness of climate interventions but also ensures the inclusion and empowerment of marginalised populations, positioning women as key agents in climate response and adaptation efforts.

Recent scholarship increasingly highlights that climate finance, while central to global climate justice, remains deeply unequal in access and impact, disproportionately marginalising women, Indigenous peoples, and other vulnerable groups, particularly in the Global South. Achampong and Officer (2023) emphasises that these populations bear the brunt of climate change impacts, yet climate finance mechanisms are often inaccessible due to systemic discrimination, structural inequities, and the persistence of gender-biased policies. The study notes that in 2019, only 2% of climate finance reached marginalised farmers and communities, inadvertently reinforcing existing social and gender disparities. Structural limitations embedded in mainstream economic paradigms, particularly the dominance of loan-based finance, exacerbate these inequities by increasing debt burdens in low- and middle-income countries. Women, frequently excluded from land ownership and credit systems, face compounded barriers that perpetuate cycles of poverty, constrain agency, and limit their capacity to adapt to climate-related shocks. Achampong argues that climate finance must shift towards grants and gender-responsive instruments while incorporating feminist economic principles to promote equitable resource allocation, advance human rights, and strengthen climate justice frameworks.

Building on this foundation, Doku and Phiri (2024) provide empirical evidence from 43 Sub-Saharan African countries (2006–2018) on the differential impacts of climate finance on women's food security. Their findings reveal that grant-based and targeted aid interventions have a significantly greater effect on reducing women's hunger than foreign direct investment, which shows weak results. The study further identifies governance quality as a critical mediating factor, where higher institutional transparency and accountability enhance the effectiveness of climate finance initiatives. The authors highlight the gendered nature of agricultural labour in the region, noting that women contribute approximately 60% of farm labour but face systemic restrictions in access to land, credit, and productive resources. These constraints not only deepen vulnerability to climate shocks but also reinforce structural inequities, exacerbating the feminisation of poverty and agriculture. By demonstrating the tangible benefits of gender-sensitive financing, Doku and Phiri reinforce the argument that equitable distribution mechanisms are critical for achieving broader development objectives, including SDG-2 on ending hunger.

Complementing these insights, Patel et al. (2023) interrogate the structural and sectoral biases in climate finance flows, revealing that male-dominated mitigation sectors, such as energy and transport, receive the majority of investment, while women-focused adaptation projects receive less than 3% of total funding. The authors note that gender policies within multilateral climate finance institutions are often superficial, functioning more as procedural add-ons than integral components of project design. They advocate for strategic, long-term investments in gender transformation, improved monitoring of financial flows, and the active inclusion of women and local actors in decision-making processes. By highlighting the disconnect between the theoretical commitment to gender equality and actual resource allocation, Patel et al. provide a critical lens for evaluating the effectiveness of climate finance interventions and their potential to support equitable low-carbon transitions.

As African countries confront escalating climate vulnerabilities, the mobilisation and equitable distribution of climate finance has never been more urgent. Yet, despite the increasing availability of international funds, a complex web of social, political, institutional, and financial obstacles continues to undermine their effectiveness. Cultural norms, gendered roles, and socioeconomic inequalities intersect to make women particularly vulnerable, often excluding them from decision-making, access to resources, and meaningful participation in adaptation initiatives (Georgalakis, 2020). Institutional mechanisms frequently fail to translate gender mandates into actionable programmes, leaving gender-responsive finance aspirational rather than operational. This tension exposes a critical paradox: while climate finance is intended to bolster resilience, existing structures risk reproducing the very inequities they aim to mitigate.

These challenges are especially pronounced in Africa due to limited financial infrastructure, geographic disparities, entrenched gender inequalities, and the difficulties of coordinating multiple funding streams. The societal roles and obligations assigned to women intensify the impacts of climate shocks on their livelihoods. Tantoh et al. (2022) reveal that rural and indigenous women disproportionately bear the brunt of inadequate climate finance, as unequal allocation of resources restricts their capacity to respond effectively to climate hazards. Patriarchal norms and distinct gender roles, including responsibilities as primary caregivers, food producers, and water collectors, exacerbate their vulnerability (Dankelman, 2002).

In effect, restricted access to financial resources represents persistent barrier to women's engagement in climate initiatives. Implementing gender-sensitive strategies requires sustained investment in capacity development and financial support, even so, many organisations and governments face limitations in both funding and expertise necessary to operationalise gender considerations effectively (Asomah, 2024). In the absence of adequate resources, even well-intentioned policies and programmes struggle to achieve meaningful gender-responsive outcomes. Collectively, these challenges highlight the need for climate finance mechanisms that are not only equitable in allocation but also attuned to the structural, social, and institutional realities shaping women's vulnerability across the continent.

Collectively, the literature highlights a persistent and multifaceted set of barriers that constrain women's participation in climate finance and adaptation initiatives across Africa. From loan-dominated funding structures and weak institutional capacity to entrenched sociocultural norms and restricted access to resources, these intersecting factors limit the effectiveness of climate interventions and perpetuate gendered inequities. Even where gender-sensitive policies exist, their implementation remains inconsistent, often reducing gender considerations to tokenistic references rather than actionable strategies. Applying an intersectionality lens further clarifies that these barriers do not affect all women equally, overlapping systems of power, including gender, class, geography, and socioeconomic status, compound vulnerabilities, particularly for rural and marginalised women.

Discussion

Inequality in Africa's Climate Finance

The discourse on climate finance in Africa is often framed around a compelling statistic, a 48% surge in flows, from USD 29.5 billion in 2019/20 to USD 43.7 billion in 2021/22 (Climate Policy Initiative (CPI), 2024). While this growth suggests rising global attention, a deeper interrogation of the data reveals a more troubling reality. Beneath the apparent progress lies a structure of inequality rooted in how this finance is sourced, distributed, and governed. Africa's climate finance architecture is not merely inadequate in scale, it is systemically flawed, perpetuating dependency, reinforcing geographic and sectoral imbalances, and misaligning with the continent's vulnerability and potential.

The origin of climate finance is a fundamental marker of agency and sovereignty. In Africa's case, it reveals profound external dependence. An overwhelming 87% of the continent's climate finance, USD 38.0 billion, originates from international sources, while domestic contributions amount to just 10% (USD 4.2 billion) (CPI, 2024). This imbalance entrenches a donor–recipient dynamic that leaves African countries' climate priorities vulnerable to the shifting interests and political currents of the Global North.

A closer look at these external flows underscores the dominance of multilateral institutions. Multilateral development finance institutions (DFIs), such as the African Development Bank and the World Bank, provide 43% (USD 18.9 billion) of all climate finance on the continent (CPI, 2024). When combined with bilateral DFIs (USD 5.7 billion) and government-to-government finance (USD 9.4 billion), public institutions account for roughly 77% of total flows. Climate action in Africa thus remains largely a publicly funded endeavour, orchestrated by international bureaucracies and concessional mechanisms.

By contrast, private sector participation remains strikingly limited. Despite nearly doubling to USD 8 billion, private finance constitutes less than 15% of total flows (CPI, 2024; FSD Africa, 2024). Even within that share, corporate investments (USD 2.7 billion) dominate, while institutional investors, pension funds, insurers, and banks contribute only about 2% (USD 0.98 billion). This chronic under-engagement of private capital signals deep structural and perception-based barriers: high risk, a lack of bankable projects, and insufficient de-risking tools. Consequently, private finance gravitates towards mitigation projects (80%) with clear revenue streams, such as renewable energy, while largely neglecting adaptation (CPI, 2024).

This sourcing pattern reveals the first layer of inequality: a structural dependency that constrains financial sovereignty. With nearly 9 out of every 10 climate dollars originating abroad, African countries face heightened exposure to currency risks, debt distress, and donor-driven agendas often misaligned with local priorities.

Gendered Architecture of Climate Finance in Africa

The global climate finance landscape is often narrated through the record-breaking pledges, surging disbursements, and ambitious new targets. In 2022, developed countries mobilised USD 115.9 billion, surpassing their annual goal, and the COP29 agreement of 2024 pledged to triple this support to USD 300 billion annually (OECD, 2024; Sasi, 2025). However, beneath this progress lies a structurally entrenched inequity, the systematic exclusion of women, particularly in Africa, from the financial resources intended to build resilience against a crisis they did little to cause.

Africa contributes only 2–3% of global emissions but bears a disproportionate share of climate impacts (Sasi, 2025). To achieve their NDCs, African countries require an estimated USD 2.8 trillion by 2030. In contrast, climate finance flows to the continent reached only USD 44 billion in 2021–2022, a 48% increase from previous years, but still merely 3.6% of global climate finance and just 23% of Africa's annual needs (CPI, 2023, as cited in Sasi, 2025).

This aggregate shortfall conceals a deeper inequity. The distribution of these limited funds is governed by an invisible fence, a structure shaped by political, socioeconomic, and institutional biases that systematically sideline women. As Sasi (2025) observes, women face cultural norms, gender unresponsive financial instruments, and a lack of understanding, exacerbating their exclusion. As such, the prevailing climate finance architecture is not merely gender-blind but actively gender-regressive, perpetuating vulnerability by failing to recognise, fund, and empower the very actors who form the backbone of community-level climate resilience. Climate-related Official Development Assistance (ODA), one of the few financial streams with gender-disaggregated data, reveals a stark imbalance. In 2022, a mere 3% of all climate ODA identified gender equality as a primary objective (Sasi, 2025). This suggests that gender equity remains peripheral within a multi-billion-dollar global finance regime.

The inequity becomes sharper when examining flows to civil society. Of the USD 2.4 billion in climate ODA channelled through civil society organisations, less than 2%, approximately USD 43 million, reached feminist, women-led, and women's rights movements, most of which were headquartered in the Global North (Sasi, 2025). This double marginalisation leaves African women excluded both from the bulk of climate finance and from the small fraction nominally intended for their empowerment. Against this backdrop, Africa's gender financing gap stands at USD 42 billion (Sasi, 2025). Initiatives designed to close this gap provide relatively small amounts of financing compared to what is needed, functioning as symbolic gestures rather than transformative interventions (Sasi, 2025). Hence, the macro-inequity thus reveals a foundational truth that the global financial system is not configured to recognise women, especially African women, as central actors in climate adaptation and resilience.

A further examination of GRCF allocation reveals a striking misalignment between funded sectors and the lived realities of women's climate vulnerability. Data from 2013–2022 demonstrate a concentration of funds in traditionally 'productive' sectors (see Table 1.1).

Table 1.1. Gender-relevant Climate Finance by Sector, 2013–2022.

Sector	Percentage of GRCF
1. Agriculture, Forestry, and Fishing	43.4
2. Energy	19.2
3. Other Social Infrastructure and Services	7.1
4. Other Multisectors	6.3
5. Water Supply and Sanitation	4.7
6. General Environment Protection	4.2
7. Government, CSO, Peace	3.3
8. Health	3.2
9. Business and Banking	3.1
10. All Other Sectors	7.1
Grand Total	**100.0**

Source: Data adapted from Development Initiative based on OECD-DAC CRS data (as cited in Sasi, 2025).

Table 1.2. Gender-Relevant Climate Finance by Select Purpose Codes, 2013–2022.

Purpose	Volume (USD millions)	Percentage of Total GRCF
Social Protection	73.6	6.9
Basic Nutrition	7.4	0.7
Women's Rights Organizations and Movements	3.0	0.3
Family Planning	2.3	0.2
Reproductive Health Care	1.9	0.2
Ending Violence Against Women and Girls	0.1	0.01

Source: Data adapted from Development Initiative based on OECD-DAC CRS data (as cited in Sasi, 2025).

While the dominance of agriculture, forestry, and fishing (43.4%) appears logical given women's pivotal role in food systems, the focus often narrows to export-oriented, male-dominated value chains. This neglects subsistence farming, seed preservation, and local food processing, where women's expertise is central. Similarly, while 19.2% of GRCF flows to energy, much of it supports large-scale infrastructure, grid expansion, or utility-scale solar projects, rather than decentralised, clean cooking, or off-grid solutions that directly improve women's health, productivity, and safety.

Most troubling, however, is the systematic underfunding of sectors women consistently identify as critical for resilience. Health receives just 3.2% of GRCF, water and sanitation 4.7%, and disaster risk management a mere 1.1% (Sasi, 2025). These omissions disregard the gendered pathways through which climate shocks exacerbate vulnerability. Droughts force women and girls to travel farther for water, increasing their exposure to gender-based violence (GBV). Floods that destroy sanitation infrastructure expose women to health risks and indignity. By privileging hard infrastructure over these soft but essential systems, climate finance overlooks the most immediate levers of resilience.

Similarly, the greatest gap appears in the funding of gender-specific programmes, where neglect becomes a serious ethical concern, as revealed from Table 1.2.

Despite extensive evidence that climate change acts as a threat multiplier for GBV, only 0.01% of gender-relevant climate finance over a decade targeted the prevention of violence against women and girls (Sasi, 2025). Climate disruptions displace communities, strain social systems, and intensify competition over scarce resources, all conditions that heighten risks of sexual violence, child marriage, and domestic abuse. However, the global climate finance architecture has devoted, on average, just USD 100,000 per year to addressing these threats.

Consequently, negligible allocations for family planning (0.2%) and reproductive health (0.2%) illustrate a dangerous fragmentation between environmental and bodily autonomy agendas. Women's reproductive agency, central to resilience and adaptive capacity, remains unrecognised as a climate issue. This compartmentalisation reflects a persistent failure to perceive women's lives as integrated systems where environmental and reproductive justice are inextricably linked. The priorities of major financial institutions further entrench this imbalance. Analysis of the World Bank's International Development Association (IDA) funding between 2013 and 2022 also reveals the persistent disconnect between climate and gender objectives.

From the data, the majority (77.6%) of IDA funding serves other objectives. While climate-related initiatives account for 14.8% and gender equality 7.6%, there is no clear evidence of overlap between these categories (Sasi, 2025). Even when climate projects are funded, they seldom embed gender analysis or responsiveness. For instance, irrigation systems may be installed without securing women's land rights, or agricultural training offered without addressing women's time poverty or access to extension services. Institutional silos thus reproduce inequity through omission. Trends of climate finance distribution have a greater tendency to produce inequity, if the sources of finance expose dependency. Climate finance in Africa exhibits asymmetrical flows, serving as a current that consolidates advantages for regions or actors while leaving others at the periphery of support.

Geographic concentration is stark. Just 10 countries, including South Africa, Egypt, and Nigeria, receive 50% of all climate finance, while 30 others share a mere 10% (CPI, 2024). The disparity is even sharper for private finance, where the top 10 recipients capture 76% of flows. This creates a feedback loop, nations with low initial capacity to attract investment fall further behind, lacking the track record to draw future capital. Most troublingly, Africa's 10 most climate-vulnerable countries receive only 10% of total flows, an inversion of justice that allocates the least support where it is needed most.

In the same vein, sectoral patterns reflect a similar imbalance. Energy systems, dominated by renewable energy projects, receive 31% (USD 13.7 billion) of total finance (CPI, 2024). While crucial for decarbonisation, this focus mirrors global mitigation priorities at the expense of Africa's urgent adaptation needs. Agriculture, forestry, and land use, sectors that sustain most African livelihoods and face the brunt of climate shocks, receive only 16% (USD 7.0 billion), while water and wastewater management attract just 7% (USD 3.2 billion).

The mitigation–adaptation divide reinforces this inequity. Mitigation projects capture 46% (USD 19.9 billion), compared to 32% (USD 13.8 billion) for adaptation (CPI, 2024). Although Africa's adaptation share exceeds the global average, it remains far below what is required, given the continent's negligible emissions and disproportionate exposure to climate impacts. The economic cost of inaction could reach 20% of Africa's GDP by 2050 (Christian Aid, 2022), underscoring the unsustainability of this mitigation-heavy bias. Equally troubling is the form this finance takes. Over half (51%) of Africa's climate finance arrives as debt – split between concessional and market-rate loans (CPI, 2024). This is more than double the loan share in East Asia (18%) or Latin America (20%). For already debt-burdened economies, such financing transforms climate aid into a liability, deepening fiscal stress and constraining future investment. In effect, countries are borrowing to address a crisis they did not create.

From the previous analysis, the inequalities in sourcing and distribution culminate in a third layer, one that undermines local agency and perpetuates gender and social exclusion. For instance, Senegal offers a vivid illustration, where women make up 70% of the agricultural workforce and produce 80% of the country's food but remain largely excluded from land ownership and formal finance (Associated Press, 2024). According to Mariama Sonko, climate funds are often centralised and loan-based, making them inaccessible to women farmers lacking collateral (Associated Press, 2024). This not only marginalises those most affected by climate change but also silences invaluable indigenous knowledge crucial to local adaptation. The result is an architecture that systematically bypasses the most effective agents of resilience.

Thus, gender disparity reflects a broader failure to harness domestic capital and agency. Africa's financial system holds an estimated USD 2.4 trillion in bank, pension, and insurance assets, largely untapped for climate investment (FSD Africa, 2024). The negligible 2% contribution from institutional investors underscores a disconnect between domestic finance and climate priorities. Mobilising this capital is not just an economic necessity but a strategic imperative for reducing currency risk, aligning investment with local needs, and strengthening ownership of Africa's climate transition.

More so, research on solar mini-grids in rural Kenya and Nigeria demonstrates that when finance is community-centred, the impact can be transformative. Following grid connection, median household incomes quadrupled, alongside measurable gains in health, security, and gender equality as women accessed new economic opportunities (Aklin et al., 2023). Such examples affirm that inclusive, decentralised finance can simultaneously advance climate action and development justice.

Gendered Dimensions of Climate Finance and Decision-Making in Africa

Having analysed and discussed the layers of inequality in climate finance in Africa and the gendered dimensions of access to such finance, this chapter finds that gender gaps also shape participation in climate decision-making, policy formulation, and implementation. Women and women-led organisations remain significantly underrepresented in advocacy, policymaking, and leadership roles (Tavenner et al., 2019). Data from the Environment and Gender Index show that within the Conferences of the Parties and the three Rio Conventions, women constitute less than one-third of decision-makers in six of the nine processes examined (International Union for Conservation of Nature [IUCN] Global Gender Office & United Nations Entity for Gender Equality and the Empowerment of Women [UN Women], 2015).

The Gender Action Plan stresses the need for full, meaningful, and equal participation of women in all aspects of the UNFCCC process and in broader climate policy and action. Building gender-responsive climate resilience therefore requires empowering women to assume leadership and decision-making positions. The capacity of women to engage in these processes is closely linked to their economic empowerment. Access to resources, affordable finance, and entrepreneurial training through multi-sectoral initiatives can enhance their participation. Economic empowerment not only improves women's financial standing but also strengthens their influence in community and household decision-making (Asomah, 2024).

Improving resilience to the effects of climate change depends on access to relevant information, resources, and technologies. However, barriers such as limited education, restricted mobility, and unequal access to finance often prevent women from obtaining these essential services (UN Women, 2018). Given their responsibilities as caregivers, food producers, and water collectors, women are disproportionately affected by climate change (Food and Agriculture Organization [FAO] et al., 2019). Addressing gender-specific challenges in climate mitigation and adaptation therefore requires gender-sensitive approaches that ensure inclusivity in the dissemination of climate information and technologies. Initiatives that expand women's access to climate resilient technologies, such as clean energy solutions, drought-resistant crops, and weather forecasting tools, can enhance their ability to adapt and reduce community vulnerability. Building women's adaptive capacity requires making climate information relevant and accessible, supported through coordinated action by governments, civil society, and the private sector to implement gender-responsive policies and initiatives (UN Women, 2018; UNFCCC, 2021).

Conclusion and Recommendation

The analysis in this chapter reveals that despite the rapid growth of climate finance flows to Africa, the system remains unequal in both structure and effect. Finance distribution is skewed towards mitigation rather than adaptation, dominated by external loans, and largely gender-insensitive in implementation. These patterns mirror the structural asymmetries within global financial governance and perpetuate dependency between the Global North and South. Although climate finance was conceived under the principles of CBDR and the PPP as a form of environmental justice, the current architecture undermines these principles by prioritising credit-based mechanisms that deepen debt and neglect the gendered realities of vulnerability and adaptation.

At the continental level, inequalities emerge through source-based, distributional, and gendered dimensions. Most climate finances originate externally, reinforcing donor dominance, flows concentrate in a few industrialised sectors and countries, marginalising adaptation projects that directly benefit women, rural populations, and indigenous communities, and women remain excluded from access, leadership, and benefits in climate investment processes. Although mechanisms such as the GCF and GEF have adopted gender policies, their implementation remains limited, with less than 4% of global climate finance addressing gender equality and only a small share reaching women-led organisations.

Adaptation financing, which is central to Africa's resilience, remains underfunded and poorly aligned with gender-responsive priorities. Despite women's vital role in agriculture and community adaptation, funding continues to favour large-scale mitigation projects over local, people-centred initiatives. To correct these disparities, the chapter concludes by recommending a rebalancing of financial flows towards adaptation and the prioritisation of gender-responsive approaches that empower women and vulnerable groups as central actors in Africa's climate response. Shifting from loan-based to grant-based mechanisms, strengthening institutional capacity for gender mainstreaming, and supporting inclusive, locally driven adaptation projects will make climate finance more equitable, effective, and transformative for sustainable development across the continent.

References

Achampong, L., & Officer, A. (2023). *Gender-responsive climate finance: the key to just climate action and tackling inequalities*. UN Women.

Aklin, M., Harish, S. P., & Urpelainen, J. (2023). *Solar mini-grids and local development in sub-Saharan Africa: Evidence from Kenya and Nigeria*. arXiv preprint arXiv:2301.01234.

Asomah, J. K. (2024). Climate change and gender in Africa: An analysis of effects and gender-sensitive approaches. *International Journal of Agriculture and Earth Science (IJAES)*, *10*(4), 84–110.

Associated Press. (2024, June 10). *Women farmers in Senegal are fighting for access to land, education, and climate finance*. AP News. https://apnews.com/article/women-agriculture-climate-change-development-senegal-africa-376734977ad99bfee82c0d-99b68e5fb8

Cho, S., Crenshaw, K. W., & McCall, L. (2013). Toward a field of intersectionality studies: Theory, applications, and praxis. Signs: *Journal of Women in Culture and Society, 38*(4), 785–810. https://doi.org/10.1086/669608

Christian Aid. (2022). T*he cost to Africa: Drastic economic damage from climate change* [Report]. https://www.christianaid.org.uk/sites/default/files/2022-11/the-cost-to-africa.pdf

Climate Finance Playbook. (2021). *Innovative strategies to finance a cooler, safer planet*. The Nature Conservancy.

Climate Policy Initiative. (2024). *Landscape of climate finance in Africa* 2024. https://www.climatepolicyinitiative.org/wp-content/uploads/2024/10/Landscape-of-Climate-Finance-in-Africa-2024.pdf

Dankelman, I. (2002). Climate change: Learning from gender analysis and women's experiences of organising for sustainable development. *Gender & Development, 10*(2), 21–29.

Doku, I., & Phiri, A. (2024). Climate finance and women-hunger alleviation in the global south: Is the Sub-Saharan Africa case any different? *Plos One, 19*(2), e0290274.

Edidah, L. A., Mariola, A., Sofia, H., Ritah, K., Perez, M., Rebecca, M., & Laurence, J. (2020). Gender in climate change, agriculture, and natural resource policies: Insights from East Africa. *Climatic Change, 158*, 43–60. https://doi.org/10.1007/S10584-019-02447-0

Food and Agriculture Organization [FAO], International Fund for Agricultural Development [IFAD], United Nations Children's Fund [UNICEF], World Food

Programme [WFP], & World Health Organization [WHO]. (2019). *The state of food security and nutrition in the world 2019: Safeguarding against economic slowdowns and downturns.* FAO.

FSD Africa. (2024). *Bridging the climate finance gap in Africa: Insights and investment pathways*. FSD Africa Publications.

Georgalakis, J. (2020). A disconnected policy network: The UK's response to the Sierra Leone Ebola epidemic. *Social Science & Medicine*, *250*, 112851.

Gerasimenko, D. (2024). *Gender and climate: How gender finance fosters climate finance*. International Institute of Green Finance.

International Union for Conservation of Nature [IUCN] Global Gender Office, & United Nations Entity for Gender Equality and the Empowerment of Women [UN Women]. (2015). *Women's participation in global environmental decision making: New research from the Environment and Gender Index (EGI)*. IUCN. https://genderandenvironment.org/egi-womens-participation-in-global-environmental-decision-making-factsheet/

Kabaseke, C. (2023). Gender responsive climate financing as a strategy to climate change mitigation and adaptation: A legal analysis. *Kabale University Interdisciplinary Research Journal (KURJ)*, *2*(2), 77–88.

Lam, S., Novović, G., Skinner, K., & Nguyen-Viet, H. (2024). Greener through gender: What climate mainstreaming can learn from gender mainstreaming. *Wiley Interdisciplinary Reviews: Climate Change*, *15*(4), e887.

Neimanis, A. (2000). *Gender mainstreaming in practice: A handbook*. UNDP RBEC.

Ngum, F., & Bastiaensen, J. (2020). Intersectional perspective of strengthening climate change adaptation of agrarian women in Cameroon. In W. Leal Filho, N. Oguge, D. Ayal, L. Adeleke, & I. da Silva (Eds.), *African handbook of climate change adaptation* (pp. 1–23). Springer. https://doi.org/10.1007/978-3-030-42091-8_213-1

OECD. (2024). *Climate finance provided and mobilised by developed countries in 2013–2022*. OECD Publishing.

Patel, S., Plutshack, V., Kajumba, T. C., Uribe, M. D. P. L., & Krishnapriya, P. P. (2023). *Gender, climate finance and inclusive low-carbon transitions*. IIED.

Renee, A. (2018). Gender mainstreaming as feminist politics: A critical analysis of the pursuit of gender equality in Swedish local government [Repro 03/2018]. Orebo University.

Sasi, I. (2025, February 5). *Climate finance flows in Africa – The gender disparity*. Agri Frontier. https://www.agrifrontier.com/case-study/climate-finance-flows-in-africa-the-gender-disparity/.

Schalatek, L., & Nakhooda, S. (2016). *Gender and climate finance*. Heinrich Böll Stiftung.

Tantoh, H. B., Ebhuoma, E. E., & Leonard, L. (2022). Indigenous women's vulnerability to climate change and adaptation strategies in Central Africa: A systematic review. In E. E. Ebhuoma & L. Leonard (Eds.), *Indigenous knowledge and climate governance: A Sub-Saharan African perspective* (pp. 53–66). Springer. https://doi.org/10.1007/978-3-030-99411-2

Tavenner, K., Mishra, A., Bryan, E., & Ringler, C. (2019). Climate change, commercialization, and collective action in East African agriculture. *Global Environmental Change*, *59*, 101997.

UK Nigeria Infrastructure Advisory Facility (UKNIAF). (2024, July 31). *Climate finance in Nigeria: An introduction*. https://ukniaf.ng/climate-finance-in-nigeria-an-introduction/UKNIAF±1

UN Women. (2018). *Turning promises into action: Gender equality in the 2030 Agenda for Sustainable Development*. UN.

UNFCCC. (1992). *United Nations Framework Convention on Climate Change*. United Nations. https://unfccc.int/resource/docs/convkp/conveng.pdf

UNFCCC. (2021). *Introduction to climate finance* [UNFCCC Policy Report]. https://unfccc.int/topics/introduction-to-climate-finance
UNFCCC. (2021, October 12). *Overrepresentation of men in UN climate process persists.* https://unfccc.int/news/overrepresentation-of-men-in-un-climate-process-persists

Chapter 2

Social Norms and Equitable Access to Climate Finance Among Women Cassava Producers in Oyo State, Nigeria

Tope I. Omirin and Yetunde A. Aluko

Social Policy Department, Nigerian Institute of Social and Economic Research (NISER), Nigeria

Abstract

In the agrifood systems (AFSs) in low- and middle-income nations, characterised by widespread small-scale production, social norms are crucial in determining the opportunities and life outcomes of individuals. Women are primary agricultural producers and are prominently involved in small-scale agriculture. Their ability to scale up production and boost value through processing and marketing, thereby improving economic independence, is shaped by access to resources. This study examined how social norms affect women cassava producers' access to climate finance. Data were collected from 70 women cassava producers using interview schedules. Descriptive (percentages, means, and standard deviation) and inferential (regression) statistics were used for the analysis. Results on roles performed by women cassava producers showed they participated more within the processing (peeling and sieving – 100.0%, packaging – 92.9%) and marketing (trading – 98.6%) value chains. Restrictive social norms were more prevalent in three norm domains: access and resource ownership (sole operation of machinery – $\bar{X}$ = 1.04); influence and decision-making (having a say in household decisions – $\bar{X}$ = 2.39); and mobility and decorum (leaving the house without husband's permission – $\bar{X}$ = 1.87, riding a bicycle/motorcycle to the market – $\bar{X}$ = 1.64). Many respondents (54.3%) were favourably disposed to the possibility of accessing climate finance, notwithstanding the prevalence of restrictive social norms in their context. Social norms within the access and resource ownership domain collectively limited the

Gender and Climate Finance in Africa: Addressing Inequalities and Bridging Gaps, 21–36

Published under exclusive licence by Emerald Publishing Limited
doi:10.1108/978-1-83742-085-820261002

chance of women cassava producers' equitable access to climate finance by 62.7%. Therefore, implications abound for policy makers to initiate deliberation on social norms and encourage changes in restrictive norms to advance gender equality, thereby engendering equitable access to resources.

Keywords: Social norms; climate finance; equity; agrifood systems; cassava producers; women

Introduction and the Problem

The AFSs encompass the full range of actors and activities in agriculture. Among the actors in the AFSs, women are prominent as they serve as a major source of employment for women. Globally, the figure of women working in the AFSs was put at 36% as of 2019, while the figure was 66% in sub-Saharan Africa (Food and Agriculture Organization of the United Nations (FAO), 2023). This makes it apparent that AFSs constitute a major source of livelihood for women. In Nigeria, women are engaged in these activities as producers, processors, and marketers of produce, where small-scale and homestead production are common within the AFSs, while the ability to produce larger quantities and increase value via processing and marketing is often dictated by individual access to resources. *Beyond this, entry for women into different nodes of the AFS is shaped by societal expectations regarding the roles that are appropriate for them, highlighting the influence of social norms even before the emergence of resource-related constraints.*

The participation and productivity of women in AFSs are low, which comes at a high economic cost to Nigeria. It is estimated that the forgone earnings resulting from the gender gap in agricultural productivity are 0.6% of the total gross domestic product (GDP), or US$2.3 billion annually (World Bank, 2022). An adducible reason to the low participation of women in AFSs is the presence of prevailing social norms, which are strong and often unfavourable to women. Such norms weaken women farmers' access to markets, opportunities for finance, and networks (MEDA, 2023), while access to resources (land, inputs, finance, services, digital technology) is crucial for women operating in AFSs. Women's participation in AFSs can also be associated with the value attached to their work. Gendered social norms prevent the contributions of women not to being well appreciated. The roles of women, for instance, are often marginalised, coupled with the likelihood of poorer working conditions (e.g. informal, irregular, part-time, labour-intensive, low-skilled) relative to those of men (FAO, 2023). *These norms also determine the division of labour in a household, who is responsible for controlling major productive assets, as well as agricultural tasks that are deemed acceptable for women.*

Similarly, low participation of women can result from gendered social norms, which in turn predispose to gender inequality. Hence, the ability of women to succeed in such contexts becomes dependent on deeply entrenched gender inequalities concerning, for example, women's roles and the division of labour within households, as well as women's freedom of movement and the livelihoods and activities viewed as acceptable for women to participate in work outside the household (FAO, 2023). All these, consequently, make the degree to which they are resilient and recover from shocks and stress typically lower than their male counterparts. *Such resilience is additionally governed by norms that determine the extent to which women can freely seek information, adopt technologies, or make financial decisions, all of which are key climate adaptation factors.* Yet, closing the gap in gender participation could lead to an estimated yearly increase of about 2% of Nigeria's GDP, which is approximately US$8.1 billion (World Bank, 2022).

The absence of gender equality in participation in agricultural value chain activities as a result of social norms may distract from the most essential development outcomes, including nutrition and poverty issues, resulting in ineffective interventions (Masamha et al., 2017). The degree of women's and men's participation in AFSs determines what they end up benefiting from the system. For instance, in a cassava value chain, differences in human capital and productive inputs made women cassava farmers achieve lower productivity of 20–30% compared to men farmers in Nigeria (Ahmadu & Idisi, 2014). The lower productivity of women was due to gender-related constraints, including reduced access to resources, family and work responsibilities, social restrictions over mobility, reduced training and extension service access, and lack of information on market access. This finding points to the fact that social norms can be restrictive to the activities of women farmers. *Particularly, the post-harvest and processing roles of women are restricted by norms bordering on mobility and access to machinery, reinforcing segmentation by gender along the cassava value chain.*

Furthermore, gendered social norms can even be more restrictive when women use certain resources independently from their spouse (Seymour et al., 2023). As such, restrictive social norms prevent women from accessing resources/technologies that could reinforce their resilience, such as climate finance, which is defined by the United Nations Development Programme (UNDP) (2017) as financial flows mobilised for mitigation and adaptation to climate change by industrialised countries to developing countries. Climate finance is considered a means to catalyse the much-needed transition to zero-carbon and climate-resilient development while also fostering equitable social policy, including gender equality and women's empowerment (UNDP, 2017). Overseas development institute (ODI, 2016) reckoned that the manner in which climate finance is structured is significantly shaped by gender norms, and that agency and decision-making power are crucial for women to benefit from financing.

By definition, social norms are referred to as the often informal, unspoken, and unwritten rules that govern which behaviours are appropriate (Cialdini et al., 1991). *Understanding these norms becomes essential given that they shape the underlying structure that limits the participation of women and eventually their access to climate finance.* Cassava, being an important food security staple in Nigeria, adds significance to the study, coupled with the fact that it aligns with Goal 5 on gender equality of the United Nations' Sustainable Development Goals (SDGs). This study, therefore, examines how social norms affect equitable access to climate finance among women within cassava AFSs in Oyo State, Nigeria.

Objective of the Study

The overall objective of the study is to examine how social norms restrict equitable access to climate finance among women within cassava AFSs in Oyo State, Nigeria. In achieving this, the study specifically:

1. identified roles performed by women cassava producers in the cassava value chain;
2. ascertained the prevalence of social norms within cassava producers' social context; and
3. examined the social norms' influence on women cassava producers' perception of access to climate finance.

Test of Hypothesis

Hypothesis tested: There is no significant correlation between social norms prevalence and cassava women's access to climate finance.

A Brief Review of Literature

In Africa, AFSs are not just central to food security but also important for rural livelihoods, and a considerable proportion of the agricultural labour force is made up of women. Yet, gendered social norms shape and, in many cases, limit women's contributions. Mobility, labour roles, access to productive resources, and decision-making are influenced by social norms, and they collectively govern the capacity of women's meaningful participation in agricultural value chains (FAO, 2023). Within the cassava systems, women are more involved and dominate post-harvest processing and marketing, while norms connected to physical strength, operation of farm machines, and preparation of land usually limit their engagement in on-farm and mechanised activities (Ahmadu & Idisi, 2014). Such division of agricultural activities reinforces inequality in gender and creates structural barriers to productivity and resilience to shocks.

Gendered constraints in AFSs are increasingly recognised by the development framework globally. The *SDGs of the United Nations, specifically Goal 5 (gender equality) and Goal 13 (climate action),* acknowledge that the access of women to land, finance, and climate-resilient technologies is restricted by discriminatory social norms, thus generally hindering development outcomes (United Nations, 2015). Likewise, the United Nations Framework Convention on Climate Change (UNFCCC, 2019) *Gender Action Plan* emphasises the need for gender-responsive climate interventions, noting that women's ability to adapt to climate change is constrained by their access to finance, information, and decision-making. Embedded social norms, lack of control over assets, and limited autonomy are identified by the framework as critical barriers to equitable climate finance.

Policy instruments similarly highlight the same concerns within the African continent. For instance, the *African Union's strategy for gender equality and women's empowerment (2018–2028)* emphasises that women's economic agency is undermined by norms restricting their ownership of land, mobility, and leadership in rural institutions (African Union, n.d.). Whereas, according to the source, the economic empowerment of women in agriculture particularly depends on access to financial services (e.g. climate finance), *secure rights to productive assets*, and the elimination of *social and institutional barriers* that restrain their *autonomy and power in making decisions*. These provisions align with findings from the African Development Bank (2018) report that mechanisms of climate finance usually demand documentation, collateral, and institutional engagement, which women are unable to fulfil as a result of normative constraints.

Similarly, in Nigeria, gendered social norms determine the roles of women within AFSs, even in smallholder cassava production. Relative to men, limitations such as restricted mobility, low decision-making power, and lopsided access to extension services result in lower productivity for women (Masamha et al., 2017). Just as such norms restrict access to cooperative membership and financial institutions, they can also do the same to women's access to climate-related funding opportunities that could boost their resilience to shocks. This claim is strengthened by evidence from other African contexts, which indicates that the ability of women to benefit from climate finance is closely linked to their autonomy, resource control, and ability to satisfy formal conditions, which are collectively and significantly shaped by social norms (African Development Bank, 2018; ODI, 2016).

Overall, the centrality of women to the cassava AFSs is apparent, and there is evidence that gendered social norms hinder the extent of their participation, access, and ownership of productive resources, notwithstanding the global and regional commitments under the SDGs, UNFCCC, and African Union frameworks. Consequently, this study empirically examined how these norms specifically influence women cassava producers' access to climate finance within AFSs in Oyo State.

Methodology

Study area: Oyo State is situated between latitudes 7°02′N and 9°10′N and longitudes 2°04′E and 4°30′E. It is geographically found in the Southwest region of Nigeria. It has a land area of 28,454 km^2. The climate of the state is tropically wet and dry, with distinct rainy (April–October) and dry (November–March) seasons, accompanied by high relative humidity. The mean annual rainfall is 1,480 mm, while the mean monthly temperature ranges between 18°C and 24°C during the rainy season and 30°C and 35°C during the dry season. The climate is quite suitable for the cultivation of cassava and other arable crops.

Sampling method: Purposive sampling was used to select two local government areas (LGAs) where cassava production is concentrated in the hands of smallholder farmers, which include Akinyele LGA and Ibarapa Central LGA in Oyo State. A total of 70 respondents were randomly selected from a list of registered women cassava producers as provided by the Agricultural Development Programme, Oyo State.

Data collection method: An interview schedule was the instrument used to collect data from the respondents. The instrument consisted of three sections: (a) division of roles in the cassava value chains; (b) prevalence of social norms within the social context of women cassava producers; and (c) social norms' influence on women cassava producers' perception of access to climate finance. Operationalisation of the variables was done as follows:

- *Division of roles in the cassava value chain*: This was measured on a 2-point scale of yes = 2 and no = 1. The percentage figures were obtained and used to assess the cassava value chain activities in terms of women's participation in them.
- *Prevalence of social norms within the social context of women cassava producers*: This was done using a 4-point scale by adapting the six gendered social norm domains provided by Seymour et al. (2023). Points on the scale include always = 4; sometimes = 3; occasionally = 2; and never = 1. Scores assigned to each point on the scale were summed and divided by the number of scale points to obtain a mean score cut-off point. Due to the framing of the scale items, a mean score less than 2.5 denoted the prevalence of restrictive social norms, while a mean score equal to or greater than 2.5 denoted the absence of restrictive social norms.
- *Perception of social norms influences access to climate finance*: A 5-point Likert scale of strongly agree = 5, agree = 4, undecided = 3, disagree = 2, and strongly disagree = 1 (scale point scores were reversed for negatively worded statements) was used to measure access to climate finance. Composite scores were then generated, via which women cassava producers' perception towards access to climate finance was categorised into unfavourable (< mean score) and favourable (≥ mean score).

Data analysis: Descriptive analysis of data was done using percentages, mean values, and standard deviation, while inferential analysis was performed using *t*-test from linear regression to test the hypothesis predicting the contribution of the six domains of social norms to access to climate finance. The model is depicted thus:

$$Y = a + b_1X_1 + b_2X_2 + \cdots + b_nX_n.$$

where Y = access to climate finance,
$X_{1\text{–}6}$ = independent variables (social norm domains),
a = constant, and
b = slope of line.

Results and Discussion of Findings

Division of Roles in the Cassava Value Chain

Table 2.1 presents the involvement of the respondents in the different cassava value chain activities, which is higher for processing when compared to production and marketing. All of them were involved in processing activities such as peeling (100.0%) and sieving (100.0%), just as an overwhelming majority were

Table 2.1. Role Division Within the Cassava Value Chain.

Cassava Value Chain	Activities	Yes (%)
Production	Land preparation	0.0
	Seed selection	0.0
	Planting	0.0
	Weed management	1.4
	Harvesting	100.0
Processing	Peeling	100.0
	Washing	92.9
	Fermentation	1.4
	Sieving	100.0
	Drying	97.1
	Grinding/milling	2.9
	Packaging	92.9
Marketing	Transportation	0.0
	Storage	0.0
	Selling/trading	98.6

Source: Researchers' fieldwork 2025.

involved in drying (97.1%), washing (92.9%), and packaging (92.9%). Similarly, all of them were involved in harvesting (100.0%) as a production activity, while their visibility in the trading (98.6%) of cassava products was equally very high. However, they were not represented in other productive activities like land preparation, seed selection, planting, and weed management.

These findings show that the lower involvement of women in on-farm activities compared to off-farm activities can be traced to existing social norms within the communities of the respondents. For instance, concerning gender roles, in many societies, women traditionally assume domestic and caregiving responsibilities, which can also extend to the processing and marketing of agricultural products. Social norms equally condition societal perception that women are less physically strong than men, which may discourage women from engaging in production activities that are deemed to be more energy demanding. This is not surprising, given that norms strongly manifest as exclusion from the production node of the cassava value chain, and inclusion in the off-farm nodes of the chain, such as processing (Pyburn & Hallin, 2023).

It is worth noting that the roles of women in off-farm work in AFSs are more likely to be in less profitable nodes of the value chain or on worse terms than those of men due to restrictive traditional social norms (FAO, 2023). This stems from the fact that though processing is a value-adding activity, the participation of women in off-farm nodes such as the peeling, washing, drying, and local-level processing of cassava is usually done at the least mechanised and least profitable section of the value chain. Apart from being less profitable, such activities are typically informal, small-scale, and labour-intensive. Social norms more or less constrain cassava women producers' participation in as well as the benefits they can derive from working in the different value chain activities. Ultimately, such exclusions can impact cassava women producers' access to climate finance.

Prevalence of Social Norms

Table 2.2 shows the organisation of the six domains of gendered social norms that are prevalent within the cassava AFS. As indicated, social norms that are restrictive to the activities of the respondents manifested in three of the domains, except the participation, leadership, and representation domains and the division of labour domain. For instance, there was a restriction in women cassava producers operating agricultural machinery on their own ($\bar{X}=1.04$) and having a say in household decisions ($\bar{X}=2.39$) as depicted by their low mean scores, within the access and ownership of resources, and influence and decision-making domains, respectively. Similarly, within the mobility and decorum domain, social norms proved restrictive to the respondents leaving the house without the permission of their husbands ($\bar{X}=1.87$) and riding a bicycle/motorcycle ($\bar{X}=1.64$).

Table 2.2. Social Norms Prevalence Within the Context of Women Cassava Producers.

Domains of Social Norms	**Mean**	**SD**
Access and ownership of resources		
Ownership of land by women cassava producers in their name in this community	2.67	1.20
Use of technology (e.g. smartphones) by women cassava producers in this community	3.96	0.36
Operation of agricultural machinery by women cassava producers on their own	1.04	0.36
Participation of women cassava producers in agricultural extension training	3.00	0.91
Own or control of husband's assets after their death	2.74	1.21
Securing credit or loan by women cassava producers without their husbands' approval	2.95	0.99
Influence and decision-making		
Women cassava producers have a say in household decisions (such as what food to buy and grow)	2.39	1.23

Table 2.2. (*Continued*)

Domains of Social Norms	**Mean**	**SD**
Ownership of personal savings by women cassava producers in this community	3.97	0.17
Can spend their wages/income on personal items	3.03	0.99
Participation, leadership, and representation		
Holding of leadership roles by women cassava producers in community groups	3.33	0.15
Women cassava producers being members of rural organisations or producer groups	3.01	0.21
Women cassava producers holding leadership positions at their workplace	3.03	0.17
Division of labour		
Women cassava producers taking care of large farms in this community	2.86	1.03
Perform most of the routine household chores (e.g. cooking, cleaning, washing clothes)	3.17	1.05
Carry out most of the childcare duties within the household (changing diapers, giving the kids a bath, feeding, etc.)	2.90	1.02
Mobility and decorum		
Working outside the home by women cassava producers in this community	3.05	0.99
Women cassava producers leaving the house without the permission of their husbands	1.87	0.90
Women cassava producers riding a bicycle/motorcycle to get to the market in this community	1.64	0.96
Bodily autonomy and freedom from violence		
Women cassava producers beaten by their husbands for any reason in this community	3.97	0.23
Use of family planning by women cassava producers in this community	2.50	1.19
Women cassava producers can determine the number of children to have	2.67	1.20

Source: Researchers' fieldwork 2025.

Regarding the operation of farm machinery, men are typically associated with the role of operating it. This is traceable to physical strength stereotypes, as women are perceived as not possessing the energy or stamina required to operate machines, regardless of whether such perception is wrong. Safety concerns may also discourage women from operating machinery, irrespective of whether they have received any necessary training. This is related to riding a bicycle/motorcycle to the market. Within the cassava value chain, this restriction will have more impact on women at the production stage (e.g. use of cassava puller for harvesting, using a bicycle/motorcycle to convey produce to the market) than at other stages that make use of less technical and energy-consuming machinery.

The finding bordering on restrictive social norms concerning decision-making is buttressed by the World Bank (2022) submission that women are 25% less likely to be the primary person responsible for making decisions about farm plots than men. Restrictions on decisions on which crop to cultivate or food to buy can determine the full or partial engagement of women in AFSs, which can limit their potential to access finance.

As regards the respondents' ability to leave the house without the permission of their spouse, this is largely what is obtained in the study area, the country and Africa at large, where traditional views informed by culture are quite important. However, sole decision-making as to leaving the home without spousal consent is considered acceptable in the absence of a partner for women-led households. There is also more acceptance of women farmers investing in farm machinery for households headed by women (Petesch, 2022).

Perception of Access to Climate Finance

As revealed in Table 2.3, more than half (54.3%) of the women cassava producers were favourably disposed towards the possibility of accessing climate finance irrespective of the manifestation of social norms in their context.

Reasons for this view stem from the outcome of their reaction to the perception statements shown in Table 2.4.

Additionally, as earlier observed under the section on the prevalence of social norms, restrictive social norms in the cassava AFS only manifested in three of the domains of gendered social norms, i.e. those related to access and ownership of resources, decision-making, and mobility and decorum. Within AFSs, norms around gender access to and control of resources and division of labour usually stand out, especially concerning how they influence productive work. However,

Table 2.3. Categorisation of Women Cassava Producers by Access to Climate Finance.

Access to Climate Finance	Percentage	Mean
Favourable	54.3	69.72±2.90
Unfavourable	45.7	

Source: Researchers' fieldwork 2025.

Table 2.4. Women Cassava Producers' Perception on Access to Climate Finance.

Domains of Social Norms	**SA**	**A**	**U**	**D**	**SD**
Access, ownership and control over productive resources					
If women cassava producers cannot own land in their own name, accessing climate finance will be difficult or impossible	34.3	28.6	0.0	21.4	15.7
The ability of women cassava producers to use technology (e.g. smartphones) can engender their access to climate finance	4.3	87.1	0.0	2.9	5.7
The ability of women cassava producers to operate agricultural machinery on their own can engender access to climate finance	0.0	4.3	0.0	12.9	82.8
Participation of women cassava producers in agricultural extension training can engender access to climate finance	0.0	0.0	0.0	5.7	94.3
Women cassava producers who can inherit their husbands' assets after death will equally have access to climate finance	35.7	50.0	0.0	4.3	10.0
As long as a woman cassava producer cannot secure creditor a loan without her husband's approval, she will not also have access to the climate finance without his approval	47.1	35.7	0.0	7.2	10.0
Influence and decision-making					
Access to climate finance will be impossible for women cassava producers who do not have a say in household decisions (such as what food to buy and grow)	28.5	42.9	0.0	21.4	7.2
Access to climate finance will be possible for women cassava producers who can own personal savings	81.4	0.0	0.0	5.7	12.9
Women cassava producers who can spend their wages/income on personal items will equally have access to climate finance	0.0	10.0	0.0	0.0	90.0

(*Continued*)

Table 2.4. (*Continued*)

Domains of Social Norms	SA	A	U	D	SD
Participation and leadership					
If women cassava producers can hold leadership roles in the community groups, it will engender access to climate finance	0.0	1.4	0.0	0.0	98.6
Membership in rural organisations or producer groups will boost women cassava producers' chances of accessing climate finance	12.8	18.6	2.9	28.6	37.1
It will be impossible for a woman cassava producer to access the climate finance in a community where most people believe that women should not hold leadership positions at their workplace	57.1	28.5	0.0	11.5	2.9
Division of labour					
If men alone can manage large farms, access to climate finance will be impossible for women cassava producers	64.2	14.3	0.0	14.3	7.2
When men and women cannot share routine household chores (e.g. cooking, cleaning, washing clothes), access to climate finance will be less for women cassava producers	42.8	28.5	7.2	7.2	14.3
Ownership or management of commercial farms by women can translate to access to climate finance	21.4	42.8	14.3	14.3	7.2
It will be difficult for women cassava producers to access climate finance if they are responsible for carrying out most childcare duties within the home	92.9	1.4	0.0	5.7	0.0
Mobility and decorum					
Access to climate finance will be impossible if women cassava producers cannot work outside the home	68.5	12.8	2.9	7.2	8.6

Table 2.4. (*Continued*)

Domains of Social Norms	SA	A	U	D	SD
Access to climate finance will be impossible if women cassava producers cannot leave their houses without the permission of their husbands	21.4	57.2	2.9	14.3	4.3
Women cassava producers who can ride a bicycle/motorcycle to get to the market will also have access to climate finance	1.4	91.4	0.0	0.0	7.2
Bodily autonomy and freedom from violence					
Women cassava producers whose husbands do not beat them for any reason will have access to climate finance	37.1	57.2	0.0	5.7	0.0
Women cassava producers who can use family planning will likewise have access to climate finance	24.3	47.1	7.2	17.1	4.3
Women cassava producers who cannot determine the number of children to have will not be able to access climate finance	22.9	74.2	2.9	0.0	0.0

Source: Researchers' fieldwork 2025.

the prevalence of such may not necessarily reflect their strength (Cislaghi et al., 2018). Accordingly, the favourable perception of the respondents towards access to climate finance partly infers that, just as restrictive norms (e.g. operation of agricultural machinery, household decision-making), are prevalent in their social context, enabling norms (e.g. participation/leadership and division of labour) likewise prevail. The reasons as to why certain social norms are restrictive while others are enabling differ from one context to another.

Relationship Between the Prevalence of Social Norms and Perception of Access to Climate Finance

As depicted in Table 2.5, the conversion of access mean values into figures in percentage indicates that the manifestation of restrictive social norms on the access and ownership of resources domain would limit women cassava producers' access to climate finance by 62.7%.

Table 2.5. Relationship Between the Prevalence of Social Norms and Perceived Influence on Access to Climate Finance.

Variables	Unstandardised coefficients	Std. Error	Standardised coefficients	*T*	Sig.
	B		*β*		
Constant	63.749	9.215		6.918	0.000**
Access and resource ownership	–0.627	0.244	–0.478	–2.564	0.013*
Influence and decision-making	0.533	0.401	0.236	1.327	0.189
Participation and leadership	0.693	0.819	0.120	0.846	0.401
Division of labour	0.306	0.329	0.245	0.930	0.356
Mobility and decorum	0.433	0.357	0.326	1.210	0.231
Bodily autonomy and freedom from violence	–0.060	0.494	–0.024	–0.122	0.903

Note: *,** denote significance at 5% and 1% levels, respectively.

It is observable from the table that social norms on the access and ownership of resources domain are the only norm domain that was significant and negatively associated with access to climate finance relative to others. This underscores the submission that the norm domain on access to, ownership of, and control over productive resources sits neatly within an AFS (Pyburn & Hallin, 2023). Such restrictive norms imply that they block access to resources and opportunities, thereby limiting women from attaining their full potential within AFSs. The engagement of women in small-scale and homestead production is quite common, and their ability to individually access and own resources strongly determines whether they can scale up production and add value to their farm.

Conclusion and Policy Recommendations

Women cassava producers' perception towards the possibility of accessing climate finance was fairly favourable, despite the manifestation of social norms in their context. This was premised on the manifestation of restrictive social norms in the cassava AFS in three of the domains of gendered social norms (access and ownership of resources, decision-making, and mobility and decorum). Social norms on the access and ownership of resources significantly and negatively influenced perceived access to climate finance, underscoring their restrictive significance within AFSs. The manifestation of such restrictive social norms blocks access to resources and opportunities, thereby limiting women from attaining their full potential within AFSs.

In the light of the foregoing, the following recommendations are therefore made:

1. Programmes with focus on addressing norms limiting the access and ownership of resources by women should be initiated, as that their likelihood of accessing climate finance was significantly reduced by norms in this domain.
2. Efforts aimed at strengthening the autonomy in *decision-making for women* in households and producer groups should be undertaken, considering its influence on their financial engagement.
3. Restrictions around mobility should be reduced to improve the ability of women to reach financial institutions and support services.
4. Initiatives on climate finance should be designed to identify and act on normative barriers for women in the AFSs, particularly as it relates to processing and marketing activities.

References

African Development Bank. (2018). *Inclusive climate-smart finance for climate-resilient development in Africa*. AfDB.

African Union. (n.d.). *AU strategy for gender equality & women's empowerment, 2018–2028*. African Union.

Ahmadu, J., & Idisi, P. O. (2014). Gendered participation in the cassava value chain in Nigeria. *Merit Research Journal of Agricultural Science and Soil Sciences*, *2*(11), 147–153.

Cialdini, R. B., Kallgren, C. A., & Reno, R. R. (1991). A focus theory of normative conduct: A theoretical refinement and reevaluation of the role of norms in human behaviour. In M. P. Zanna (Ed.), *Advances in experimental social psychology* (Vol. 24, pp. 201–234). Academic Press. https://doi.org/10.1016/S0065-2601(08)60330-5

Cislaghi, B., Manji, K., & Heise, L. (2018). *Social norms and gender-related harmful practices. Learning Report 2: Theory in support of better practice*. Learning Group on Social Norms and Gender-Related Harmful Practices of the London School of Hygiene and Tropical Medicine. http://strive.lshtm.ac.uk/system/files/attachments/STRIVE%20Norms%20Report%202.pdf

Food and Agriculture Organization of the United Nations (FAO). (2023). *The status of women in agrifood systems*. https://doi.org/10.4060/cc5343en

Masamha, B., Uzokwe, V. N. E., Ntagwabira, F. E., Gabagambi, D., & Mamiro, P. (2017). Gender influence on participation in cassava value chains in smallholder farming sectors: Evidence from Kigoma region, Tanzania. *Experimental Agriculture*, *55*(1), 1–16. https://doi.org/10.1017/S0014479717000552

MEDA. (2023). *Alliances and innovation: Strengthening women's resilience and food security in Nigeria*. Mennonite Economic Development Associates. https://www.meda.org/news/blog/alliances-and-innovation-strengthening-womens-resilience-and-food-security-in-nigeria/

Overseas Development Institute (ODI). (2016). *Climate finance briefing: Gender and climate finance*. ODI.

Petesch, P. (2022). *Gender norms, agency, and trajectories of social change and development in agricultural communities* [Doctoral dissertation, Wageningen University].

Pyburn, R., & Hallin, R. (2023). *Gendered social norms in agrifood systems: Conceptual framework*. CGIAR Initiative on Gender Equality.

Seymour, G., Cole, S., Costenbader, E., Mwakanyamale, E., Adeyeye, O., Feleke, S., Ferguson, N., Heckert, J., Msita, S., Litvin, K., & Johnson, T. P. (2023). *Measuring gender and social norms in agrifood systems: Evidence from Nigeria and Tanzania*. CGIAR Initiative on Gender Equality.

United Nations. (2015). *Transforming our world: The 2030 agenda for sustainable development*. United Nations.

United Nations Development Programme (UNDP). (2017). *Gender and climate finance*. UNDP. https://www.undp.org/publications/gender-and-climate-finance

United Nations Framework Convention on Climate Change (UNFCCC). (2019). *Enhanced Lima work programme on gender and its gender action plan*. UNFCCC. https://unfccc.int/topics/gender/workstreams/gender-action-plan

World Bank. (2022). *Gender gaps in agriculture productivity and public spending in Nigeria*. The World Bank Group.

Chapter 3

The Role of Climate Finance in Addressing Contemporary Challenges and Enhancing Prospects for Women in Zimbabwe's Fragile Agricultural Economy

Prince Dzingirayi[a] *and Alison Nyaradzo Zuva*[b]

[a]*Department of Languages and Communications, Women's University in Africa, Zimbabwe*
[b]*Centre for the Study on Race, Gender and Class, University of Johannesburg, South Africa*

Abstract

Developing countries, particularly in Sub-Saharan Africa, face significant challenges due to economic fragility, social inequality, and the impacts of climate change. Women's empowerment is a cornerstone of achieving sustainable and equitable development, yet women in Zimbabwe's fragile agricultural economy continue to face pervasive gender inequalities. Zimbabwe's economic hardships marked by high unemployment, poverty, corruption, and inflation have intensified the vulnerability of women, who bear the brunt of the social responsibility of caring for their families. The agricultural sector, which many women depend on for their livelihoods, is particularly affected by climate change, exacerbating economic challenges and limiting growth opportunities. Climate finance, aimed at mitigating and adapting to climate impacts, holds the potential for addressing these challenges and empowering women. This chapter explores the role of climate finance in supporting women in Zimbabwe's agricultural sector, identifying how targeted financial mechanisms can help enhance their prospects and alleviate gender-specific challenges. The study utilises a mixed research method and auto-ethnographic research design to assess how climate finance can be integrated into women's livelihoods in vulnerable

Gender and Climate Finance in Africa: Addressing Inequalities and Bridging Gaps, 37–55

doi:10.1108/978-1-83742-085-820261003

agricultural communities. Purposive and convenience sampling techniques were employed to select participants. Findings indicate that access to climate finance can significantly improve women's adaptive capacity, empowering them to adopt sustainable agricultural practices and diversify income sources. The study recommends the development of climate finance strategies that specifically target women, ensuring they have the tools and resources to thrive in Zimbabwe's fragile agricultural economy.

Keywords: Climate finance; gender inequality; agricultural economy; Zimbabwe; women's empowerment; climate change adaptation; sustainable development

Introduction

Globally, agriculture is at a crossroads due to the effects of climate change. Climate change is currently threatening the livelihoods of ecology in many communities. It has caused a complex, multifaceted web of challenges in developing countries, including Zimbabwe. The mainstay of the economy of Zimbabwe is anchored on agriculture, and it has been tasked with the portfolio of ensuring food security in the Southern African Development Committee. Zimbabwe's economy is currently in a 'sorry state' precipitated by a high inflation rate, high unemployment rate, corruption, and political instability. The economic status of Zimbabwe has a significant impact on women who have the mandate to feed the family. Climate change is political and has worsened the vulnerability of women in a fragile agriculture economy of Zimbabwe. This concept of climate change has been brought to light through the hand of Euro-Western hegemony. The concept of climate had attracted foreign aid, and the aid is a neo-colonial tool used as a checkmate to control the operations of weaker countries. Many factors trigger climate change, including technological advancement, industrialisation, experimentation, and more. Women play a pivotal role in agricultural production in all parts of the world. There are so many ways in which women can engage in agribusiness. Agriculture is the production of crops and the rearing of animals to boost economic development. For instance, an individual can engage in aquatic farming, dairy production, apiculture, horticulture, and animal husbandry both for subsistence and commercial purposes. Agriculture is one of the major sectors of the economy that encompasses all activities related to the production, processing, and distribution of agricultural products and services in Zimbabwe. The country has experienced different climatic threats, such as cyclones, hailstorms, floods, droughts, acute fluctuation of temperatures, and heat waves that have a significant impact on the agricultural sector. The powder of climate change has caused unprecedented damage to the infrastructure, which ultimately has a great negative effect on economic development. For instance, in 2019, Zimbabwe was hit hard by tropical Cyclone Idai, which affected almost 250,000 individuals and destroyed infrastructure such as shelters, roads, powerlines, bridges, fauna, and flora. The gap left by Cyclone Idai has not yet been bridged due to the limping economy in the country. The United Nations (2024) estimated that women make up 80% of people forcibly displaced by climate-related disasters in developing countries. Imran et al. (2018) reveal that agriculture is a major economic driver of many developing countries. It is against this background that this chapter seeks to assess the role of climate finance in addressing the contemporary challenges faced by women in Zimbabwe's fragile agricultural-backed economy. The land reform programme of 2000 in Zimbabwe has been negatively downplayed by economic sanctions, developmental sabotage, political instability, mismanagement, and corruption. This has caused trails of economic cracks in the country. Women are a fractured and fluid vulnerable population trapped in a double tragedy of socio-economic responsibilities due to the status of Zimbabwe's economy. Women constitute two-thirds of the world's population, but they are not involved in the economic decision-making process. The Zimbabwe National Statistics Agency (ZimStat, 2019) reveals that 2% of women are documented agricultural landowners in Zimbabwe. This justified the vulnerability of women in an agriculture-supported economy. Inequality against women is a global pandemic which can be equated to coronavirus and needs funding to curb it. Universally, women are active individuals who are productive and reproductive. Surviving in a fragile economic environment is a mammoth task for women who are facing multiedged swords of seeking economic development, social presence, and caring and protecting the family. In support of that, Gaidzanwa (2011) urges that women shoulder the responsibilities of domestic services, family care, and nutritional security. Life in a fragile economic environment has forced women to squeeze their way to overcome daily challenges in Zimbabwe. Muzorewa (2021) argues that agriculture is a dominant industry providing employment and daily livelihood for many women across African countries. This shows that women are key stakeholders in an agrarian-supported economy like Zimbabwe. The main challenge is that women lack financial support to ensure productivity.

Women are at the epicentre of socio-economic development in Africa. Meinzen-Dick (2019) argues that over 60% of employed women in Africa work in Agriculture. They represent the continent's major (60%–80%) food producers (Njobe & Kaaria, 2015). Their contribution to economic development in Africa cannot be overemphasised, as they represent a formidable force in the African agricultural sectors, spending significant time planting, weeding, ridging, and harvesting while simultaneously doing other household tasks (Dinkelman & Ngai, 2021; Mukasa & Salami, 2016). The prevalence rate of women in agriculture justifies that women are the central nerve of economic development in society. However, climate change has emerged as a developmental hindrance in agriculture. There are counter approaches to address climate change in the field of agriculture, and climate finance is the contemporary impromptu strategy. The availability of adequate financial resources is the solution of addressing climate change in the field of agriculture.

Climate finance is an emerging tool for ensuring progressive transformation to counter the fragility of the agriculture-based economy in Zimbabwe. CPI (2024) climate finance refers to the financial resources allocated to projects and initiatives that aim to mitigate climate change and adapt to its impacts. This is such a noble initiative that can support women to adapt and curb the effects of climate change to ensure productivity. Climate finance is a sustainable approach to empowering women to be innovative by encouraging them to start fast-growing projects such as the adoption of drought-resistant crops, improving irrigation systems, or implementing agroforestry practices that enrich the soil and enhance biodiversity. Climate finance fosters innovation mechanisms in agriculture through the adoption of new technologies and practices that boost economic productivity, hence spraying off economic fragility in a way to transform the future generation. Numerous threats emanate from climate change, which pose a direct challenge to food security, water resources, public health, and economic stability across the globe (World Bank, 2021). This study intends to understand climate change challenges and opportunities for women to survive without being abused.

Characteristics of a Fragile Economy

There is no single definition of a fragile economic situation because of varying and complex environments. Climate change is also not universal; hence, different communities experience diverse climate change. Therefore, climate change and climate finance are dyadic. Hearle (2023) postulates that women living in fragile economic countries are more likely to lose their livelihoods, experience displacement, and have education interrupted during times of crisis. The World Bank (2021, p. 301) characterises fragile economic situations as 'high levels of exclusion, lack of capacity, and limited provision of basic services' and an 'inability or unwillingness of the state to manage or mitigate risks'. This clearly shows that fragile economic environments are less able to respond to unprecedented emergencies of climate change and are often unable to deliver basic social, economic, legal, and security services.

Countries with fragile economies often have complex political systems. Nyabasa and Peng (2024) argue that the financial sector in a fragile economy is dominated by a small elite with close ties to political circles. This is a clear replica of what is currently happening in Zimbabwe. Very few individuals own the means of production, and the majority are suffering. Women in Zimbabwe are less likely to save or borrow from formal financial institutions due to the lack of collateral security demanded by financial institutions. For example, individuals who acquired land in 2000 were given offer letters that were not suitable for an individual to access loans from financial institutions. This shows that agriculture in Zimbabwe is limping because of a lack of funding.

An Overview of Climate Finance in Agriculture

The role of women in agriculture is key in enhancing food productivity as women constitute an important role in the agricultural workforce. Women play a crucial role in managing household food production, small-scale and commercial farming. Despite their noble contributions, they face numerous challenges, including limited access to land, credit, and farming skills. Empowering women in agriculture is essential for enhancing resilience and improving food security. Climate finance in Zimbabwe's agriculture sector is a critical tool for addressing the pressing challenges posed by climate change. Climate finance serves as a lifeline, offering the necessary resources to adapt to climate change-related challenges and sustain agricultural productivity. Matsito and Magaraba (2024) point out that climate finance initiatives can empower women through training, resource allocation, and technology support. This was supported by Hearle (2023), who indicates that climate finance initiatives facilitate women's access to credit and financial services. By providing microloans tailored for women farmers, these programmes help them invest in their farms, purchase tools, and expand their businesses. Financial independence allows women to support their families better and contribute to their communities. Climate finance can be used to improve irrigation systems, roads, and storage facilities, enabling farmers to adapt to climate variability and reduce post-harvest losses. Climate finance can fund workshops and training programmes that equip farmers with the knowledge they need to make informed decisions about crop management and resource utilisation (World Bank, 2021). Climate finance encourages innovation in agriculture by funding research and development of new technologies and practices. This can include drought-resistant crop varieties or renewable energy solutions for irrigation, helping farmers to be more adaptive and sustainable. Climate finance can help women in fragile situations manage risks, preserve what gains are made, and help them have positive mental health.

Challenges Faced by Women in the Fragile Agribusiness of Zimbabwe

A fragile economic environment is associated with a lot of challenges. The fragility of the economy of Zimbabwe is precipitated by corruption, mismanagement, the conspiracy of sanctions, climate change, political instability, and inconsistency of policies. The concept of a fragile agriculture economy is complex, and it is difficult to make sustainable interventions. According to Nneli and Livingstone (2024), fragility is still not universally understood, and scholars, practitioners, and policymakers have various ideas about it. They further explain that countries with fragile economies are failing to deliver essential social services to their citizens, which compromises legitimacy. In the Zimbabwean context, there is only a handful of social services offered, leaving the rest crumbling in mucky waters. Fragility entwines risk exposure and insufficient coping capacity for the state to manage, absorb, and reduce risks (Chianca, 2008). This chapter dwells much on challenges related to climate change that affect the agricultural business in Zimbabwe. The role played by women in African society is a pure representation of the general populace. Men and children are supported by the umbilical code of the women for them to survive in the community. Therefore, empowering women is enlightening the whole community. The challenges encountered by women can limit the impact of funding and impede progress towards climate resilience and sustainable development. Dzingirayi et al. (2020) noted that women in rural areas lack access to information on available climate finance opportunities. This knowledge gap is a hindrance for women to apply for funding to boost their start-up businesses. The poor road network is another big hindrance that blocks potential organisations from successfully deploying climate finance projects in other rural areas. There are so many areas that are inaccessible due to poor road infrastructure in the country, and this has made women vulnerable to climate finance. For example, some areas of Chiendambuya are not accessible during the rainy season due to a lack of bridges. Social and cultural norms are some of the challenges faced by women to independently venture into climate finance. Gaidzanwa (2011) argues that in other African communities, women are viewed as objects of development. Some of the obstacles faced by women are gender norms, prejudice, discrimination, lack of party support, biased media coverage that favours males, gender wage discrepancies, and few possibilities for leadership. Therefore, traditional practices may hinder women from engaging in modern, sustainable climate finance initiatives. A lack of monitoring and evaluation metrics can hinder the proper utilisation of climate finance projects.

Women in Zimbabwe are exhausted by the prolonged economic challenges in the country. Most women are fleeing the country, going to neighbouring countries like South Africa, Botswana, Mozambique, Zambia, Malawi, Namibia, and Lesotho to look for better living conditions. Chikwira (2024) estimates that almost 2 million Zimbabweans are living in the diaspora and 85% of them are in South Africa. This shows that the hostile economic environment in Zimbabwe is a cancer to human survival. The push factor is triggered by high inflation, devaluation of the currency, and reduced consumption amid a hostile environment precipitated by many factors like climate change and lack of good governance. Marriages are breaking down due to prolonged distance between couples. Some women cross the border using undesignated entry points such as the perennial crocodile-infested Limpopo river, hence risking their lives. According to Dzingirayi et al. (2020), children are left alone as parents are forced to go to neighbouring countries to look for greener pastures. This parental gap has caused young children to drop out of school, child marriages, child prostitution, the abuse of drugs, and high juvenile offenders. All these challenges are leaving a painful scar on the face of the women both directly and indirectly. Therefore, climate finance is an insurance of hope for indigenous Zimbabweans to remain and develop their country. Therefore, women play a critical role in shaping the behaviour of the community. Biblically, women are the first teachers on earth. It is important to fund all projects done by women should be supported to ensure development.

The other challenge faced by women in the agriculture-supported economy is that they are treated as second-class citizens without control of the land. This shows that women do not have equal ownership rights to immovable property, equal rights to inherit assets, or equal authority over the administration of assets. This is triggered by the African indigenous culture, which is lopsided towards the patriarchal system. Zimbabwe's fragile economy is currently male-dominated, and women occupy a small fraction. For instance, in most Zimbabwean societies, land belongs to the man, despite having laws that advocate for gender equality. This has created a developmental gap in ensuring food security, reducing poverty, and responding to climate change without depletion of the natural resource base. Climate finance can be a saviour to challenges faced by women in the fragile economy of Zimbabwe.

The Dimensions of Climate Change in Fragile Environments

This chapter has outlined five main dimensions of fragile environments encountered during climate change. The economic, political, social, environmental, and technological are the characteristics of fragility.

Table 3.1 dimensions of climate change are a threat multiplier (De Lorenzi et al., 2017) that has increased stress among women with no likelihood of taking action. The changes that emanate from climate change are complex and devastating. Climate change has heightened the vulnerability of women in countries

Table 3.1. Multiple Dimensions of Contemporary Fragility in the Context of Climate Change.

Dimensions	Brief Explanation
Economic	This has resulted in slow macroeconomic growth. Economic fragility has caused high unemployment, dependency syndrome, vulnerability, conflict, corruption, and social instability.
Political	Politics is the umbrella of social settings. Political instability led to a lack of transparency, political terror, resistance, corruption, and mismanagement.
Social	Societal fragility leads to inequality and gender-based social inequality. It affects the cultural identity of the society and it creates social cleavages. It compromises, harmony, resilience, and adaptability to climate challenges. It can lead to high crime rates in the community as a survival strategy.
Environmental	This exposes the populations to climatic and health threats. The threats include natural disasters, air, water, and sanitation quality, infectious disease, uprooted people, and household livelihoods. Climate change raises environmental risks in vulnerable contexts.
Technological	Technological development has disturbed the ecological balance due to a lot of experiments. The smooth movement of waves is consistently being disrupted due to technological inventions. This has drastically affected the agriculture-backed economy, leading to catastrophic events such as cyclones, heatwaves, floods, drought, earthquakes, earth traumas, and more.

Source: Adaptation Fund (2024).

with economic challenges, such as Zimbabwe. This indicates that there is a need to support women because of their social roles in the community. Women are the engine of humanity in the African culture. Climate finance is the potential solution to counter climate change. However, a lot of financial institutions are hesitant to invest in a country with political discord and economic meltdown like Zimbabwe. There are a lot of conspiracy theories that justify the fragility of the economy. Other scholars had traced the economic meltdown from Zimbabwe's participation in the war of Democratic Republic of Congo in 1997 and the fast land reform programme. However, other scholars blame poor governance as the main culprit that led to the economic meltdown. The above arguments justify that Zimbabwe's economy is in a mercy that needs serious intervention strategies such as climate finance.

Empowering Women Farmers

Women in agriculture need to be empowered through several initiatives. They can be empowered as both owners of the means of production and as employees in the agricultural sector. Women in the current fragile economic environment are struggling to access funding to start sustainable projects that could enable them to cope with unprecedented climate change. The socio-cultural responsibility of women in Zimbabwe has made them vulnerable due to the harsh and hostile economic environment. Climate finance has been identified as the solution to address climate change-induced economic fragility. Climate finance is a mechanism that provides the necessary resources to empower women to invest in climate-resilient crops, the use of efficient irrigation systems, and sustainable farming techniques (CPI, 2024). Therefore, climate finance is an initiative that can bridge the gender gap in the agrarian economy of Zimbabwe. Zimbabwe is a multicultural community, and the role of women is to take care of the family. For instance, it is prudent to support and encourage women to start horticulture businesses so that they can be economically relevant in the fragile environment. The horticulture project is a multifold approach that can help to enhance nutritional value in the family as well as boost the economy. The support can be in the form of training women to start nutritional gardens of organic crops to reduce the use of chemical fertilisers that are believed to cause health challenges. Climate finance can bolster their resilience by supporting projects that promote the diversification of crops, the development of community-based resource management, and access to climate information services. This not only helps women adapt to climate change but also strengthens their role in community leadership and decision-making. Through climate finance, women can also network, collaborate, and share their business resilience and experience. For example, a group of women farmers, supported by climate finance, might come together to share best practices, market their produce collectively, or advocate for their needs within local governance structures. This sense of community can amplify their voices to create a sense of belonging that can lead to agricultural productivity. In this case, climate finance is a catalyst for economic change in the community. Through empowerment, resilience, and community engagement, climate finance initiatives can help create a more equitable and sustainable agricultural future.

Zimbabwe's Agriculture Hardships

Zimbabwe's economy is agriculture-based, which is vulnerable to climate change. The climate conditions in Zimbabwe are favourable to agriculture. There are a lot of hardships that are threatening the agricultural productivity in the country, and these threats need to be addressed so that Zimbabwe can reclaim its title of being 'a jewel of Africa' in food security. Some of the challenges encountered in agriculture are lack of resources, diseases, and climate change-induced problems such as droughts, cyclones, floods, heatwaves, lack of knowledge, skills, and lack of financial support. These hardships have caused untold suffering to indigenous people and are a threat to food security in the country. Persistent drought has caused most communities to rely on food aid support systems. The food aid syndrome has caused some individuals not to take agriculture seriously. This has pushed agriculture partners to support women through climate finance. However, climate finance had its own shortcomings which are centred on discrimination, lack of monitoring and evaluation, and top-down approach without the involvement of women implementing the projects. Climate finance is an initiative that can support farmers with access to climate-resilient seeds, irrigation systems, and training in sustainable farming practices. This enables them to adapt to changing weather patterns, ensuring food security for their families and communities. Zimbabwe, once known as the 'breadbasket of Africa', has faced profound challenges in its agricultural sector over the past few decades. In the early 2000s, Zimbabwe underwent a controversial land reform programme that aimed to redistribute land from white commercial farmers to black Zimbabweans. The purpose of land reform was to rectify historical injustices. During the land reform programme, very few women managed to be allocated land, and the few who got land through political connections did not have access to modern agricultural technology. This causes them to struggle to break the yoke of climate change; they keep on relying on compromised traditional farming methods. Muzorewa (2021) indicates that Zimbabwe's agrarian economy started to deteriorate soon after the fast-track land reform programme, and it has affected the lives of many, especially women. This constant struggle to secure resources can lead to despair and frustration. As time progresses, climate change has added another layer of complexity to the agricultural economy of Zimbabwe due to erratic rainfall patterns, prolonged droughts, and severe flooding.

Objectives

To evaluate how climate finance initiatives specifically support women farmers in improving agricultural productivity and resilience.

To identify the barriers faced by women in accessing information about climate finance opportunities.

To document successful climate finance initiatives that have positively impacted women in agriculture.

Research Gaps in Climate Finance

The role of climate finance in addressing contemporary challenges faced by women in Zimbabwe's fragile economy reveals that there is a lack of in-depth studies focusing specifically on how these initiatives impact women. Understanding the nuances of how climate finance affects women differently from men is crucial for developing targeted interventions. The other research gap is on strategies of empowering women through climate finance for them to have better health and improve nutrition for their families. There are a lot of research gaps concerning climate finances, and some of the gaps are the underexplored roles of the community dynamics and inadequate focus on the indigenous community.

Theoretical Framework

This chapter used the climate justice theoretical framework to understand the role of climate finance in addressing contemporary challenges for women in Zimbabwe's hostile economic environment. This theoretical framework provides a comprehensive lens through which to analyse the role of climate finance in addressing the contemporary challenges faced by women in Zimbabwe's fragile agricultural economy. Kumar Rai and Kumar (2025) argue that climate justice is an essential component of contemporary environmental discourse, emphasising the fair distribution of climate-related burdens. Setzer and Vanhala (2020) explain that the climate justice system advocates for the fair distribution of climate finance and resources to vulnerable groups. It underscores the need for inclusive decision-making processes that consider women's voices and perspectives in climate finance initiatives. Climate justice is an evolving concept, and its core assumptions include epistemic justice, justice as recognition, procedural justice, and distributive justice. It determines whether the allocation of funds and projects mirrors fairness and justice. Climate justice focuses on halting climate change through financial contributions based on the idea of retribution for caused injustice. Setzer and Vanhala (2020) posit that climate justice also focuses on human rights, economic disparity, and social justice. This explains that climate justice is a multidimensional ethical principle that emphasises the fair and equitable distribution of environmental benefits and burdens. Therefore, it is a people-centred practice that focuses on empowering vulnerable individuals during difficult times. Climate justice is becoming increasingly established as a theory capable of navigating the complex challenges and rising gender inequalities of climate change.

Methodology

A qualitative research paradigm was instituted to fish out an in-depth understanding of the context of climate finance among the women living in the hostile agriculture-based economic environment of Zimbabwe. This chapter was triggered to unpack climate change-related challenges and opportunities faced by women in Zimbabwe. The objectives were the main drivers that ensured accuracy of the research findings.

Research Design

The multipronged research design was collaboratively used with a comprehensive literature review, rigorous document analysis, and thematic analysis to develop the conceptions of intertwined climate finance and climate change issues within the Zimbabwean context. The qualitative research method advocates for using multiple data sources and analytical techniques to enhance the depth and validity of findings (Creswell & Poth, 2018; Yin, 2017). It allows researchers to gather diverse data of both qualitative and quantitative metrics in a way to form an accurate decision-making process. Multipronged research designs allow for flexibility in the research process. It can combine secondary and primary data to understand complex phenomena affecting women in the quest for a fragile climate change-induced economy.

Literature Review

This study's pillar was the use of secondary data established from peer-reviewed journal articles, books, and book chapters. The secondary review data covered topics related to climate finance, climate change adaptation, socio-economic status, political influence, and monitoring and evaluation of projects run by women.

Document Analysis

The researchers examined key policies of women empowerment, climate finance, and climate change in Zimbabwe. This included a thorough review of the literature and other relevant information on climate finance. The analysis assessed the coverage, effectiveness, and alignment of these documents with the needs and perspectives of local communities, in line with the recommendations of policy analysis scholars (Patton et al., 2015; Ritchie & Spencer, 1994). In this context, data related to women's empowerment, climate change, and climate finance shape the spine analysis of this study.

Thematic Analysis

Thematic data analysis was used to generate themes from the interconnected literature and observations. The analysis focused on five key areas: climate change vulnerabilities, climate finance, supporting resources, challenges faced by women, and decision-making processes. This approach, as advocated by Braun and Clarke (2006), enabled the researchers to develop a comprehensive understanding of the multifaceted nature of the climate change-related challenges and opportunities faced by women in Zimbabwe.

Ethical Considerations

The researchers considered all the ethical principles, including the acknowledgement of sources, accurate representation of findings, and avoidance of bias or misrepresentation. The researchers ensured that the analysis and the presentation of the findings remained objective and truthful, contributing to the credibility and reliability of the research, as recommended by qualitative research ethics guidelines (Creswell, 2013; Merriam & Tisdell, 2015). The combination of a rigorous literature review, in-depth document analysis, and thematic analysis allowed the researchers to develop a comprehensive understanding of climate finance and come out with potential solutions.

Findings

The chapter brought to surface three main themes, which are climate finance initiatives used to support women in the business of farming, the barriers, and the impact of climate finance in the fragile agricultural economy of Zimbabwe. Subthemes also emerged from each main theme. The themes were informed by the objectives of the research study. The following themes emerged.

Climate Finance Initiatives to Support Women Farmers

Empowering the Voices of Women

Women in agriculture deserve for their voices to be heard. They usually encounter diverse challenges in carrying out their agricultural business. In climate finance initiatives, women's voices need to be heard so that they can come up with solutions to address their needs. This will enable women to have an opportunity to share their experiences and knowledge. Ferguson (2022) outlines that the voice of women matters most in decision-making on all developmental issues, such as agriculture. This will unlock economic dividends that have been caused by climate change in affecting food security. Miles (2025) explains that the voice of women in agriculture plays a vital role in climate finance to a unique perspective. Their understanding of local ecosystems and farming practices can lead to more effective climate solutions that are tailored to the specific needs of their communities. By amplifying their voices in climate finance discussions, initiatives can ensure that the needs and priorities of entire communities are considered, leading to more inclusive and impactful outcomes (Anon, 2024). Inclusive climate finance initiatives that value women's voices can build trust and collaboration among stakeholders, making it easier to implement effective solutions. Women's voices can lead to investments in sustainable practices that ensure food security and environmental health for future generations. Recognising and elevating women's voices helps address gender inequalities in agriculture. This focus can lead to more equitable access to resources, training, and opportunities, benefiting the agricultural sector as a whole. Elevating the voices of women in agriculture enriches climate finance efforts, leading to more effective, inclusive, and sustainable solutions that benefit entire communities. The poor involvement of women in decision-making and their weak negotiating power, coupled with rigid patriarchal social norms and value systems, can prevent women from actively participating in climate action or Disaster risk response initiatives (DRR) initiatives and/or saving themselves in disaster situations (Dasgupta et al., 2010).

Empowering Women Through Access to Resources

Access to resources is the key climate finance initiative that can help women to survive in the fragile agrarian economy. Women in agriculture should have access to basic resources such as adequate land, financial support, seeds, tools, and technology. The most finite resource is the funds to start up the business. Adequate financial resources help in the smooth running of the operations of the project. It has been noted that in Zimbabwe, a lack of financial support is a hindrance to starting a sustainable agriculture project. The availability of funds can help to buy modern technological agriculture equipment such as irrigation systems (Nyabasa & Peng, 2024). Climate finance can support initiatives that provide women with access to clean water and irrigation systems. This support helps them to produce quality products that enhance food security for their families and communities. The availability of and access to finance play a fundamental role in the establishment, development, and survival of businesses (Pavlova & Gvetadze, 2023). Financial backing allows businesses to explore new methods, crops, and technologies, helping them stay competitive and adapt to changing market demands. Agriculture in Zimbabwe is a rain-based system that can be easily affected by climate change. Anon (2024) postulates that the availability of financial resources enables women in agriculture to implement risk management strategies, such as insurance or diversification of crops, to safeguard their investments. This helps to increase productivity. Nyabasa and Peng (2024) put that adequate financial resources enable women in agriculture to advertise their agricultural produce and have access to the market. Marketing helps the farmers to establish the expectations of the customers. Access to financial resources not only benefits individual farmers but also strengthens the entire community. The financial support can be accessed from the government, banks, non-governmental organisations, and agricultural partners. The funds can be accessed through mobilisation and networking; hence, women in agriculture from hostile economic environments need to be supported financially without conditions.

Promoting Sustainable Practices

Climate finance can encourage businesses to adopt sustainable practices. For example, funds can support companies in transitioning to eco-friendly technologies, thus reducing their carbon footprint. This not only benefits the environment but also positions businesses for future growth in a global market increasingly focused on sustainability. Education and training are initiatives that can be used to promote sustainable practices. For instance, women can be trained to venture into value addition of agricultural produce. Educating women about sustainable practices empowers them with the skills and knowledge to make informed decisions. This can enhance their confidence and leadership in agricultural enterprises. The other financial climate initiative linked to the promotion of sustainable practices is developing environmental stewardship. This helps women to improve soil fertility and conserve water through practicing farming techniques such as crop rotation, organic farming, and integrated pest management, which can reduce dependency on expensive chemicals and inputs, increasing profitability (United Nations, 2015). Such education and skills help to benefit the future generations. Miles (2025) reveals that the promotion of sustainable agricultural practices helps to improve community health through producing healthier food and ensuring food security. The implementation of sustainable practices helps women in a fragile economic environment to adapt to climate change through planting drought-resistant crops such as rapoko, sorghum, and millet. This will enable women to embrace the use of the indigenous knowledge system in agriculture, such as pfumvudza/itwasa, to counter climate-related challenges.

Networking and Collaboration

Networking and collaboration are the contemporary strategies that can be used to support entrepreneurial women in the fragile economic environment. Linking women to each other leads to knowledge sharing, collaboration on projects, and increased visibility in agricultural markets (Muzorewa, 2021). Networking helps women to share experiences and how to solve challenges faced in running an agricultural business. This can also enable women to advocate for pro-gender equality initiatives policies. Miles (2025) alludes to the fact that networking provides emotional and practical support, helping women navigate challenges in agriculture. Collective approach can make it easier for women to access what they need to grow their businesses. Women in agriculture can collaborate to create cooperatives or collectives, increasing their bargaining power in markets. Therefore, collaboration of women in climate finance is a pipeline of generational leadership through mentorship. It was noted that networking and collaboration of women in the fragile agriculture economy encourage creativity and innovation of new ideas related to addressing challenges encountered in agriculture. Networking enabled women to showcase their skills, contributions, and successes in agriculture.

Building Capacity

Climate finance can also be directed towards education and training programmes that build local capacity. By enhancing knowledge about climate change and sustainable practices, communities become more resilient and better equipped to face challenges. Climate finance can lure international players to support climate-resilient activities such as embracing indigenous farming methods like zero tillage (pfumvudza/Itwasa). Building strong partnerships between governments, international organisations, civil society, and the private sector is essential for adequate climate financing in fragile and conflict-affected states

(Pavlova & Gvetadze, 2023). Monitoring and evaluation are critical for climate financing projects in fragile and conflict-affected countries like Zimbabwe. This may help to solve the economic challenges leading to sustainable projects. Therefore, climate finance is a weapon of hope that shapes the future of vulnerable women in hostile economic environments. Ferguson (2022) states that capacity-building initiatives equip women with essential skills and knowledge in climate finance to take active roles in decision-making processes that affect their communities and livelihoods. Capacity building helps women to improve with financial literacy in climate finance and to understand funding mechanisms, budgeting, and investment strategies. This knowledge allows them to manage resources effectively and make informed choices that benefit their families and businesses. Successful initiatives can create jobs, improve livelihoods, and enhance food security in fragile economies. Capacity building for women in climate finance in fragile economies not only empowers individuals but also fosters community resilience, drives sustainable development, and promotes gender equality, creating a positive ripple effect throughout society.

Celebrating Success Stories for Women in Agriculture

Heralding the success stories for women in agriculture is a noble initiative of climate finance. This is a positive way of inspiring other women to engage in agricultural business. Personal achievements give hope and guidance to potential women to participate in agriculture. This strategy is a solution to climate change and can help to improve the fragile economy.

The Barriers Faced by Women in Accessing Climate Finance Information

Limited Resource Capacity and Infrastructure Deficit

The findings indicate that Zimbabwe's financial constraints severely limit its ability to implement robust infrastructure projects and technological advancements crucial for building climate resilience (World Bank, 2021). This lack of resources has a cascading effect, hindering the implementation of effective climate change policies and community-level adaptation efforts, as highlighted in the policy analysis (Government of Zimbabwe, 2021). It was found that women lack awareness of climate finance–related projects, especially those who reside in rural areas. Even if they get information, they are usually affected by nepotism and corruption. For instance, corruption is now a norm in which women would be asked to pay a bribe for them to be involved in climate finance initiatives. This is difficult for poor women from disadvantaged communities. Climate finance is therefore mostly accessed by women who are politically connected. Lack of financial literacy is another barrier that is common amongst women in fragile agrarian economic situations. This means most women have no sustainable capacity to budget and effectively utilise their finances. Financial literacy is a key complex phenomenon of business management, especially in agriculture.

Cultural Norms

Cultural norms are a significant barrier faced by women to access climate finance. The cultural norms are entwined in the traditional roles and responsibilities of women in their diverse communities. In many African cultures, women play the primary role of caring for the family as a mother or wife. This philosophy treats women as undervalued objects of development with limited access to climate finance opportunities. Although some laws support the elevation of women into business, there are still societies that do not allow women to make decisions independently about cultural norms. Matsito and Magaraba (2024) state that this lack of decision-making power can hinder her ability to pursue funding for her projects, and man usually controls financial resources as women are believed not to have financial skills. World Bank (2021) alludes that social discrimination and stigma are the labels given to deep-rooted cultural areas for women pursuing climate finance opportunities. This shows that women receive limited social support to engage in climate finance initiatives. Therefore, cultural conformity can affect women's desire to pursue climate finance projects in a fragile agrarian economic environment. Conversely, cultural norms are impediments for women to participate confidently in climate finance initiatives.

Insufficient Networking Opportunities and Socio-economic Constraints

Lack of networks of climate finance is another challenge faced by women in the fragile economic environment. For instance, women might struggle to find mentors to offer guidance and counselling in climate finance. This will affect business confidence amongst women in agricultural initiatives under a climate change environment. Socio-economic constraints require women to prioritise family needs over climate finance.

Educational and Communication Barriers

Women with limited education are looked down upon, and this will affect women's pursuit of climate finance projects. This lack of education can create a sense of inadequacy when trying to engage in business discussions. Anon (2024) puts that lack of communication can affect women's access to information regarding climate finance due to dominant language. For instance, in the scenario where the Chinese nationals are the funders, this means there will be language discrepancies.

Chronic Economic Instability and Foreign Investment Constraints

The study reveals that Zimbabwe's chronic economic instability, marked by a history of hyperinflation and political unrest, discourages foreign investment and hinders the mobilisation of financial resources necessary for large-scale climate change initiatives (Moyo et al., 2016; Transparency International, n.d.). This creates a vicious cycle that undermines the effectiveness of climate change policies, as discussed in the scholarly literature on the interplay between climate change, economic instability, and social cohesion (Eriksen & Lind, 2009; Moyo et al., 2014).

The Impact of Climate Finance Initiatives on Women in Agriculture

Zimbabwe's Climate Change Vulnerabilities

The analysis reveals that Zimbabwe's vulnerability to climate change stems from a confluence of factors, including limited financial resources, economic instability, and heavy reliance on climate-sensitive economic activities, particularly rain-fed agriculture (Transparency International, n.d.; World Bank, 2021). This 'perfect storm' of vulnerabilities threatens the country's future prosperity and overall well-being, as evidenced by the scholarly literature (Eriksen & Lind, 2009; Moyo et al., 2014).

Supporting Health and Nutrition

By investing in sustainable agricultural practices through climate finance, women can grow a diverse range of crops. This diversity improves family nutrition and health outcomes. When women are empowered to produce nutritious food, they contribute to the well-being of their families and communities.

Conclusion and Recommendations

The hardships faced by Zimbabwe's agricultural sector are deeply human, affecting families, communities, and the nation as a whole. Climate finance plays a crucial role in paving the way for a brighter future by addressing the contemporary economic challenges in Zimbabwe, particularly those emanating from climate change. Climate finance plays a vital role in addressing the challenges faced by women in Zimbabwe's fragile agricultural economy. Climate finance is instrumental in uplifting the well-being of women by addressing their unique challenges and providing the necessary resources; it empowers them to thrive, ensuring food security, economic stability, and community resilience. This ultimately creates a positive ripple effect, benefiting families and communities throughout Zimbabwe. The empowerment of women in agriculture is not merely a goal but an imperative for achieving sustainable development goals.

The study recommends the following:

- Financial protection to farmers, including women.
- Supporting female entrepreneurship to promote positive change.
- Inclusive access to funding in agricultural business.
- Women to create agriculture networking and collaborative business platforms to strengthen social safety nets.
- The provision of financial literacy skills to women.
- The use of indigenous knowledge farming systems to adapt to climate change.

References

Adaptation Fund. (2024, January). *Addressing climate change adaptation in fragile settings and conflict-affected countries: Lessons learned from the Adaptation Fund's portfolio*. Adaptation Fund. https://www.adaptation-fund.org/wp-content/uploads/2024/02/climate-change-adaptation-in-fragile-settings-2024.pdf

Anon. (2024). *World economic situation and prospects 2024*. United Nations. Retrieved September 25, 2024, from https://www.un.org/development/desa/dpad/wpcontent/uploads/sites/45/WESP_2024_Web.pdf

Braun, V., & Clarke, V. (2006). Using thematic analysis in psychology. *Qualitative Research in Psychology*, *3*(2), 77–101. https://doi.org/10.1191/1478088706qp0630a

CPI. (2024). *Landscape of climate finance in Africa 2024*. https://www.climatepolicyinitiative

Chianca, T. (2008). The OECD/DAC criteria for international development evaluations: An assessment and ideas for improvement. *Journal of Multidisciplinary Evaluation*, *5*(9), 41–51. https:doi.org/10.56645/jmde.v5i9.167

Chikwira, C. (2024). Impact of remittances on foreign currency supply in developing economies: A case of Zimbabwe from 2009 to 2022. *Dinasti International Journal of Economics, Finance and Accounting*, *5*, 5515–5526.

Creswell, J. W. (2013). *Qualitative inquiry and research design: Choosing among five approaches* (3rd ed.). Sage.

Creswell, J. W., & Poth, C. N. (2018). *Qualitative inquiry and research design: Choosing among five approaches* (4th ed.). Sage.

Dasgupta, N., Asgari, S., & Stout, J. G. (2010). When does contact with successful in group members change self-stereotypes? A longitudinal study. *Journal of Personality and Social Psychology*, *99*(3), 491–511.

De Lorenzi, M., Filippone, M., Fridoni, G. B., Alexander, D. C., & Ourselin, S. (2017). Probabilistic disease progression modeling to characterize diagnostic uncertainty: Application to staging and prediction in Alzheimer's disease. *NeuroImage*, *190*, 56–68.

Dinkleman, T., & Ngai, L. R. (2021). *Time use and gender in Africa in times of structural transformation* [Discussion paper 16792, RePEc:cpr:ceprdp:16792]. CEPR.

Dzingirayi, P., Mutete, F., & Maunganidze, L. (2020). Young women and adolescent girls lived experiences of COVID-19 lockdown in Zimbabwe. *International Journal of Law, Humanities & Social Science*, *4*(6), 56–68 (ISSN: 2521-0793).

Eriksen, K., & Lind, J. (2009). The role of a survey-based scenario planning process in corporate strategic decision-making. *European Journal of Operational Research*, *194*(3), 557–573.

Ferguson, S. (2022). *The key to change: Women's voice and influence*. UN Women India Office. hindustantimes.com

Gaidzanwa, R. B. (2011). *Why women matter in agriculture*. Faculty of Social Studies, University of Zimbabwe.

Government of Zimbabwe. (2021). *Zimbabwe revised nationally determined contribution*. Government of Zimbabwe.

Hearle, C. (2023). *What works to promote women's economic empowerment overcoming barriers to women's economic participation, progression, voice and agency*. Work and Opportunities for Women. publishing.service.gov.uk

Imran, M., Khan, N., Shah, A. A., & Ahmad, I. (2018). Overweight and obesity prevalence pattern and associated risk factors among the people of Malakand Division, Khyber Pakhtunkhwa, Pakistan. *Arabian Journal of Sciences and Engineering*, *43*(7), 3745–3755.

Kumar Rai, A., & Kumar, S. (2025). *Legal dimensions of climate justice: Challenges and prospects in the era of climate change* (ISSN: 3048-9539). www.theinfinite.in

Matsito, J. T., & Magaraba, O. (2024). Climate justice in Zimbabwe: An exploration of equity, adaptation, and sustainable development. *The Fountain – Journal of Interdisciplinary Studies*, *8*(1), 54–68.

Meinzen-Dick, R. (2019). Women's land rights as a pathway to poverty reduction: Framework and review of available evidence. *Agricultural Systems*, *172*, 72–82.

Merriam, S. B., & Tisdell, E. J. (2015). *Qualitative research: A guide to design and implementation*. Wiley.

Miles, K. (2025). *Global North and Global South | Definition, countries, differences, history, map, & facts*. Britannica. Retrieved January 7, 2025, from https://www.britannica.com/topic/GlobalNorth-and-Global-South

Moyo, B., Matsika, B. J., & Muchenje, V. (2014). Effect of feeding Moringa (*Moringa oleifera*) leaf meal on the physic-chemical characteristics and sensory properties of goat meat. *South African Journal of Animal Science*, *44*(1), 64–70.

Moyo, M., Goodyear-Smith, F. A., Weller, J., Robb, G., & Shulruf, B. (2016). Healthcare practitioners' personal and professional values. *Advances in Health Sciences Education: Theory and Practice*, *21*(2), 257–286.

Mukasa, A. N., & Salami, A. O. (2016). Gender equality in agriculture: What are really the benefits for sub-Saharan Africa? *Africa Economic Brief*, *7*(3), 1–12.

Muzorewa, W. (2021). Evaluating the role of climate smart agriculture towards sustainable livelihoods in Mutare District, Zimbabwe. *Significances of Bioengineering & Biosciences*, *4*(5). https://doi.org/10.31031/SBB.2021.04.000597

Njobe, B., & Kaaria, S. (2015). *Women and agriculture: The untapped opportunity in the wave of transformation* [Bakground paper]. Feeding Africa Conference, Dakar-Senegal.

Nneli, O. V., & Livingstone, D. (2024). *Women's economic empowerment in fragile and conflict-affected states*. UKAID.

Nyabasa, M., & Peng, Z. (2024). The impacts of green credit financing on climate change in Zimbabwe. *Open Access Library Journal*, *11*, 1–16. https://doi.org/10.4236/oalib.1111512

Patton, M. (2015). *Qualitative research and evaluation methods* (4th ed.). Sage.

Pavlova, E., & Gvetadze, S. (2023). Female access to finance: A survey of literature. *Journal of Financial Economics*, *142*(1), 1–22.

Ritchie, J., & Spencer, L. (1994). *Qualitative data analysis for applied policy research* (pp. 173–194). Routledge.

Setzer, J., & Vanhala, L. (2020). Climate change litigation: A review of trends and directions. *Wiley Interdisciplinary Reviews: Climate Change*, *11*(3), e660. https://doi.org/10.1002/wcc.660

Transparency International. (n.d.). *Annual report*. https://www.transparency.org.uk

United Nations Department of Economic and Social Affairs. (2024). *United Nations statistical yearbook*. ISBN (PDF) 9789213588642.

United Nations. (2015). *Paris agreement*. https://unfccc.int/process-andmeetings/the-paris-agreement

World Bank. (2021). *Accelerating climate-resilient and low-carbon development: The Africa climate business plan (second phase) – Strategy note*. https://openknowledge.worldbank.org/handle/10986/36386

Yin, R. K. (2017). *Case study research and applications: Design and methods* (6th ed.). Sage.

Zimbabwe National Statistics Agency (ZIMSTAT). (2019). *2019 Labour Force and Child Labour Survey (LFCLS)*. https://Zimstat.co.zw/mics-2019

Chapter 4

Gender, Climate, and Finance in Africa: Strategies for a More Equitable Future

Anthonia Folasade Ibitoye

Centre for Study of Race, Gender and Class, University of Johannesburg, South Africa

Abstract

This chapter examines the complex relationships between gender, climate, and finance in Africa, highlighting the inequalities that limit marginalised groups' access to climate change mitigation and adaptation resources. Existing policies and institutional frameworks are analysed, assessing the implementation of global frameworks and agreements such as the Green Climate Fund (GCF) and the African Union's Agenda 2063. This study aims to assess the intersectional dynamics of gender, climate vulnerability, and access to financial services across three African countries namely Kenya, Senegal, and South Africa, using selected World Development Indicators (WDIs). The study's findings reveal persistent barriers to equitable access for women and highlight innovative financing mechanisms, such as green bonds and digital financial tools that could enhance women's participation. This research also examines intersectional factors, including race, ethnicity, and socio-economic status, that exacerbate the vulnerability of certain populations to climate-related economic challenges. Using descriptive statistics and visual representations, disparities in access to climate finance are illustrated. This chapter aims to provide evidence-based insights to inform policy and practice, fostering an interdisciplinary dialogue that addresses gender inequalities in climate finance across Africa. Bridging the gaps in climate finance will promote more inclusive and equitable climate change mitigation and adaptation strategies. These three countries were purposefully selected because they represent diverse subregions of Africa with differing levels of economic development, financial inclusion, and climate vulnerability, providing a balanced comparative perspective.

Keywords: Gender inequality; climate change mitigation; adaptation strategies; intersectionality; digital finance tools; green bonds; climate justice; sustainable development

Gender and Climate Finance in Africa: Addressing Inequalities and Bridging Gaps, 57–76

doi:10.1108/978-1-83742-085-820261004

1. Introduction

The intersection of gender, climate, and finance is pivotal in addressing the unique vulnerabilities faced by women, particularly in African contexts, where socio-economic disparities are pronounced. Women's roles as managers of natural resources and their unique experiences with climate change necessitate inclusive frameworks that not only acknowledge but also actively integrate gender considerations into climate finance policies. This approach is vital to advancing sustainable development goals and achieving equitable climate action across the continent. Given the backdrop of international commitments, such as the Paris Agreement, and regional frameworks like the African Union's Agenda 2063, there is a need for a structured examination of existing policies and institutional mechanisms designed to support gender-responsive climate finance in Africa.

Despite international pledges to incorporate gender considerations into climate finance, the reality on ground reflects substantial shortcomings in policy frameworks. The GCF Gender Policy, established to promote gender equality and empower women in climate action, offers a foundational guideline. However, its effectiveness in various African nations remains contingent on local adaptation and enforcement of gender-responsive policies. Some countries have made strides; for example, Rwanda has integrated gender considerations into its national climate strategy, recognising women's contributions to agricultural sustainability and climate resilience (Hirsch, 2018). However, such national frameworks must be developed and supported across all African nations to create a cohesive approach that addresses gender-specific climate vulnerabilities.

The African Union's Agenda 2063 emphasises inclusive growth and sustainable development while explicitly acknowledging the need to leverage women's participation in all sectors. The various frameworks outlined in Agenda 2063, such as the African Regional Strategy for Disaster Risk Reduction, provide a roadmap for integrating gender into disaster risk reduction and climate resilience initiatives (African Union, 2015). However, the success of these policies depends on their domestic implementation, effective monitoring, and the establishment of accountability mechanisms at both national and local levels.

The intersection of gender and climate finance in Africa is a critical area of research that seeks to understand how financial resources are allocated and utilised in the context of climate change, particularly concerning gender inequalities. This study aims to explore the dynamics of climate finance in Africa, focusing on how gender considerations are integrated into funding mechanisms and the implications for women and marginalised communities. This chapter examines various climate finance mechanisms, including international funds such as the GCF and regional initiatives. It aims to assess how these mechanisms incorporate gender-responsive approaches and the extent to which they address the specific needs of women and vulnerable populations (Baker et al., 2018). The study also evaluates the impact of climate finance on gender equality in Africa. This includes analysing case studies where climate finance has been directed towards projects that empower women, enhance their resilience to climate change, and promote sustainable livelihoods.

In addition, this chapter identifies barriers that women face in accessing climate finance. Based on the findings, the chapter proposes actionable recommendations for policymakers, financial institutions, and civil society organisations to enhance the integration of gender considerations in climate finance. The chapter also reviews existing policies and frameworks at national and regional levels that govern climate finance and gender equality by assessing the effectiveness of these policies in promoting gender-responsive climate action and identify gaps that need to be addressed (UN Women, 2020). Some of the identified challenges experienced by women in accessing climate finance include institutional, cultural, and economic obstacles that hinder women's participation in climate-related projects and decision-making processes (Oxfam, 2019). This study assesses the intersectional dynamics of gender, climate vulnerability, and access to financial services across three African countries namely Kenya, Senegal, and South Africa, using selected WDIs. These three countries were purposefully selected because they represent diverse sub-regions of Africa with differing levels of economic development, financial inclusion, and climate vulnerability, providing a balanced comparative perspective.

The significance of this study lies in its potential to contribute to the understanding of how gender dynamics influence climate finance in Africa with emphasis on Kenya, Senegal, and South Africa, and to inform policies that promote gender equality in climate action. By addressing the inequalities and gaps in climate finance, the research aims to contribute to a more equitable and sustainable future for all, particularly for women and marginalised communities who are disproportionately affected by climate change. The findings will not only enhance the understanding of gender dynamics in climate finance but also provide actionable recommendations for promoting gender equality in climate action across the continent.

2. Research Objectives, Questions, and Indicators

2.1. Objective 1

To assess gender disparities in access to financial services and resources in selected African countries.

- *RQ 1*: How does access to formal financial services differ between men and women in selected African countries?
- *WDI*: Account ownership at a financial institution or with a mobile-money-service provider (% of population ages 15+) – female and male.

- *Statistical tools/charts*:
  - Descriptive statistics (mean, percentage gap).
  - Line chart (male vs female account ownership by country).

2.2. Objective 2

To evaluate the impact of climate vulnerability on women's livelihoods and economic participation.

- *RQ 2*: What is the relationship between climate-related shocks and the economic activity of women in agriculture and informal sectors?
- *WDI*: Employment in agriculture, female (% of female employment) (modelled ILO estimate).
- (Optional complement: ND-GAIN Climate Vulnerability Index for broader context).
- *Statistical tools/charts*:
  - ANOVA: The ANOVA test was employed to determine whether mean differences across the three countries are statistically significant, making it suitable for comparative multi-country analysis. The ANOVA is typically used to compare three or more sample means to determine if they are statistically significance.
  - Cluster bar chart.

3. Case Studies on Successful Gender-inclusive Climate Finance Initiatives

In recent years, there were numerous projects that have validated the significance of gender-inclusive climate finance in promoting sustainable development and addressing climate change. These case studies offer precious insights into the potential effect of targeting women and marginalised agencies in climate finance packages and spotlight the advantages of advancing gender equality in environmental investment. The ladies' climate fund offers financing and technical help to ladies-led community companies to put into effect climate edition projects, empowering women to take management roles in weather resilience efforts and enhancing their resilience to weather trade influences. The ladies' climate fund in Uganda is an example of a gender-inclusive climate finance initiative (UN Women, 2018).

There is a fund on women-led tasks that deal with weather alternate and promote sustainable development in susceptible groups that specialise in women as beneficiaries of climate finance; the Gender-Responsive Weather Fund has expanded women's participation in decision-making processes, improved access to resources and technologies, and better community resilience to weather alternate (Rehman et al., 2026). This is a gender inclusive climate finance initiatives known as Gender-Responsive Weather Fund in Bangladesh (UNDP, 2018). These case studies demonstrate the positive effects of gender-inclusive climate finance tasks in advancing sustainable development and addressing weather trade by means of focusing on women and marginalised organisations in environmental funding packages.

4. Assessment of Alternative Financing Models to Enhance Women's Participation in Climate Finance in Africa

In recent years, the intersection of gender and climate finance has garnered growing attention, especially in the context of Africa, where women are disproportionately affected by weather alternate. Addressing these inequalities requires progressive financing models that not only support weather resilience but also additionally empower women economically. This chapter explores alternative financing fashions, which include green bonds, microfinance, and blended finance, and assesses their ability to beautify women's participation in climate finance initiatives throughout the continent.

Green bonds have emerged as a considerable tool for financing environmentally sustainable tasks. These monetary units are designed to elevate finances particularly for projects that have tremendous environmental effects, such as renewable strength, power performance, and sustainable agriculture. In Africa, the inexperienced bond marketplace is still in its infancy; however, it holds vast promise for promoting gender fairness in climate finance. A first-rate example is the issuance of green bonds by the African development bank (AfDB, 2020a), with the objective to mobilise sources for weather-resilient initiatives by integrating gender issues into undertaking selection and implementation for the benefit of women. Moreover, the potential for green bonds to draw institutional buyers can be leveraged to create gender-centred investment opportunities by organising frameworks that prioritise gender-responsive initiatives; inexperienced bonds can serve as a catalyst for growing women's participation in climate finance (World Bank, 2019). However, demanding situations including limited recognition and capacity among girls-led establishments to access those funds have to be addressed to fully recognise this capacity.

Microfinance has long been identified as a powerful device for empowering women, in particular in developing international locations by means of imparting small loans and monetary services to people who lack get entry to traditional banking. Microfinance institutions (MFIs) enable women to put money into sustainable livelihoods and weather-resilient practices. In Africa, wherein women play a vital function in agriculture and natural resource control, microfinance facilitates their participation in weather version and mitigation efforts. Research has proven that women who have access to microfinance are much more likely to invest in environmentally sustainable practices, inclusive of organic farming and water conservation (Kumar & Singh, 2021). As an example, the Grameen bank version, which has been replicated in diverse African countries, demonstrates how microfinance can empower women to adopt sustainable agricultural practices, thereby improving meals protection and resilience to climate alternate. The effectiveness of microfinance in promoting gender equity in climate finance is contingent upon the design of the economic merchandise supplied. MFIs have to make certain that their offerings are tailor-made to the unique desires of women, which include flexible repayment terms and monetary literacy training; additionally, integrating weather training into microfinance applications will improve women's capability to have interaction in weather-resilient practices (UN Women, 2020).

Blended finance is also an alternative financing model that mixes public and personal funding to aid development dreams, and further enhances women's participation in climate finance. This version can leverage philanthropic capital and improvement useful resource to de-hazard investments in gender-responsive weather initiatives, thereby attracting private zone funding. In Africa, blended finance initiatives have proven promise in helping women-led agencies within the renewable power quarter. As an instance, the worldwide surroundings facility (GEF, 2021) has implemented blended finance mechanisms that offer concessional loans to women marketers in easy power, by means of reducing the monetary barriers that women face in accessing capital, combined finance can facilitate their participation in climate finance and sell gender equality. Furthermore, mixed finance can foster partnerships between governments, NGOs, and the non-public sector to create opportunities for women in climate finance. Collaborative efforts can cause the development of gender-responsive rules and investment frameworks that prioritise women's needs and contributions to climate resilience (OECD, 2018).

The assessment of alternative financing reveals huge capacity for enhancing women's participation in climate finance in Africa. By addressing the precise challenges that women face in accessing financial sources, these models can empower girls to interact in weather-resilient practices and make a contribution to sustainable development. To completely comprehend this capacity, it's far vital to implement supportive rules, financial literacy, and foster partnerships among stakeholders in developing gender-responsive investment frameworks that prioritise women's needs. As Africa maintains to grapple with the effects of climate change, integrating gender concerns into climate finance will be essential for attaining equitable and sustainable results.

5. Role of Digital Financial Inclusion in Bridging Gender Gaps in Climate Finance

In the context of climate finance, gender disparities remain a considerable barrier to accomplishing equitable and sustainable improvement in Africa. Leach et al. (2025) opine that women are considered as managers of natural resources, but they face numerous demanding situations in gaining access to monetary assets necessary for climate edition and mitigation. Digital monetary inclusion has emerged as a transformative device that can bridge these gender gaps by permitting women to participate more absolutely in climate finance projects. This chapter explores the function of digital financial inclusion in improving women's access to climate finance in Africa, highlighting recent developments and evidence.

Digital financial inclusion refers to the usage of digital technology to offer financial contributions to underserved populations, particularly individuals who lack entry to traditional banking systems. In Africa, mobile cash structures have revolutionised the economic landscape, permitting individuals to conduct transactions, shop, and access credit score through their mobile gadgets. Consistent with the GSMA (2021), cellular money bills in Sub-Saharan Africa reached 469 million in 2020, with women representing a widespread portion of this boom. This shift closer to virtual finance presents the possibility to curb the gender disparities that exist in climate finance. Digital economic inclusion bridges gender gaps in climate finance by improving women's admittance to monetary assets. Traditional financial establishments often impose stringent requirements that women, mainly the ones in rural areas, go through. Virtual platforms, then again, can provide opportunity for microloans and savings merchandise which can be brought through cell packages, permitting women to manipulate their finances and invest in climate-resilient practices. A study of the International Finance Corporation (IFC, 2021) determined that ladies who use digital monetary offerings are more likely to put money into sustainable agricultural practices, including natural farming and water conservation. Through presenting ladies with the monetary manner to adopt these practices, digital economic inclusion empowers them economically and also contributes to their weather resilience.

Virtual financial inclusion also performs a critical function in enhancing economic literacy among women, which is vital for powerful participation in climate finance (Guerra-Leal et al., 2021). Many women lack the knowledge and skills that are vital to navigate economic structures, leading to underutilisation. Digital structures provide educational resources that empower ladies to make informed financial choices.

Digital monetary inclusion also helps in the improvement of gender-responsive financial merchandise in the context of climate finance (Tailor 2024). Monetary establishments can leverage information analytics to recognise the specific challenges faced by women. As an instance, insurance merchandise that covers climate-associated risks, which includes crop failure due to drought or flooding, can be tailor-made to satisfy the desires of female farmers (AfDB, 2020). Moreover, digital systems can facilitate peer-to-peer lending and network-based totally financing models that empower girls to guide each other in accessing climate finance. By means of creating networks of women entrepreneurs and farmers, those structures can foster collaboration and knowledge sharing, in the long run enhancing women's capability to interact in weather-resilient practices (Kumar & Singh, 2021).

Even as digital economic inclusion holds superb promise for bridging gender gaps in climate finance, numerous demanding situations have to be addressed. First, the digital divide stays a massive barrier, especially in rural areas where access to era and internet connectivity is restrained. Efforts must be made to ensure that women in those areas can access digital financial services. Second, there is a need for strong regulatory frameworks that shield ladies from capacity dangers associated with digital finance, which includes fraud and statistics private concerns. Policymakers need to prioritise the improvement of policies that promote safe and inclusive virtual financial ecosystems (OECD, 2021). It is also important to engage women in the design and implementation of virtual monetary offerings by inculcating women in the decision-making procedure; financial institutions can make certain that the goods and offerings developed in reality meet their desires and options. Climate finance is a critical aspect in the global reaction to climate exchange, specifically in Africa, where the effects of climate trade are felt acutely; however, access to climate finance is not uniform; it is motivated by means of various intersectional factors, along with race, ethnicity, and socio-monetary repute. Know-how those dynamics is crucial for creating equitable climate finance mechanisms that deal with the desires of the most inclined populations.

6. Institutional Mechanisms for Gender-responsive Climate Finance

Institutional mechanisms play an important role in the execution of gender-responsive climate finance initiatives. The effectiveness of climate finance institutions frequently hinges on their capability to interact with nearby groups, mainly women, who are important stakeholders in weather motion. Establishments such as the African improvement financial institution (AfDB) and various united international location bodies have evolved gender-touchy frameworks geared towards fostering gender equality in climate projects. The AfDB's (2019) Integrated Approach to weather alternate seeks to deal with gender disparities through centred investments in sectors wherein women are disproportionately affected. However, participatory techniques in task design and implementation to determine the effectiveness of interventions through ensuring that women's voices are heard and prioritised (Arora-Jonsson, 2016).

Despite the existence of international frameworks and regional policies, significant challenges impede the practical implementation of gender-responsive climate finance initiatives. One major challenge rests in the lack of robust data and monitoring systems that disaggregate information by gender. Limited access to gender-sensitive data hampers the ability of policymakers and practitioners to design targeted interventions that address the specific needs of women (UN Women, 2021). The Gender-Responsive Climate Action Project suggests that improved data collection and analysis can help inform better policy decisions and resource allocation. Additionally, there is often a disconnect between policymakers and grassroots organisations. While national policies might reflect gender considerations, local communities may remain unaware of such policies or lack the means to access available resources. Strengthening collaborations between governmental bodies, civil society organisations, and local communities is essential to bridge this gap. Women's groups must be adequately represented in decision-making forums to ensure that their needs and perspectives are incorporated into climate finance strategies (MacGregor, 2021).

To address these challenges and advance gender-responsive climate finance, innovative strategies must be implemented. One approach is the establishment of dedicated funding mechanisms aimed specifically at empowering women in climate action. Such mechanisms will provide direct support for women's initiatives, enhancing their roles as leaders and decision-makers in climate resilience efforts. In addition, integrating gender considerations into all climate finance projects regardless of sector will help ensure that women benefit from funding. Capacity building is another critical strategy. Training programmes designed to empower women and enhance their technical skills in climate resilience and adaptation initiatives can bolster their capacity to engage in climate finance effectively. Programmes that promote women's leadership in climate governance can also enhance gender representation and ensure that women's voices are central in climate action discussions (Dankelman, 2020).

7. Exploration of Barriers to Equitable Access to Climate Finance for Women and Marginalised Groups

Climate finance plays a critical position in assisting countries adapt to and mitigate the influences of weather trade. However, access to climate finance is often unequal, with women and marginalised organisations dealing with enormous obstacles in getting access to those budgets. Numerous factors make a contribution to this inequality, which include socio-economic constraints, lack of education, discriminatory guidelines and practices, and restricted illustration in selection-making processes. According to Haider (2026), women face lots of challenges on environmental issues due to cultural norms that prioritise male gender. One of the primary barriers to equitable access to climate finance for women and marginalised groups is their limited get admittance to monetary resources and assets (Galabuzi, 2018). Women, specifically, often face challenges inclusive of decrease incomes, constrained get access to credit score, and less property as compared to men, making it tough for them to invest in climate-resilient technology and practices (UN Women, 2020). This lack of monetary sources hinders their potential to conform to the influences of climate exchange correctly.

Discriminatory rules and practices additionally contribute to the inequality in access to climate finance. Moreover, ladies and marginalised companies often face discriminatory rules and practices that save them from having access to climate finance. Restrained education also poses considerable barriers for women and marginalised groups (UNEP, 2016). Many women lack knowledge and abilities to navigate the complex software tactics (UNFCCC, 2017). This lack of facts and ability-constructing aid in addition hinders their ability to get right of entry to these finances and put in force powerful climate model tasks. Addressing these obstacles to equitable access to climate finance for women and marginalised organisations requires a multi-faceted method. Governments and global companies have to cast off discriminatory regulations and practices that prevent women from accessing economic assets and property. Moreover, cultural norms and stereotypes may restrict women's participation in choice-making methods related to climate finance, similarly marginalising them from getting access to these funds (Fernandez & Nambi, 2020). By addressing these obstacles and promoting gender equality in climate finance, we are able to ensure that women and marginalised corporations will not be left behind within the fight against climate alternate.

8. Strategies for Empowering Women as Key Stakeholders in Climate Finance Decision-making Processes

This section concludes the conceptual discussion and bridges to the subsequent analytical sections, linking theory with the empirical examination of gender and climate finance.

The intersection of gender and climate finance in Africa presents demanding situations and possibilities. Women, who are disproportionately stricken by climate exchange, often lack illustration in selection-making strategies associated with climate finance. Empowering women as key stakeholders is important for creating equitable and effective climate finance techniques. This section explores various techniques to enhance women's participation in climate finance selection-making procedures, making sure that their voices are heard and their needs are addressed.

One of the foundational techniques for empowering women in climate finance is the development and implementation of gender-responsive guidelines. These policies will explicitly apprehend the particular demanding situations women face in the context of climate alternate and displacement. Following the African Union's agenda 2063 emphasises on the significance of gender equality and women's empowerment in attaining sustainable development (African Union, 2015). Furthermore, integrating gender analysis into climate finance checks will assist in empowering women as stakeholders.

Capacity building and education are crucial for empowering women to interact efficiently in climate finance decision-making. Training applications that focus on monetary literacy, assignment management, and negotiation capabilities will also equip women with the vital tools to participate in discussions. Organisations such as the United Nations Development Programme (UNDP, 2020) have applied tasks aimed at enhancing women's capabilities in climate finance control. Additionally, mentorship applications that connect women with skilled leaders in climate finance will offer precious guidance and help. These programmes will help women to navigate the complexities of climate finance and build networks that will have effect on in choice-making strategies.

Constructing sturdy networks and coalitions among women can increase their voices in climate finance discussions. Collaborative efforts can decorate advocacy and create a unified front for addressing gender inequalities in climate finance. Women's organisations, consisting of the African Women's Development Fund (AWDF, 2021), play a vital role in mobilising resources and facilitating talk among women stakeholders. While empowering women is essential, inclusion of men as allies in the combat for gender equality in climate finance is similarly vital. Men can play a vital function in challenging gender norms and advocating for women's participation in choice-making processes. Projects that promote gender equity in climate finance ought to include recognition-raising campaigns targeting men and emphasising the blessings of inclusive choice-making. Applications such as the 'MenEngage Alliance' awareness on involving men in gender equality efforts, highlighting how their help can result in more equitable effects in climate finance (MenEngage, 2019) can be used to foster a tradition of collaboration between the male and female genders.

Access to monetary resources is also an important aspect in empowering women as stakeholders in climate finance. Women often face huge obstacles in having access to credit and investment for weather-associated initiatives. Monetary establishments ought to develop gender-sensitive financing mechanisms that cater for women. This consists of imparting microfinance alternatives, grants, and coffee-interest loans designed for girls-led initiatives. The AfDB (2021a) has diagnosed the importance of gender-responsive financing and has initiated programmes aimed towards growing women's access to financial sources. By supplying centred economic aid, establishments can permit women to put into effect climate model and mitigation initiatives, thereby enhancing their function in climate finance selection-making.

To ensure that women's participation in climate finance decision-making is significant, it is vital to establish robust monitoring and assessment frameworks. These frameworks will verify the effectiveness of gender-responsive regulations and initiatives, tracking progress towards gender equality in climate finance by using gathered statistics on women's participation and outcomes, stakeholders can discover gaps and areas for development. Such information can provide insights into the effect of climate finance on ladies and assist shape future strategies to decorate their participation. Flowing from above, empowering women as key stakeholders in climate finance decision-making approaches is critical for addressing gender inequalities and improving the effectiveness of climate finance projects in Africa. With the aid of promoting gender-responsive regulations, imparting potential-constructing possibilities, strengthening networks, encouraging men as allies, ensuring access to financial resources, and enforcing strong monitoring frameworks, stakeholders can create an inclusive environment that amplifies women's voices. As weather exchange continues to pose vast challenges, prioritising women's participation in climate finance is not always most effective a matter of equity, however, additionally a crucial step in the direction of building resilient and sustainable groups.

9. Intersectionality and Climate Finance

Building upon the preceding conceptual insights, this section connects them with empirical analysis, illustrating how overlapping identities such as gender, class, and ethnicity influence women's access to climate finance.

9.1. Intersectionality and Weather Finance

Intersectionality, a term coined by an American critical legal race scholar Kimberlé Crenshaw, refers to how numerous social identities along with race, gender, and class interact to create precise modes of discrimination and privilege within the context of climate finance (Hankivsky, 2022b). This framework is important because it examines how women, especially the ones from marginalised ethnic backgrounds, frequently face compounded challenges that restrict their ability to comfortable climate finance. With the aid of the United Nations Environment Programme (UNEP, 2021), women in Africa are disproportionately affected by weather exchange, and they lack entry to financial assets that might help them adapt and mitigate its influences. Race and ethnicity play giant roles in figuring out access to climate finance in Africa. Traditionally marginalised corporations, inclusive of indigenous populations and ethnic minorities, frequently lack representation in selection-making methods associated with climate finance. This exclusion can lead to a misalignment between the funding priorities of climate finance establishments and the actual needs of these groups. AfDB (2020b) cites that many smallholder farmers, who are predominantly from marginalised ethnic organisations, find it difficult to navigate the technical requirements for getting access to climate finance. This situation underscores the need for more inclusive investment mechanisms that consider the specific demanding situations confronted with the aid of those groups. The International Institute for Environment and Development (IIED) (2019) also highlights that indigenous groups in Africa regularly have conventional know-how and practices which are vital for weather resilience but are regularly not noted in funding allocations.

Furthermore, systemic racism occurs in the bureaucratic methods of climate finance establishments, in which complex application tactics and stringent eligibility criteria disproportionately disadvantage racial and ethnic minorities. For example, a report via the socio-financial popularity is another important challenge confronting access to climate finance. Low-income communities often lack the essential sources, with technical know-how and monetary literacy, to apply for and control climate finance efficiently. In addition, socio-economic inequalities intensify the consequences of weather trade, for instance, communities with limited economic resources are unable to invest in weather-resilient infrastructure or sustainable agricultural practices, making them more vulnerable to climate-related shocks. A document by the UNDP (2022) emphasises the importance of integrating socio-financial concerns into climate finance techniques to ensure that most susceptible populations get hold of the aid they need. A 2021 study also affirms that households inside the lowest earnings brackets are less likely to get hold of climate finance aid, in spite of being very prone to weather impacts (World Bank, 2021).

To respond to the highlighted inequalities and bridge the gaps in climate finance access, numerous techniques can be carried out. First, it is essential to undertake an intersectional approach in climate finance rules and programmes, this means recognising the various needs and also enhancing ability-constructing projects. Imparting education and assets to marginalised communities will empower them to navigate the complexities of climate finance. A GEF (2020b) record highlights the fulfilment of potential-building applications in increasing the participation of women and marginalised companies in climate finance projects. Fostering collaboration between governments, civil society, and the private region will create an extra inclusive climate finance prospect.

Addressing the intersectional factors that influence access to climate finance in Africa is critical for creating equitable and effective climate solutions. By recognising the roles of race, ethnicity, and socio-financial repute, stakeholders can broaden focused strategies that empower marginalised groups and ensure that climate finance gets to individuals who need it maximally.

10. Methodology

Following the conceptual discussions, this chapter employs quantitative techniques to analyse gender disparities in climate finance access across the selected countries.

This chapter employs quantitative research methodology by relying on secondary data with the use of numerical data, statistical analysis, and objective measurements. Data are collected from AfDB, World Bank Fender Data Portal so as to do justice to the objectives of this study. The analyses are divided into sections as in Tables 4.1 and 4.2.

Table 4.1. Account Ownership at a Financial Institution or with a Mobile-Money-Service Provider (% of Population Ages 15+) – Female and Male.

Year	Kenya	Senegal	South Africa
2011	42.34	5.82	53.65
2014	74.66	15.42	70.32
2017	81.57	42.34	69.22
2021	79.2	55.96	85.38

Source: World Bank (2025).

Table 4.2. Descriptive Statistics of Account Ownership at a Financial Institution or with a Mobile-Money-Service Provider (% of Population Ages 15+) – Female and Male.

Analysis and Interpretation of Objective 1: Gender Disparities in Financial Access

Descriptive Statistics Summary

Country	Mean (%)	Std. Dev.	Min (%)	Max (%)
Kenya	69.44	18.29	42.34	81.57
Senegal	29.89	23.26	5.82	55.96
South Africa	69.64	12.96	53.65	85.38

Source: World Bank (2025).

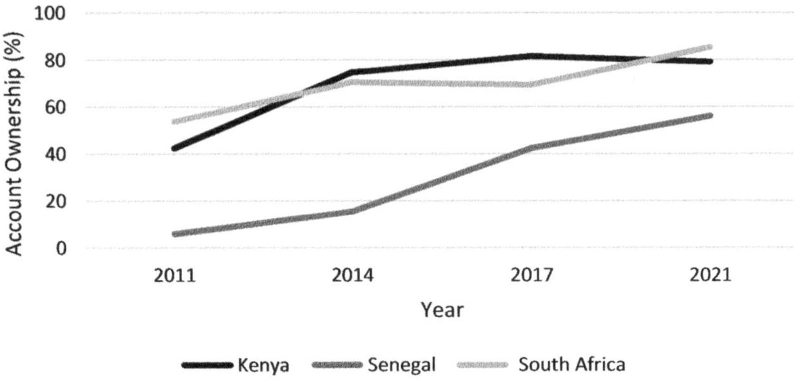

Fig. 4.1. Line Chart of Account Ownership at a Financial Institution or with a Mobile-Money-Service Provider (% of Population Ages 15+). *Notes*: The chart shows the progression of female account ownership (% of population ages 15+) in Kenya, Senegal, and South Africa from 2011 to 2021. These three countries were purposefully selected because they represent diverse sub-regions of Africa with differing levels of economic development, financial inclusion, and climate vulnerability, providing a balanced comparative perspective.

10.1. Data Presentation, Analysis, and Interpretations

KE Kenya:

- Significant growth from **42.34% (2011)** to **81.57% (2017)**, then a slight dip to **79.2% (2021)**.
- **Average ownership**: ~69.44%
- This high rate reflects strong mobile-money penetration (e.g., M-PESA).

SN Senegal:

- Lowest starting point in 2011 (**5.82%**) but remarkable growth over time to **55.96% (2021)**.
- **Highest average yearly growth rate**: ~**16.7 percentage points**.
- Indicates increasing but still lagging access compared to others.

ZA South Africa:

- Consistently high account ownership across all years.
- Grew from **53.65% (2011)** to **85.38% (2021)**.
- **Average ownership**: ~69.64%, similar to Kenya but with steadier growth.

From Fig. 4.1, it becomes apparent that Senegal has the widest gender gap but also the fastest improvement, while Kenya and South Africa show greater financial inclusion for women, especially post-2014. Kenya's progress was mobile-finance driven, while South Africa benefitted from formal banking access. This implies that countries with strong digital infrastructure and financial innovation (like Kenya) lead in gendered financial inclusion. Policy efforts and financial education also contributed to Senegal's improvements, though a significant gap remains. Despite similar average access rates, South Africa's financial inclusion is more stable than Kenya's, whose 2021 rate slightly declined (see Tables 4.3 and 4.4).

11. Analysis and Interpretation of Objective 2: Climate Vulnerability and Women's Economic Participation

- The F-value = 68.22 is significantly greater than the F-critical = 3.354.
- The P-value < 0.05 indicates statistical significance.

Conclusion: There is a significant difference in the average impact of climate vulnerability on women's livelihoods and economic participation among Kenya, Senegal, and South Africa. These three countries were purposefully selected because they represent diverse sub-regions of Africa with differing levels of economic development, financial inclusion, and climate vulnerability, providing a balanced comparative perspective.

From the analysis, climate vulnerability and women's economic participation (see Tables 4.3 and 4.4, and Fig. 4.2), Kenya has the highest average (37.04) with the least variance, indicating a consistent and relatively high exposure of women's livelihoods to climate risks. Senegal has a lower average (21.30) but the highest variance (31.79), showing uneven impacts of climate vulnerability while South Africa shows the lowest average impact (18.33), but with moderate variability.

Table 4.3. Employment in Agriculture, Female (% of Female Employment) (Modelled ILO Estimate).

Country Name	Kenya	Senegal	South Africa
2014	40.89645	29.53407	14.68190399
2015	39.83525	26.94008	16.06019422
2016	38.85411	30.2829	16.27879104
2017	37.89609	23.08229	17.59193104
2018	36.80006	16.77371	16.51410667
2019	35.73935	17.72426	17.3811263
2020	35.61694	17.76842	22.81615849
2021	35.66789	17.59101	22.40276809
2022	34.80057	16.78994	19.84994776
2023	34.24907	16.52321	19.76736188

Source: World Bank (2025).

Table 4.4. Anova Table Showing the Difference Between the Means Impact of Climate Vulnerability on Women's Livelihood and Economic Participation Among Kenya, Senegal, and South Africa.

Anova: Single Factor

Summary

Groups	*Count*	*Sum*	*Average*	*Variance*
Kenya	10	370.3558	37.03558	5.018964
Senegal	10	213.0099	21.30099	31.7933
South Africa	10	183.3443	18.33443	7.611085

Source of Variation	*SS*	*df*	*MS*	*F*	*P-value*	*F crit*
Between Groups	2,020.369	2	1,010.185	68.21985	< 0.05	3.354131
Within Groups	399.8101	27	14.80778			
Total	2,420.179	29				

Source: World Bank (2025).

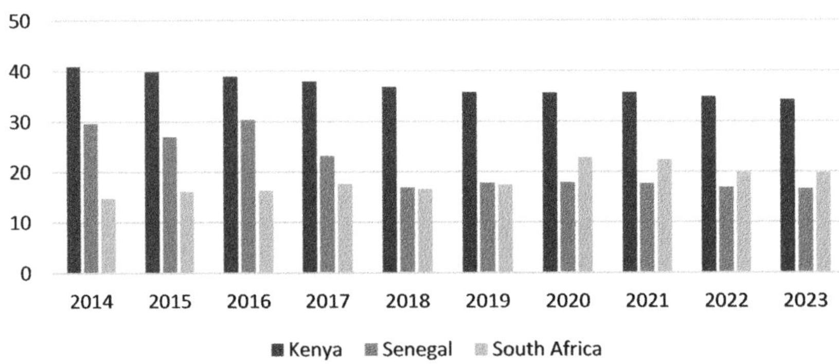

Fig. 4.2. Cluster Bar Chart of Employment in Agriculture, Female (% of Female Employment) (Modelled ILO Estimate).

This implies that women in Kenya are consistently more vulnerable to climate impacts, potentially due to agriculture-dependence and limited adaptive infrastructure. In Senegal, vulnerability is heterogeneous, as a result of regional and socio-economic disparities while South Africa, with more developed infrastructure and climate adaptation systems, shows relatively lower vulnerability, although disparities still exist. Targeted Interventions are needed based on each country's profile as evident above. Kenya should support women's adaptive capacities (e.g., climate-resilient agriculture, access to water, insurance schemes), for Senegal, interventions should be region-specific due to the wide variability while South Africa should focus on maintaining current adaptation while closing localised gaps in rural or under-resourced areas.

12. Conclusions and Recommendations

This study assessed the intersectional dynamics of gender, climate vulnerability, and access to financial services across three African countries namely Kenya, Senegal, and South Africa, using selected WDI. Key findings under each objective reveal critical patterns: On gender disparities in financial access, analysis of the indicator shows that account ownership at a financial institution or with a mobile-money-service provider (% of population ages 15+), it further reveals that Kenya and South Africa have achieved relatively high financial inclusion for women, averaging over 69% while Senegal lags significantly but has made remarkable progress, increasing from just 5.82% in 2011 to 55.96% in 2021. The Bar chart and trend analysis revealed that digital finance innovations and policy shifts contributed to these gains, especially in Kenya. Conclusively, while financial inclusion is rising, gender gaps persist, especially in lower-income or less digitised economies like Senegal. These three countries were purposefully selected because they represent diverse sub-regions of Africa with differing levels of economic development, financial inclusion, and climate vulnerability, providing a balanced comparative perspective.

As regards the second objective on climate vulnerability and women's economic participation, the ANOVA analysis of the impact of climate vulnerability on women's livelihoods showed statistically significant differences across countries ($F = 68.22$, $P < 0.05$). From the analysis, Kenya has the highest average climate impact on women (37.04%) with low variance, indicating consistently high exposure, Senegal showed moderate average exposure (21.30%) but very high variance, suggesting uneven regional vulnerability. While South Africa recorded the lowest average exposure (18.33%), reflecting better adaptive infrastructure, though challenges remain in marginalised areas. The author concludes that women's economic resilience to climate shocks is highly context-dependent and women in agriculture-dependent and infrastructure-poor regions face disproportionately high climate risks. While employment rates do not differ significantly across countries statistically, the real-world disparities highlight the ongoing structural barriers, including gender norms and host-country policies that shape migrant women's labour experiences. The ANOVA test was employed to determine whether mean differences across the three countries are statistically significant, making it suitable for comparative multi-country analysis.

This chapter on gender, climate, and finance in Africa: Strategies for a more equitable future examined case studies on successful gender-inclusive climate finance initiatives in Africa and also assessed alternative financing models to enhance women's participation in climate finance in Africa followed by the role of digital financial inclusion in bridging gender gaps in climate finance while the institutional mechanisms for gender-responsive climate finance was also reviewed. From the findings of this study, gender disparities have been identified. The analyses highlight significant gender disparities in access to climate finance, with women facing unique barriers due to socio-economic factors, cultural norms, and institutional limitations.

Flowing from above, this study recommends that digital financial inclusion should be enhanced by expanding mobile banking initiatives in countries like Senegal, building on Kenya's M-PESA model. There should be promotion of gender-sensitive financial literacy programmes targeting rural and low-income women while regulatory reforms should ensure that women can access, control, and benefit from financial services equally. In addition, gender should be integrated into climate adaptation policies by embedding gender-responsive planning in national climate action frameworks, increasing investment in climate-resilient livelihoods, especially in agriculture, where women constitute a major workforce and also strengthening early-warning systems and microinsurance schemes tailored to women's needs. Furthermore, there should be improvement in gender data collection and disaggregation; by so doing, governments and international bodies should collect sex-disaggregated data on climate impact, financial services, and employment and also invest in longitudinal studies to track the evolving impact of climate on women's economic participation. Governments in Africa should also promote inclusive labour market policies by facilitating formalisation of work for migrant and domestic workers, providing legal protections and social safety nets for women working in precarious or informal sectors, especially migrants and tailoring employment programmes to support upskilling and reskilling of women in climate-affected regions. Lastly, cross-sectoral partnerships should be strengthened by encouraging collaboration between government agencies, financial institutions, civil society, and climate actors to promote integrated gender and climate solutions and also mobilising climate finance specifically targeted at women entrepreneurs and farmers to foster long-term resilience.

References

African Development Bank (AfDB). (2019). *Integrated approach to climate change*. https://www.afdb.org/en/topics-and-sectors/sectors/climate-change

African Development Bank (AfDB). (2020a). *Gender strategy 2020–2024*. https://www.afdb.org

African Development Bank (AfDB). (2020b). *Green bonds: Financing climate resilience in Africa*. https://www.afdb.org
African Development Bank (AfDB). (2020c). *Gender and climate change: A review of the evidence*. https://www.afdb.org
African Development Bank (AfDB). (2021a). *Enhancing financial literacy among women entrepreneurs in Africa*. https://www.afdb.org
African Development Bank (AfDB). (2021b). *Empowering women in climate-resilient agriculture*. https://www.afdb.org
African Women's Development Fund (AWDF). (2020). *Capacity building for women's organizations in Africa*. https://awdf.org.
African Women's Development Fund (AWDF). (2021). *Empowering women for climate justice in Africa*. https://awdf.org.
African Union. (2015). *Agenda 2063: The Africa we want*. https://au.int/en/agenda2063
Arora-Jonsson, S. (2013). *Gender, development and environmental governance: Theorizing connections*. https://doi.org/10.4324/9780203106808
Baker, S., Newell, P., & Phillips, J. (2018). The political economy of climate finance. *Climate Policy, 18*(4), 447–461
Dankelman, I. (2020). Gender and climate finance: Bridging the gap. *Environmental Science & Policy, 107,* 1–8.
Fernandez, L., & Nambi, P. (2020). Gender mainstreaming in climate finance: Challenges and opportunities. *Journal of Gender, Agriculture, and Climate Change, 1*(1), 78–92.
Galabuzi, G. (2018). Gender, climate change, and adaptation. *African Journal of Environmental Science and Technology, 12*(7), 247–254.
GSMA (Groupe Spec. Mob. Assoc.). (2021). *Mobile money regulation index*. GSMA.
Guerra-Leal, E. M., Arredondo-Trapero, F. G., &Vázquez-Parra, J. C. (2021). Financial inclusion and digital banking on an emergent economy. *Review of Behavioral Finance, 15*(2), 257–272.
Haider, Z., Rocklöv, J., Berry, P., Jobanputra, K., Ebi, K. L., Ngo, T. A., & Schwerdtle, P. N. (2026). Barriers to climate finance for local communities. *Environmental Science & Policy, 89*, 1–10.
Hankivsky, O. (2022). *Intersectionality 101*. The Institute for Intersectionality Research & Policy, SFU.
Hirsch, A. (2018). Rwanda: Leading the way on gender and climate. *International Journal of Climate Change Strategies and Management, 10*(4), 669–686.
International Finance Corporation (IFC). (2021). *Digital financial services and women's economic empowerment*. https://www.ifc.org
International Institute for Environment and Development (IIED). (2019). *Indigenous peoples and climate finance: A review of the evidence*. https://www.iied.org
Kumar, A., & Singh, R. (2021). Microfinance and women's empowerment: Evidence from Africa. *Journal of Development Studies, 57*(3), 456–472.
Leach, M., Joekes, S., & Green, C. (2025). *Gender relations and environmental change*. Routledge.
MacGregor, S. (2021). Women and climate change: Voices from the field. *Environmental Politics, 30*(3), 395–413.
MenEngage. (2019). *MenEngage alliance: Engaging men and boys for gender equality*. https://menengage.org.
Organisation for Economic Co-operation and Development (OECD). (2018). *Climate finance and gender equality*. https://www.oecd.org
Organisation for Economic Co-operation and Development (OECD). (2021). *Digital financial inclusion policies*. https://www.oecd.org
Oxfam. (2019). *Gender inequalities and climate finance*. https://www.oxfam.org

Rehman, M. T., Farooq, M. I., Rizvi, S. A. A., & Anis, H. (2026). Climate finance in Pakistan: Access, utilization, and governance challenges. *Pakistan Journal of Social Science Review*, *5*(3), 296–328.

Tailor, N. (2024).Women and digital green finance. In *Fintech and green investment: Transforming challenges into opportunities* (pp. 255–281). Springer.

United Nations Development Programme (UNDP). (2018). *Gender-responsive climate fund: Case study from Bangladesh*. https://www.undp.org

United Nations Development Programme (UNDP). (2020). *Women's leadership in climate change: A global perspective*. https://www.undp.org

United Nations Development Programme (UNDP). (2022). *Climate finance tracking tool*. https://www.undp.org

United Nations Framework Convention on Climate Change (UNFCCC). (2017). *Enhancing women's access to climate finance*. https://unfccc.int

United Nations Environment Programme (UNEP). (2016). *Gender and climate change finance*. https://www.unep.org

United Nations Environment Programme (UNEP). (2021). *Gender and climate change: A global perspective*. https://www.unep.org

UN Women. (2018). *Women's climate fund*. https://www.unwomen.org

UN Women. (2020). *Financing for gender equality*. https://www.unwomen.org

UN Women. (2021). *Gender and climate change*. https://www.unwomen.org

World Bank. (2019). *Green bonds: A tool for climate finance in Africa*. https://www.worldbank.org

World Bank. (2025). https://data.worldbank.org/indicator/FX.OWN.TOTL.ZS

World Bank. (2021). *Climate finance and the poor*. https://www.worldbank.org

Note: All quantitative data were obtained from open-access databases including the WDI (World Bank) and the AfDB Data Portal to ensure transparency and reproducibility.

Chapter 5

Gender Differentials in Climate Impacts: Experience from Nigeria

Adebukola Yewande Daramola

Nigerian Institute of Social and Economic Research (NISER), Ibadan, Nigeria

Abstract

Climate variabilities and its profound impacts on earth systems and livelihoods are widespread globally but are more severe for vulnerable populations. Nigeria is a developing lower middle-income country with low adaptive capacities across most of its populations and systems. An estimated 133 million of the country's 200+ million people are classified multidimensionally poor. Beyond this country-wide vulnerability, deeper vulnerabilities exist for women as they have constrained access to resources, power, and, perhaps more fundamentally, to information. Many of these women are engaged in climate-sensitive sectors such as agriculture or informal enterprise. Consequently, the impacts of climate variability, while are felt by both males and females, further deepen vulnerabilities for the female gender. Further complications and differentials in vulnerability are found among females in the northern and southern divides of the country, while those in urban and rural areas also exhibit peculiar deprivations. The study explores how intersectionalities in demographics deepen vulnerabilities to climate impacts in Nigeria for females, drawing on extant literature, complemented with findings from a previous survey conducted 2023. The survey covered eight states in five of Nigeria's six geopolitical zones. The progression of vulnerability rises sharply from the female demographic (60.2%) to the northern female resident in rural areas, with no formal education, engaged in farming and earning a low income (90%). This confirms findings from extant literature that intersectionalities amplify vulnerabilities. The findings point climate fund managers to the need for intentional beneficiary targeting in dispensing benefits.

Keywords: Climate variability; gender vulnerability; intersectionality; Nigeria; adaptive capacity

Gender and Climate Finance in Africa: Addressing Inequalities and Bridging Gaps, 77–99

doi:10.1108/978-1-83742-085-820261005

Introduction

West Africa is one of the world's most vulnerable regions to climate variability and change. The sub-region experiences warming greater than the global average and this trend is expected to persist with the greatest warming occurring in the Sahel (USAID, 2018). Nigeria, the most populous country in Africa, and indeed in the continent has its own share of vulnerability and risk with climate variability characterised by changing rainfall patterns, drought occurrences, and increasing temperatures. Nigeria has three distinct climatic zones – a tropical wet climate in the south, a tropical savannah climate in much of the central region, and a Sahelian hot and semi-arid zone in the north. All the country's climatic zones are susceptible to climate variability. This includes changes in rainfall patterns, temperature swings, and severe weather occurrences like floods and droughts (Haider, 2019). Additionally, Nigeria's socio-economic context is one of a large population (200 million, plus), over 60% of which are categorised multidimensionally poor (National Bureau of Statistics (NBS), 2022). This further exacerbates the population's vulnerabilities to the impacts of extreme climate events. Aside hazard exposure and geographical susceptibility, social vulnerability (as defined by the country's socioeconomic context) is a critical factor determining the impacts of climate variability or extreme climatic events.

This chapter interrogates intersectionality in social vulnerabilities of Nigerians and analyses how these intersections influence impacts of climate variability and of extreme climatic events for different demographics. The study approach includes document reviews (from literature) and survey data analysis. The discussions relate to SDG 5 (Gender Equality), SDG 13 (Climate Action), SDG 10 (Reduced Inequalities), SDG 1 (No Poverty), and SDG 2 (Zero Hunger). The narratives also encapsulate the Africa Union's long-term development blueprint – AU Agenda 2063, specifically aspiration 6, which has gender equality as a core objective (AU Commission, 2015).

Theory and Literature

Theoretical Underpinning

The study utilises a hybrid theory christened 'Social Vulnerability and Intersectionality Theory'. This merger combines the Intersectionality theory (Collins, 2000; Crenshaw, 1989) and the Social Vulnerability theory (Cutter, 1996; Wisner et al., 2004). The combination allows us to map the structural inequalities that shape climate impacts across gender and other demographic lines. The basic tenets of the two theories is that social and economic conditions breed inequalities and that the overlaps of multiple social conditions further exacerbate social inequalities which influence people's experiences with respect to impacts from hazards or disasters.

Intersectionality Theory, introduced by Kimberlé Crenshaw in 1989 and further developed by Patricia Hill Collins around 2000, provides a framework for understanding how multiple social identities and systems of oppression overlap and interact to shape the experiences of individuals. Crenshaw (1989) coined the term 'intersectionality' to highlight the limitations of traditional single-axis frameworks (focusing on race or gender alone), and how they failed to capture the unique experiences of Black women, who face overlapping oppressions due to both race and gender. Crenshaw emphasised that these intersecting identities create complex, simultaneous forms of discrimination that cannot be understood by examining each identity separately. Her work originally focused on legal contexts, showing how Black women were marginalised by laws and policies that did not recognise their compounded experiences of racism and sexism.

Collins (2000) expanded intersectionality into a broader critical social theory. She introduced concepts like the 'matrix of domination', which explains how intersecting oppressions (including race, gender, class, and sexuality) are organised and maintained through structural, disciplinary, cultural, and interpersonal domains of power. Collins emphasised that intersectionality is not just about individual identities but about understanding how systemic power relations interlock to produce social inequalities.

Taken together, Crenshaw and Collins frame intersectionality as:

- A recognition that social identities (race, gender, class, sexuality, ability, etc.) are mutually constitutive and cannot be separated when analysing oppression or privilege.
- An analytical tool to reveal how interlocking systems of power create complex, interdependent social inequalities.
- A critical praxis aimed at addressing structural inequalities rather than only individual experiences.
- A framework that highlights how marginalised groups experience unique forms of discrimination that are often overlooked by single-axis approaches.

In summary, intersectionality theory elucidates how overlapping identities and power structures produce distinct experiences of marginalisation and privilege, calling for nuanced analysis and social justice efforts that address these complexities comprehensively.

For the purpose of this study, our interest is about the unique forms of vulnerability resulting from overlaps in gender (Male/Female), location (North/South; Rural/Urban divides), livelihood source (Agriculture-based or other), and income levels, and how these complex vulnerabilities influence climate impacts on these demographic groups.

Authors such as Cutter (1996) and Wisner et al. (2004) in elucidating the Social Vulnerability theory focus on the susceptibility of social groups and societies to harm from hazards and their capacity to cope, resist, and recover from such impacts (resilience).

Cutter (1996) conceptualised social vulnerability as the susceptibility of social groups or society at large to potential losses from hazard events and disasters, emphasising that vulnerability is shaped by social, economic, demographic, and infrastructural characteristics rather than just physical exposure to hazards. Cutter introduced the 'hazards-of-place' model, which integrates biophysical and social factors to explain how vulnerability is geographically situated and influenced by socioeconomic conditions, political power, and community resilience. Her work highlights that vulnerability is not uniform but varies across communities depending on factors like poverty, race, age, and housing quality.

Wisner et al. (2004) expanded on this by defining social vulnerability as the capacity of individuals or groups to anticipate, cope with, resist, and recover from the impacts of natural or human-caused hazards. They emphasise that social vulnerability results from systemic inequalities embedded in social structures, institutions, and cultural values, which affect people's access to resources, political power, and social networks. In their framework (Pressure and Release Model), the authors conceive of the disaster as a combined effect resulting from the magnitude of hazard and the level of vulnerability. Vulnerability was seen as an amplification factor for the hazard element, the results of which determine climate disaster impacts. An insightful lesson from the model is that hazards cannot be controlled, but socioeconomic conditions, which are perhaps more critical in determining vulnerability, fall within the ambit of human control. Their approach links vulnerability directly to resilience, focusing on how social factors influence not only susceptibility to harm but also the ability to recover and adapt after disasters.

Together, the authors' contributions frame social vulnerability as:

- A structural condition rooted in socioeconomic inequalities and power relations that determine differential exposure and sensitivity to hazards.
- A multidimensional concept involving economic status, age, gender, race/ethnicity, health, social capital, and access to services.
- A dynamic process influenced by social systems that affect both the risk of harm and the capacity for recovery.
- An analytical tool for disaster risk reduction that calls for addressing underlying social inequalities to reduce vulnerability and enhance resilience.

In summary, Social Vulnerability Theory underscores that disasters are not just natural events but are socially constructed through existing inequalities that shape who is most at risk and how well communities can respond and recover.

Review of Literature

The review of literature adopts a cross-country approach with Nigeria in core focus. Two comparator countries (Philippines and Haiti) are included in the review. While Nigeria is categorised low on the Human Development Index (HDI), Haiti is classified medium HDI, while Philippines ranks as high HDI. These differences presuppose varying levels of socioeconomic vulnerability.

A common feature in the three countries is the prevalence of climate hazards over the years.

Sociodemographic Influences on Vulnerability and Climate Impacts

Sociodemographic characteristics such as gender, rural and urban location, income levels, employment patterns, and resource availability determine how individuals and communities are impacted by climate hazards.

Gender and Its Role in Climate Vulnerability: Gender stands as a key sociodemographic factor determining climate vulnerability, as it extends beyond human biology to include societal constructs of gender roles, power imbalances, and differences in resource accessibility. Primarily, Nigerian women spend their time managing natural resources while executing their roles of fetching water, collecting fuelwood, and producing 70% agricultural food for the nation, yet are faced with challenges that increase their exposure to climate hazards. According to Oseni et al. (2013), women possess less than 16% of agricultural land control despite contributing substantial farm labour due to patriarchal inheritance laws which limit their access to loans and adaptive technology acquisition. The Nigerian social system based on patriarchy prevents women from taking charge of rain-fed farming activities therefore preventing their ability to adapt to droughts or floods (Onwutuebe, 2019). These system outcomes negate the principles of gender equality (SDG 5).

The lack of engagement in decision-making processes, uneven land tenure, and exclusion from extension services all contribute to gender-based climate vulnerability (Chah et al., 2018; Oseni et al., 2013). Because of their caregiving responsibilities and reliance on natural resources for survival, women in other nations, including the Philippines, are more susceptible to climate threats. This problem is not unique to Nigeria. For instance, the 2013 Typhoon Haiyan (Yolanda) forced nearly 4 million people to flee their homes, with female-headed families suffering the most because of their limited mobility and gendered economic reliance (Neumayer & Plümper, 2007; Oxfam, 2014). Analysis conducted after the crisis revealed that women had a lower likelihood of receiving help or being included in recovery governance (Gaillard et al., 2017). This pattern mirrors what is observed in Nigeria's flood-prone regions.

Gendered vulnerability in women is also intensified because they lack authority in making decisions and accessing vital networks of information. Findings from Enugu State showed that the extension services is dominated by men since women livestock farmers received only 20% of climate forecasts whereas men received 50% (Chah et al., 2018). Terry (2009) reported that women faced prohibitive gender norms in sub-Saharan Africa as they are restricted from formal adaptation programmes; this is similar to Nigeria's 10% community adaptation planning participation of women (Anugwa et al., 2023). During drought periods in Kwara State, men were able to shift to off-farm employment because of their societal breadwinner role but this caused women farmers to experience a 25% reduction in farm production levels (Ayanlade et al., 2023). However, Rettig et al. (2020) argued that it is important not to assume standard gender-based adaptive ability because educated or wealthy women tend to adapt better than other women; thus, gender adaptability is influenced by sociodemographic factors.

This issue of limited agency and women's exclusion from decision-making has also been observed in Haiti, where the 2010 earthquakes and events related to climate disturbances revealed severe gender gaps in exposure and resilience. Madi (2017) also opined that the 2016 Hurricane Matthew further exacerbated poverty among women, with nearly 679,000 affected, including 106,180 female heads of household. According to UN Women (2021), although women participated in humanitarian responses, their influence in decision-making was at 22%, whereas that of men was at 52%. This highlights a persistent exclusion from formal planning and aid governance. According to Daramola (2023), who analysed risk factors in natural disaster impacts across 18 countries, Haiti's vulnerabilities are notable; it has one of the lowest HDI scores globally at 0.535 and recorded the highest Disaster Risk Index among the countries studied. This country experienced significant disaster impacts due to pre-existing gender and poverty inequalities. Female-headed households, which constitute about 45% of the population, were unable to access aid or relocate due to social norms and a lack of decision-making power. The intersection of gender, poverty, and institutional weakness, therefore, increased women's vulnerability to hazard impacts and also prolonged their recovery, similar to the situation in Nigeria, where exclusion from adaptation frameworks limits women's climate resilience. These intersectionalities further deepen inequalities.

Rural Versus Urban Location and Associated Risks: Climate vulnerability is determined in part by location, such as rural and urban areas; as women in these locations face different challenges regarding access to resources, infrastructures, and economic opportunities. About 70% of female population currently living in rural Nigeria (NBS, 2022) depend heavily on agriculture and natural resources which makes them more susceptible to climate risks such as desertification in the North and flooding in the South. According to Ayanlade et al. (2023), women in Kwara's rural areas show only 8% adoption of drought-resistant seeds while men have reached 25% adoption because women lack access to extension services that provide technology. The 2022 floods which displaced 1.4 million people created additional challenges for rural women in their recovery process because they have less savings combined with limited access to infrastructure (only 20% electricity reach compared to urban areas' 60%; United Nations Office for the Coordination of Humanitarian Affairs (OCHA), 2022; World Bank, 2023b). These outcomes are inconsistent with the AU's agenda 2063 which prioritises economic empowerment, access to resources and technology.

Urban women experience climate hazards that impact their jobs in the informal sector where 80% of urban female workers are employed (Joseph & Nduka, 2022). Heatwaves in Lagos caused a 30% decline in daily profits for petty traders due to declining customer numbers, yet urban infrastructure, including electricity and improved literacy rates (70% urban vs 40% rural), provided some protective effect (NBS, 2022, World Bank, 2023b). Rural isolation leads to increased vulnerability because it creates barriers for women to access relief and adaptation programmes, yet urban exclusion occurs because women receive less support than men in development initiatives (Adeosun & Owolabi, 2021).

The north–south divide in Nigeria also creates differential risks making rural women face drought-induced crop failures in the North while their southern counterparts in the urban areas consistently battle with heatwaves and water scarcity (Ayanlade et al., 2023). The disparity between urban and rural vulnerability is particularly noticeable in Haiti, where there is low rural adaptive capacities even though rural agricultural livelihoods are extremely vulnerable to climate change. Rural agricultural communities were devastated by the 2010 earthquake and subsequent storms, such as Hurricane Matthew in 2016, with women and children suffering the greatest losses in terms of both economic losses and casualties because of the lack of adequate infrastructure and isolation (UN Women, 2017). Due to market closures and climate-related disruptions, Port-au-Prince's urban informal sector workers, many of whom are women, experienced income shocks (Mercy Corps, 2017).

Similar difficulties are faced by rural women in the Philippines. For example, women farmers in rural Mindanao stated that crop failures brought on by climate change had cost them an average of half of their household income (World Bank, 2021). According to Daramola (2023), the Philippines had 310 hazard occurrences between 2003 and 2022, most of which occurred in rural regions vulnerable to landslides, floods, and typhoons. Populations with inadequate adaptation skills were disproportionately affected. Because heatwaves and floods interrupt informal sector activities like street selling and market trade, urban poor women in Metro Manila are also at risk from climate change. However, compared to males, they still have less access to insurance and disaster assistance (Asian Development Bank (ADB), 2013). The findings in Lagos, Nigeria, where urban women vendors lose up to 30–35% of their revenue during heatwaves, are consistent with this reality (Joseph & Nduka, 2022).

Tanyanyiwa and Mufunda (2019) demonstrated the situation in Zimbabwe where rural women face increased water and fuelwood collection duties leading to climate-induced scarcity; this is similar to Nigerian rural sectors, particularly the North-based 4-hour water gathering in Borno and South flooding impacts (UNICEF, 2021).

Income Levels and Economic Resilience to Climate Impacts: Economic resilience depends heavily on income levels. In Nigeria multidimensional poverty affects 133 million people or 63% of the population (NBS, 2022); and its ecological differences create diverse vulnerability patterns that place women at the forefront of vulnerability.

Northern Nigerians make up 70% of poverty-stricken people while southern Nigerians account for 42% of those living in poverty (NBS, 2022); this poverty level prevents low-income women in climate-sensitive roles from creating protection against shocks. The study by Joseph and Nduka (2022) discovered that female urban informal traders in Kano suffered a 35% decline in income earnings during heatwaves because they did not have access to loans or achieve income diversification like men in this sector. The adoption of irrigation technologies by female farmers in rural Kwara stands at 5% whereas 10% of male farmers because of their higher socioeconomic status and access to resources and interventions (Ayanlade et al., 2023). Tschakert et al. (2013) demonstrated globally how limited income prevents people from investing in climate-resilient practices and this pattern exists throughout Nigeria's basic economy.

Just as it is in Nigeria, the same situation also obtains in the Philippines, which is a lower-middle income country. Here women dominate the informal sector, and those located in informal settlements are particularly more exposed to urban flooding and stress from heat. This leads to a reduction in their daily earnings and then long term economic security (ADB, 2013). In Haiti, the relationship between income and disaster vulnerability is even more alarming; Haiti is a country where a major percentage (59%) of its population live below the poverty line. The country's women are poor, have little or no savings, low insurance coverage, and weak institutional protection (United Nations Development Programme (UNDP), 2020). According to Daramola (2023), Haiti's high Disaster Risk Index is a result of both inadequate adaptation ability and hazard exposure, which reflects the country's pervasive socioeconomic fragility.

Household income creates better adaptive capabilities within women-headed households. During floods, Lagos's upper-income women relocated their business activities indoors using their financial savings along with their high literacy rate (70%) compared to rural areas (40%) (NBS, 2022). Rao et al. (2017) confirmed this pattern in semi-arid regions of Africa and Asia because women with economic resources develop diverse livelihoods to cope with gender-based risks. The majority of Nigerian women stay within low-income, climate-susceptible economic spheres because such resilience is rare, thereby showcasing the important role of income in vulnerability.

Employment in Climate-Sensitive Sectors (e.g., Agriculture, Fishing): Individuals working in climate-sensitive sectors such as agriculture, fishing, water management, and forestry face increased vulnerability, particularly for women employees who dominate these sectors without having enough control over resources. The majority of smallholder farmers are women (70%) who take care of about 60–80% planting, weeding and harvesting; yet their output remains 30% below par due to the lack of access to fertilisers and agricultural machinery (Anugwa et al., 2023; World Bank, 2023b). The 2022 floods caused $1.5 billion worth of damage to southern female farmers because they did not have insurance or savings to regain their losses (OCHA, 2022). In the northern state of Nassarawa, the experience showed a 25% yield decrease for women farmers due to drought conditions; because only 10% of women farmers used irrigation systems due to high costs (Ayanlade et al., 2023). The lack of access to technology and resources further deepens poverty for women, undermining attainment of SDG 1 (No Poverty).

In coastal Ondo State, Nigeria, women who made up 65% of the fishing workforce lost one-and-a-half times more money through lowered fishing profits as they depend on shore-based fishing with limited access to boats (Akinsemolu & Olukoya, 2020). According to Chowdhury et al. (2022), Bangladesh experienced similar gender-related weaknesses because women depend on their fishing earnings to survive disasters. In the coastal Philippines, where women predominate in onshore fishing and seaweed cultivation, a similar situation exists. Due to damaged boats and post-harvest facilities that they lacked the funds to repair, women fishers suffered severe livelihood losses as a result of Typhoon Haiyan's disruption of coastal economies (Philippine Commission on Women, 2014). Despite their efforts, women were frequently left out of recovery planning and post-disaster financial help; this institutional deficiency was also noted in Nigeria's adaption programmes (Adeosun & Owolabi, 2021).

In Nigeria, 80% of the rural women gather fuelwood which leads to health issues linked to deforestation, while Fruttero et al. (2024) documented the same pattern in Mali's forestry sector. Hence, the combined effect of women's greater presence in high-risk areas that produce minimal profits while denying them access to resources leads to higher exposure and vulnerabilities.

Access to Resources and Its Effect on Coping with Climate Variability: The key resources needed to address climate change adaptation which includes land, credit, technology, and information remain inaccessible for Nigerian women who experience significant resource inequalities. The low 16% of land ownership among women prevents them from obtaining loans and thus from making investments that would help them implement adaptive measures (Oseni et al., 2013). The study by Chah et al. (2018) indicated that only 20% of female farmers in Enugu State received climate forecast information while 50% of male farmers received same; due to traditional extension services that prioritise men. The lack of access to information naturally deters women from taking necessary adaptive climate action. This resulted in 15% more yield losses for women during droughts (Ayanlade et al., 2023). The limited smartphone access (25%) among women in urban areas (compared to men's 45% ownership) limits them from getting relevant climate information (World Bank, 2023b) while rural women must spend 2–4 hours per day fetching water due to drought conditions (UNICEF, 2021).

Assefa and Gebrehiwot (2023) identified this community-based resource distribution in Ethiopia because it reduces women's vulnerability but Nigeria lacks study on this path. Government agricultural programmes allocate fewer training opportunities to women since they support male farmers over female farmers (Adeosun & Owolabi, 2021), leading women to maintain obsolete farming methods.

According to Gaillard et al. (2008), women in the Philippines' rural agricultural areas frequently lacked access to early warning systems and knowledge about disaster risk, which increased the number of injuries and fatalities during extreme events. Additionally, following Typhoon Haiyan, women were unable to restore their livelihoods due to unequal access to resources, which resulted in long-term economic disempowerment (Resurrección, 2013). These findings support the notion that improving gendered climate resilience in Nigeria and the Philippines requires fair resource governance. Women experience increase risks due to resource access inequalities which control their ability to cope with climate changes.

Intersectionality and Amplified Vulnerability to Climate Impacts

According to Crenshaw (1989) and Kaijser and Kronsell (2014) on intersectionality, gender relationship with employment, geographical location, income, and other characteristics lead to increased exposure. The overlapping factors in Nigeria develop complex risk territories that need complex multiple-factor analysis methods beyond simplistic analysis approach.

Female Gender Combined with Employment in Climate-Sensitive Sectors: Female employment in climate-sensitive sector increases vulnerability through an increased risk level. Women's 70% control of farming outputs is impacted by their 16% land ownership which results in a 30% production gap and 25% higher yield loss during droughts in northern regions (Anugwa et al., 2023; Ayanlade et al., 2023). The Ilaje community in Ondo State showed how 65% female involvement in fishery meets resource barriers and creates an income reduction of 50% from coastal erosion since women cannot use the boats that men use (Akinsemolu & Olukoya, 2020). The study by Fruttero et al. (2024) indicated that women in Mali experience restricted diversification opportunities due to their distribution across specific labour sectors; similar patterns of restriction are seen in Nigeria where traditional patriarchal systems devalue female work (Onwutuebe, 2019).

The Philippines, where women make up a sizable percentage of smallholder farmers and fishers, replicates Nigeria's female agricultural dominant sector, where women account for up to 70% of the workforce (Anugwa et al., 2023). According to the Philippine Commission on Women (2021), 35% of agricultural labourers are women; yet, similar to Nigeria, these women have limited access to land rights, insurance, and finance (Oseni et al., 2013). In 2013, Typhoon Haiyan (Yolanda) caused disproportionately large losses to the livelihoods of female farmers and fishers. According to the Philippines case study in Daramola (2023), women employed in agriculture had a lower chance of recovering quickly due to long-standing gender-based disparities in post-disaster support services and resource availability, even though the country witnessed 310 hazard occurrences over a period of 20 years.

The trend is more pronounced in Haiti. Despite being involved in subsistence farming and informal trading, women have limited access to formal sector jobs, land tenure, and rehabilitation money. Women were disproportionately affected by the 2010 earthquake; women headed 26% of the displaced families, and many of them lacked access to finance or help (UN Women, 2010). Despite having fewer disasters than nations like China, Haiti had disproportionately larger impacts. This was largely due to the country's high poverty, gendered informal economy, and poor HDI (0.535).

Globally, Terry (2009) showed that occupational gender segregation breeds increased vulnerability without adequate adaptation strategies since 80% of Nigerian rural women experience health problems related to deforestation (Joseph & Nduka, 2022). The participation of women makes up 60% of the workforce in urban informal trading yet they experience economic loss of 35% during heatwave periods when uninsured (Joseph & Nduka, 2022). The relationship demonstrates that employment enables gender-based risks to cause poor economic security for women.

Female Gender in Rural Locations and Heightened Exposure to Climate Risks: Living in the rural areas and being a female creates extra exposure to climate change factors due to Nigeria's geological and gender-related differences. Women in rural areas of the North use rain-fed agriculture since 70% of them lack irrigation access which results in decreased crop yields of 20% compared to men (Ayanlade et al., 2023; NBS, 2022). Women in Borno dedicate four extra hours each day to fetch water because of desertification which reduces their adaptive capabilities (UNICEF, 2021). More than 80% of rural households in Bayelsa who experienced flooding are led by women (OCHA, 2022). A study from Ethiopia discovered that female agricultural workers experience greater workload expansion when climate stress occurs in rural communities (Assefa & Gebrehiwot, 2023).

Similar vulnerabilities may be seen in Haiti's rural areas, where 60% of the population lives and where adaptation is significantly hampered by inadequate infrastructure. According to the World Bank (2017), 90% of the crops in the impacted regions were lost, causing extreme food insecurity for women-headed rural households. Rural women in the Philippines are also disproportionately affected by climate change. Because of their reliance on subsistence farming and exclusion from official disaster preparedness, rural women in areas like Eastern Visayas were more likely experience relocation and sustained income loss, according to the ADB (2020). Despite having a medium HDI (0.699), the Philippines' high population density and frequent typhoon exposure have increased the effects on vulnerable rural women, especially in island communities.

According to Adeosun and Owolabi (2021), rural isolation prevents women from accessing relief support, and Kaijser and Kronsell (2014) showed how spatial isolation strengthens existing gender inequalities. The findings on rural women in Nigeria demonstrated how low literacy levels of 40% while having only 20% electricity access indicates how geographic positioning increases their susceptibility to gender-based climate threats (NBS, 2022; World Bank, 2023b), throughout Nigeria's regional diversity.

Other Intersecting Identities (e.g., Low-income Rural Populations, Genders, and Resource Access) and Their Cumulative Effects on Climate Vulnerability: The intersection of social factors including low income, gender, rural location, and more generate multiple vulnerabilities which increases the impacts of climate change. Nigerian low-income rural women comprising 70% of its multidimensionally poor northern population face multiple challenges which include using irrigation by just 5%, having literacy rates at 18% in Borno and limited control over Adaptation Funds (AF) at 15% (Ayanlade et al., 2023; NBS, 2022). According to Tschakert et al. (2013) poverty and gender creates challenges for adopting technology innovations yet Nigeria's rural women experience the worst impacts when they face heatwaves because they lose 35% of their trading income (Joseph & Nduka, 2022).

This is comparable to Haiti, where women are structurally excluded from economic involvement and decision-making, and more than 60% of the population lives below the poverty line (UNDP, 2022). Despite having fewer hazards (119 events were recorded between 2003 and 2022), Haiti's disaster impacts are still severe, as Daramola (2023) notes. The 2010 earthquake alone claimed over 316,000 lives, illustrating how poverty, poor governance, and gender-based exclusion combine to exacerbate disaster outcomes. Similar to this, gender and intersectionalities like age and disability combine to make people more vulnerable in the Philippines. According to research by HelpAge International (2021), older women in regions that are prone to disasters were less likely to use early warning systems or leave quickly during floods, which increased the chance of fatalities. By using exposure and susceptibility variables like population density and governance quality, which are still lacking in places with a high concentration of impoverished and disadvantaged people.

The intersection between marital status and age makes the analysis more difficult. Female adults who are married to rural males face dependency on their spouses for resources despite keeping minimal control (15%) because widowed women have separated from all support networks (Oseni et al., 2013). Nigerian young women in the age bracket of 15–24 exhibits lower adoption rates of climate-smart practices of 10% in comparison to the older adult population with 20% (Ayanlade et al., 2023; UNICEF, 2021; World Bank, 2023a) and face unemployment rates of 53% and early marriage rates of 38%. Rao et al. (2017) highlighted that education serve as a protective factor but Nigeria exhibits a clear difference between its uneducated northern population and educated metro women building multiple income streams (Rettig et al., 2020). The limited research study of ethnicity and disability risks (Adeosun & Owolabi, 2021) illustrates the importance of conducting thorough intersectional research.

Climate Variability Impacts on Conflict and How These Affect Males and Females

Major pathways of climate insecurity include deteriorating livelihood conditions, increasing migration and shifts in pastoral mobility patterns, tactical consideration by armed groups, and elite exploitation of local grievances (Tarif, 2022). Anthonia et al. (2021) also agree that climate change has an impact on resource conflicts thus recommending future studies to concentrate on developing climate-sensitive solutions to address farmers herders' clashes in Nigeria. Research shows that livelihoods that are heavily dependent on climate-sensitive natural resources are less resilient to the effects of climate change and usually lead to forced migration (Kamta et al., 2020). For instance, communities in north-eastern Nigeria are more susceptible to conflict and more likely to be displaced than populations with alternative sources of income (Tarif, 2022). In the Philippines, floods constituted 56% of the total natural hazard events in the last two decades impacting lives and properties (Daramola, 2023). The Bangsamoro Autonomous Region in Muslim Mindanao in the Philippines, for instance, is saddled with land rights disputes, conflict, and economic vulnerabilities leading to increased displacement, reduced crop yields, food insecurity, and environmental degradation owing to floods and drought (Cheeseman, 2024). Thus, climate variability impacts water and land system and affects people by disrupting their livelihoods and causing conflict over scare resources (CGIAR, 2023).

Haiti is prone to the ravages of climate variability and change as a result of its location on the Atlantic hurricane belt making it vulnerable to tropical storms and seismic activity, thereby experiencing frequent natural disasters. In a country where agriculture is basically rain-fed climate variability impacts livelihood, climate and conflict induced migration affecting over 90% of the population (Planetary Security Initiative, 2025).

Beyond establishing the impact of climate variability on conflict, climate variability affects males and females in varying ways due to social, economic, and physiological pathways. A link exists between gender inequalities and vulnerability to the effects of climate change (Pearse, 2017). These vulnerabilities are expressions of existing gender inequalities and power relations in societies across the world rather than mere natural characteristics of women. As a result of increased scarcity of natural resources brought about by climate change, women must now look for and carry water and firewood farther to cater for household needs (Meyiwa et al., 2014; Singh et al., 2013). Societal norms, reproductive responsibilities, and gender inequality are reasons why women in Bangladesh are disproportionately impacted by climate change and particularly vulnerable to climate-related disasters like droughts, cyclones, and floods. This is further aggravated by socioeconomic factors such as poverty, lack of decision-making power, and lack of access to resources (Reggers, 2019).

In Nigeria, women and girls suffer more from climate variability and conflict as they are tasked getting water for both the household and farms and work on farmlands. For instance, women in Benue face gender-based violence, farmer–herder conflict, and destroyed farmlands. While those in Nasarawa state have to walk longer distances to get water as a result of extreme heat, droughts, and food shortages making them vulnerable. Men also faced issues of violence as most deceased families turned out to be over 70% males as opposed to 22.22% females (Actionaid Nigeria, 2025). Apart from helping their mothers, over 60% of girls have dropped out of school and forced into child-marriages as a result of climate conflict and poverty (Actionaid Nigeria, 2025). Men are also forced to joined armed gangs such as boko haram group in the north and skilled labours migrate from the north to the south in search of natural resources causing further crisis in host communities (CGIAR, 2023; Team Research Project, 2023).

Just as the case is in Nigeria, women in the Philippines suffer due to loss of land-rights loss and face discrimination in conflict areas and take up the breadwinner roles. They are also saddle with the motherly roles of providing care and support to the children (CGIAR, 2023; Chandra et al., 2017). Men on the other hand join armed groups following the loss of their farmlands (CGIAR, 2023). Haiti is no different from Nigeria and the Philippines, women being key actors in the agric value chain even though holding just 25.3% of land become economically vulnerable after losing their source of livelihood, they become exposed to heightened violence and the burdens of caregiving increases (Inter-American Development Bank Climate Change Division, 2020). Addressing the inequalities that exist between gender will go a long way in improving the adaptive capacity of societies and the world at large (Andrijevic et al., 2020).

Climate Finance Targeting – Do These Consider the Most Vulnerable Groups?

Climate financing is one area of climate policy with gendered implications (Global Gender and Climate Alliance (GGCA), 2016). These are interventions provided in a bid to improve the adaptive capacity of climate-vulnerable people towards climate variability and change, Climate finance is a mechanism developed towards the funding of projects designed towards mitigating and adapting to the effects of climate change particularly in developing countries that are most vulnerable. Over two decades there have been several climate finance projects including the Green Climate Fund (GCF), the Global Environment Facility, the Climate Investment Funds, and the AF. Despite these moves, there are questions about their effectiveness in targeting the most vulnerable groups.

The GCF though targeted at vulnerable countries like least developed countries and small island developing states are largely inaccessible due to the weaknesses of institutions, which limit direct access and ownership (Garschagen & Doshi, 2022). This is in agreement with the stance of Doshi and Garschagen (2020), who opined countries with better project management prowess tend to attract more funding to the disadvantage of the most vulnerable. Islam (2022) believes that there is some justice in climate finance with greater funding for countries more vulnerable to climate change; however, overlaps may occur which negates the principles of distributive justice.

Basty and Ghachem (2022) on the other hand provide evidence of distributive justice in terms of the allocation of more funding to the most vulnerable sectors. In other words, financing is allocated according to the level of need in the recipient country and sector thus ensuring distributive justice. The study by Alcayna and O'Donnell (2022) on the health sector revealed this sector, despite its critical nature, receives a disproportionately small share of climate adaptation finance. When it comes to gender, most of the earlier listed climate financing mechanisms have adopted specific gender policies and action plans that are designed towards achieving stronger outcomes for women and men (GGCA, 2016). Because women and other marginalised groups face difficulties in accessing finance, it is important to employ an inclusive approach so it gets to the most vulnerable – women to ensure gender equality when it comes to climate mitigation measures (Price, 2021). It is therefore important for gender data to showcase women's contributions to climate action and include them in climate finance as they are often overlooked (Ezirigwe, 2024).

Nigeria is rich in policy frameworks; however, it usually faces issues of proper implementation. Although the National Action Plan on Gender and Climate Change mandates gender-responsive climate finance, adaptation finance remains insufficient (an average USD 1.9 billion per year of public and private capital in 2019/2020 compared to USD 17.7 billion that is actually needed), very little (23%) climate finance from private sector investment limiting coverage (Climate Policy Initiative, 2022).

Haiti's Gender and Climate Change Action Plan (2022–2030) prioritises gender-sensitive budgeting, funding mobilisation, and training gender focal points in climate institutions (Ministry of the Environment, 2024); but just like Nigeria, it lacks measurable targets and evidence for directing funds to high-risk groups like displaced women in gang-controlled areas (Ministry of the Environment, 2024). The Philippines has strong climate finance laws and between 2013 and 2016, averagely 42% of adaptation projects reported gender equality objectives. However, only 6% of adaptation finance is found to target gender equality.[1] From the foregoing, women, indigenous peoples, and the impoverished in rural areas are not given enough priority in climate finance systems, despite the fact that vulnerable groups are recognised by policy in all three nations. While Haiti's gender action plan is the best organised, though underfunded, the implementation gaps between policy and financial priorities are more pronounced in Nigeria and the Philippines.

Empirical Data and Discussions

The empirical data presented here relates to a 2023 study on climate variability and resource conflicts in Nigeria (Adesanya et al., 2023). The survey respondents include 1,374 individuals from the countries of six geopolitical zones, 40% (550) of which were females. The author attempts to draw out gender and intersectionality dimensions for discussions in this chapter.

Sociodemographic Characteristics

Survey respondents consisted of 80% rural and 20% urban residents. This is because the first stage of the sampling was purposive and targeted locations with a history of climate-related resource conflicts. These happened to fall mostly within rural locations. About 66% of respondents earned below N30,000 monthly and the mean age was 40.4 years. Majority of the survey respondents (64%) were engaged in climate-sensitive-dependent activities for livelihood earnings. These include farming (crop and livestock) and food crop processing. About 12% of respondents were engaged in informal trading; these are equally vulnerable to climate elements as much of the transactions are conducted in open market spaces. This means trading naturally shuts down when there is rain or other forms of unfavourable weather. Essentially as much as 76% of respondents were engaged in climate-sensitive sectors. The sociodemographic picture reflects a profile of pre-existing vulnerabilities.

Gender Differentials in Climate Impact

Respondents assessed how climate variability affected their livelihood (severe, not severe). In their assessment, some differing patterns were observed among males and females; this is presented in Table 5.1.

---

[1]https://careclimatechange.org/wp-content/uploads/2021/01/Philippines-Climate-Adaptation-Finance-Tracking-.pdf

Table 5.1. Impacts of Climate Variability on Livelihood Components (Male/Female).

Livelihood Components	**Severe Impacts (% of Respondents)**			
	Male	**Female**	X^2	**Probability (sig <0.05)**
Land for agricultural activities	70.9	71.5	139.70*	0.000
Food security	63.6	64.7	87.36*	0.000
Income generation	65.9	65.1	107.16*	0.000
Land for housing/ business enterprise	56.2	39.8	179.4*	0.000
Average (%)	64.15	60.2		

Source: Fieldwork, 2023. (Fieldwork conducted on the study 'Climate Variability and Resource Conflicts in Nigeria' by the Nigerian Institute of Social C Economic Research.)

*Significant at 5% ($P<0.05$).

While more females reported severe impacts on agricultural land and food security, more males reported same for income generation and land for housing (Table 5.1). Anecdotal evidence shows that females do not actually own land but are preponderant in use for farm labour. Hence females are not likely to suffer impacts on land for non-agriculture use, such as for housing. The results from the chi-square tests show there is a statistically significant difference in the severe impact experience on all livelihood components from climate variability for males and females.

The pattern, however, changes slightly when we consider intersections of gender by location – Urban/Rural (Table 5.2). Rural females had the highest proportion of respondents who reported severe impacts for three out of the four livelihood components considered.

Generally, more rural respondents reported severe impacts than their urban counterparts. The results show higher chi-square values when variables are combined (intersected) as seen in Table 5.2. The vulnerability of the female gender to climate impacts unfolds when gender is intersected with other variables such as location and is more pronounced for females in the rural areas. The chi-square tests show there is a statistically significant difference in the severe impact experience on all livelihood components from climate variability for urban/rural males versus urban/rural females.

In the sub-section below, we attempt to build up vulnerabilities by layers for the female gender.

Intersectionality and the Vulnerability Gradient for Females

The layered intersections of vulnerability show that a larger proportion of each subsequent demographic experiences severe climate impacts on their livelihoods.

Table 5.2. Impacts of Climate Variability on Livelihood Components (Urban/Rural).

Livelihood Components	**Severe Impacts (% of Respondents)**					
	Urban Male	**Urban Female**	**Rural Male**	**Rural Female**	X^2	**Probability (sig <0.05)**
Land for agricultural activities	60.9	52.1	72.5	78.8	452.51*	0.000
Food security	45.9	57.0	67.0	67.4	369.99*	0.000
Income generation	60.9	45.8	66.6	72.3	433.21*	0.000
Land for housing/business enterprise	42.1	40.8	58.6	39.8	441.12*	0.000
Average (%)	52.4	48.9	66.1	64.5		

Source: Fieldwork, 2023.

*Significant at 5% ($P<0.05$).

The proportion of respondents (Fig. 5.1) refers to the average proportion who reported severe impacts across the livelihood components considered.

The progressive escalation in proportion of respondents severely impacted by climate variability reflects progressive vulnerabilities with each demographic layer. The intersectionalities are further illustrated in a venn diagram (Fig. 5.2).

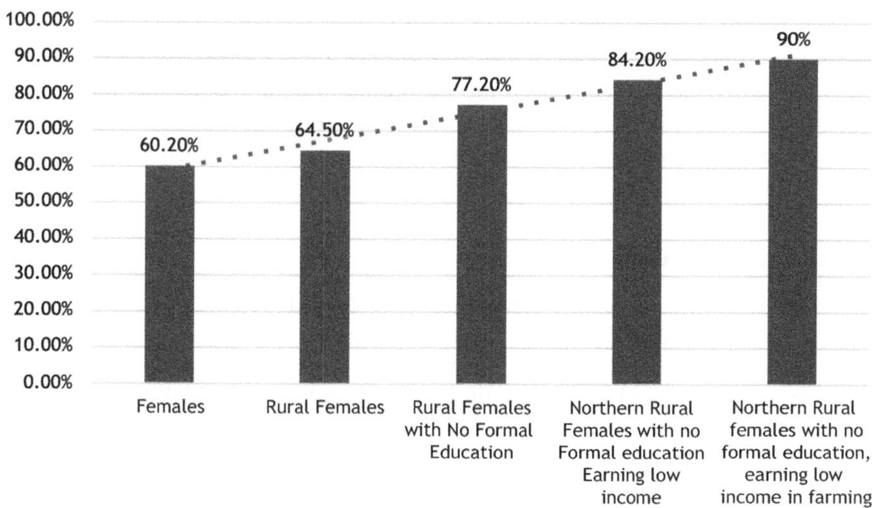

Fig. 5.1. Progression of Vulnerability with Additional Demographic Layer.

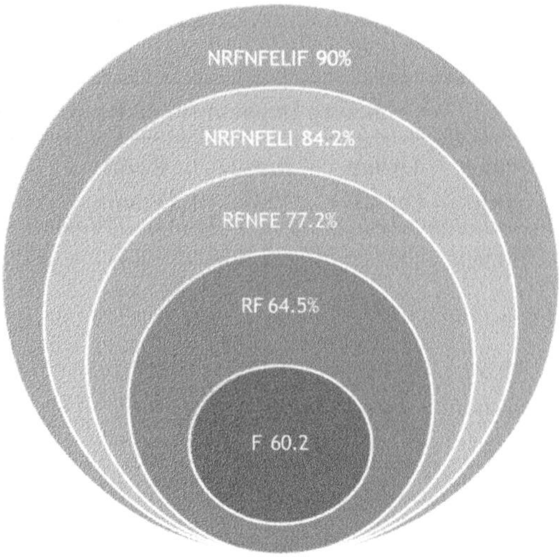

Fig. 5.2. Intersectionality and Increasing Vulnerability.
Legend: F=Females. RF=Rural Females. RFNFE=Rural Females with No Formal Education. NRFNFELI=Northern Rural Females with No Formal Education Earning Low Income. NRFNFELIF=Northern Rural Females with No Formal Education Earning Low Income in Farming.

Conclusion

Findings from extant literature and the Nigerian survey converge on the point that intersectionalities amplify vulnerability to climate impacts. This provides policy makers and programme managers a template to prioritise benefits when designing and implementing climate interventions. The depth of vulnerability (layers of intersections) appears to correspond to the scope of vulnerability (numbers affected) and evidence on these should inform the demographics targeted for the most interventions. Beneficiary targeting should thus be driven by context specific evidence to ensure that interventions are focused on those that need it the most.

Acknowledgements

The author acknowledges the contributions of NISER researchers – Drs Modinat Adekunle and Joy Folorunso to the literature review section of the chapter; and that of Mr Emmanuel Onimisi who helped with data extraction and analysis. The author also acknowledges the Environment and Physical Infrastructure Policy Department (NISER) that conducted the survey from which the data for this study were drawn.

References

ActionAid Nigeria. (2025). *The gendered face of climate chaos: How women in Nigeria are fighting two battles at once!* https://nigeria.actionaid.org/publications/2025/gendered-face-climate-chaos#downloads

Adeosun, O. T., & Owolabi, K. E. (2021). Gender inequality: Determinants and outcomes in Nigeria. *Journal of Business and Socio-economic Development, 1*(2). https://doi.org/10.1108/JBSED-01-2021-0007

Adesanya, A. O., Onwuemele, A., Daramola, A. Y., Adeagbo, A. L., Oke, M. O., Onyebuchi, N., Joseph, S. A., Onimisi, E. O., Adekunle, M. M., & Folorunso, J. O. (2023). *Climate variability and resource conflicts in Nigeria.* Nigerian Institute of Social and Economic Research (NISER). ISBN 978181767-0

African Union Commission, Strategic Planning, Monitoring, Evaluation, & Resource Mobilization. (2015). *Agenda 2063: The Africa we want.* African Union (akb.au.int).

Akinsemolu, A. A., & Olukoya, O. A. P. (2020). The vulnerability of women to climate change in coastal regions of Nigeria: A case of the Ilaje community in Ondo State. *Journal of Cleaner Production, 246*, 119015. https://doi.org/10.1016/j.jclepro.2019.119015

Alcayna, T., & O'Donnell, D. (2022). How much global climate adaptation finance is targeting the health sector? *The European Journal of Public Health, 32*. https://doi.org/10.1093/eurpub/ckac129.146

Andrijevic, M., Crespo Cuaresma, J., Lissner, T., Thomas, A., & Schleussner, C. F. (2020). Overcoming gender inequality for climate resilient development. *Nature Communications, 11*, 6261. https://doi.org/10.1038/s41467-020-16185-2

Anthonia, A. N., Bello, Y. A., Oliatan, O. M., & Macaulay, I. A. (2021). Reviewing the links between climate change and resource conflict. *Global Journal of Pure and Applied Sciences, 27*(2), 243–252.

Anugwa, I. Q., Obossou, E. A. R., Onyeneke, R. U., & Chah, J. M. (2023). Gender perspectives in vulnerability of Nigeria's agriculture to climate change impacts: A systematic review. *GeoJournal, 88*(4), 1139–1155. https://doi.org/10.1007/s10708-022-10638-z

Asian Development Bank (ADB). (2013). *Gender and urban poverty in the Philippines.* https://www.adb.org/publications/gender-and-urban-poverty-philippines

Asian Development Bank (ADB). (2020). *Gender and disaster risk management in the Philippines.* https://www.adb.org/sites/default/files/publication/576741/gender-drm-philippines.pdf

Assefa, E., & Gebrehiwot, G. (2023). Gender dimensions of climate change adaptation in Tigray, Ethiopia. *Global Environmental Change, 82*, 102737. https://doi.org/10.1016/j.gloenvcha.2023.102737

Ayanlade, A., Oluwatimilehin, I. A., Ayanlade, O. S., Adeyeye, O., & Abatemi-Usman, S. (2023). Gendered vulnerabilities to climate change and farmers' adaptation responses in Kwara and Nassarawa States, Nigeria. *Humanities and Social Sciences Communications, 10,* 911. https://doi.org/10.1057/s41599-023-02380-9

Basty, N., & Ghachem, D. (2022). A sectoral approach of adaptation finance in developing countries: Does climate justice apply? *Sustainability, 14*(17), 10835. https://doi.org/10.3390/su141710835

CGIAR. (2023). *How does climate exacerbate root causes of conflict in the Philippines? Climate security pathway analysis.* Climate Security Observatory Series. https://cgspace.cgiar.org/server/api/core/bitstreams/32dfa0ce-5f5e-4737-a928-452ee87cb565/content

Chah, J. M., Attamah, C. O., & Odoh, E. M. (2018). Differences in climate change effects and adaptation strategies between male and female livestock entrepreneurs in Nsukka Agricultural Zone of Enugu State, Nigeria. *Journal of Agricultural Extension*, *22*(1), 105. https://doi.org/10.4314/jae.v22i1.10

Chandra, A., McNamara, K. E., Dargusch, P., Caspe, A. M., & Dalabajan, D. (2017). Gendered vulnerabilities of smallholder farmers to climate change in conflict-prone areas: A case study from Mindanao, Philippines. *Journal of Rural Studies*, *50*, 45–59. https://doi.org/10.1016/j.jrurstud.2016.12.011

Cheeseman, K. (2024). *Disaster preparedness in the Bangsamoro Autonomous Region in Muslim Mindanao (K4DD Rapid Evidence Review 60)*. Institute of Development Studies. https://doi.org/10.19088/K4DD.2024.030

Chowdhury, M. A., Hasan, M. K., & Islam, S. L. U. (2022). Climate change adaptation in Bangladesh: Current practices, challenges and the way forward. *The Journal of Climate Change and Health*, *6*, 100108. https://doi.org/10.1016/j.joclim.2021.100108

Climate Policy Initiative. (2022). *Landscape of climate finance in Nigeria*. https://www.climatepolicyinitiative.org/wp-content/uploads/2022/10/Landscape-of-Climate-Finance-in-Nigeria.pdf

Collins, P. H. (2000). *Black feminist thought: Knowledge, consciousness, and the politics of empowerment* (2nd ed.). Routledge.

Crenshaw, K. (1989). Demarginalizing the intersection of race and sex: A Black feminist critique of antidiscrimination doctrine, feminist theory and antiracist politics. *University of Chicago Legal Forum*, *1989*(1), 139–167.

Cutter, S. L. (1996). Vulnerability to environmental hazards. *Progress in Human Geography*, *20*(4), 529–539. https://doi.org/10.1177/030913259602000407

Daramola, A. Y. (2023). *Case studies in natural hazards and disaster mitigation*. NISER Monograph Series No. 5. Nigerian Institute of Social & Economic Research. ISBN 978-978-181-737-3

Doshi, D., & Garschagen, M. (2020). Understanding adaptation finance allocation: Which factors enable or constrain vulnerable countries to access funding? *Sustainability*, *12*(10), 4308. https://doi.org/10.3390/su12104308

Ezirigwe, J. (2024). Advancing new governance models for gender data in climate resilience funding. *Law and Development Review*, *17*(2). https://doi.org/10.1515/ldr-2024-0110

Fruttero, A., Halim, D., Broccolini, C., Coelho, B., Gninafon, H., & Muller, N. (2024). Gendered impacts of climate change: Evidence from weather shocks. *Environmental Research: Climate*, *3*, 045018. https://doi.org/10.1088/2752-5295/ad3c69

Gaillard, J. C., Sanz, K., Balgos, B., & Dalisay, S. (2017). Beyond men and women: A critical perspective on gender and disaster. *Disasters*, *41*(3), 429–447. https://doi.org/10.1111/disa.12209

Gaillard, J. C., Sanz, K., Balgos, B., Dorotheo, E. U., & Pangilinan, M. L. C. J. D. (2008). Typhoon Haiyan: The untold story of the Philippines' most deadly storm. *Disaster Prevention and Management: An International Journal*, *26*(3), 254–267. https://doi.org/10.1108/DPM-09-2016-0193

Garschagen, M., & Doshi, D. (2022). Does funds-based adaptation finance reach the most vulnerable countries? *Global Environmental Change*, *72*, 102450. https://doi.org/10.1016/j.gloenvcha.2021.102450

Global Gender and Climate Alliance (GGCA). (2016). *Gender and climate change: A closer look at existing evidence*. Oak Foundation.

Haider H. (2019). *Climate change in Nigeria: Impacts and responses* [K4D Helpdesk Report 675]. Institute of Development Studies.

HelpAge International. (2021). *Older people in climate-related disasters: The need for inclusive risk reduction and response*. https://www.helpage.org/resources

Inter-American Development Bank Climate Change Division. (2020). *Study of the impacts of climate change on the women and men of the Caribbean: Pilot programme for climate resilience countries* [Technical Note No. IDB-TN-02064].

Islam, M. (2022). Distributive justice in global climate finance – Recipients' climate vulnerability and the allocation of climate funds. *Global Environmental Change*, *73*, 102475. https://doi.org/10.1016/j.gloenvcha.2022.102475

Joseph, U., & Nduka, O. (2022). Gender-sensitive responses to climate change in Nigeria: The role of multinationals' corporate social responsibility in oil host communities. *Journal of Global Responsibility*. https://doi.org/10.1108/JGR-05-2022-0040

Kaijser, A., & Kronsell, A. (2014). Climate change through the lens of intersectionality. *Environmental Politics*, *23*(3), 417–433. https://doi.org/10.1080/09644016.2013.835203

Kamta, F. N., Schilling, J., & Scheffran, J. (2020). Insecurity, resource scarcity, and migration to camps of internally displaced persons in northeast Nigeria. *Sustainability*, *12*(17), 6882. https://doi.org/10.3390/su12176882

Madi, M. (2017). *Hurricane Matthew and its gendered impacts in Haiti: A humanitarian response analysis* [Briefing paper]. UN Women.

Mercy Corps. (2017). *Lessons from urban Haiti: Increasing resilience through improved infrastructure and economic development*. https://www.mercycorps.org/research-resources

Meyiwa, T., Maseti, T., Ngubane, S., Letsekha, T., & Rozani, C. (2014). Women in selected rural municipalities: Resilience and agency against vulnerabilities to climate change. *Agenda*, *28*(3), 102–114. https://doi.org/10.1080/10130950.2014.951823

Ministry of the Environment. (2024). *Gender and climate change action plan of the Republic of Haiti*. https://napglobalnetwork.org/wp-content/uploads/2025/05/haiti-country-report-en-V2.pdf

National Bureau of Statistics (NBS). (2022). *Nigeria multidimensional poverty index 2022*. https://www.nigeriastat.gov.ng/pdfuploads/Nigeria_MPI_2022.pdf

Neumayer, E., & Plümper, T. (2007). The gendered nature of natural disasters: The impact of catastrophic events on the gender gap in life expectancy, 1981–2002. *Annals of the Association of American Geographers*, *97*(3), 551–566. https://doi.org/10.1111/j.1467-8306.2007.00563.x

Onwutuebe, C. J. (2019). Patriarchy and women vulnerability to adverse climate change in Nigeria. *SAGE Open*, *9*(1), 1–9. https://doi.org/10.1177/2158244019825914

Oseni, G., Goldstein, M., & Utah, A. (2013). *Gender dimensions in Nigerian agriculture* [Policy brief]. World Bank. https://openknowledge.worldbank.org/handle/10986/25459

Oxfam. (2014). *The right to be heard: Typhoon Yolanda and the peoples' recovery*. https://www.oxfam.org/en/research/right-be-heard

Pearse, R. (2017). Gender and climate change. *Wiley Interdisciplinary Reviews: Climate Change*, *8*(2), e451. https://doi.org/10.1002/wcc.451

Philippine Commission on Women. (2014). *Women and Typhoon Yolanda: Gender snapshot*. https://pcw.gov.ph/publication/women-and-typhoon-yolanda-gender-snapshot/

Philippine Commission on Women. (2021). *Women in agriculture and rural development*. https://pcw.gov.ph

Planetary Security Initiative. (2025). *Climate, peace and security fact sheet: Haiti*. Stockholm International Peace Research Institute. https://www.planetarysecurityinitiative.org/news/climate-peace-and-security-fact-sheet-haiti

Price, R. (2021). *Access to climate finance by women and marginalised groups in the Global South*. https://doi.org/10.19088/K4D.2021.083

Rao, N., Lawson, E. T., Raditloaneng, W. N., Solomon, D., & Angula, M. N. (2017). Gendered vulnerabilities to climate change: Insights from the semi-arid regions of Africa and Asia. *Climate and Development*, *11*(1), 14–26. https://doi.org/10.1080/17565529.2017.1372266

Reggers, A. (2019). Climate change is not gender neutral: Gender inequality, rights and vulnerabilities in Bangladesh. In M. M. Q. Mirza, Q. K. Ahmad, & N. Nishat (Eds.), *Confronting climate change in Bangladesh: Policy strategies for adaptation and resilience* (pp. 103–118). Springer. https://doi.org/10.1007/978-3-030-05237-9_7

Resurrección, B. P. (2013). Persistent women and environment linkages in climate change and sustainable development agendas. *Women's Studies International Forum, 40*, 33–43. https://doi.org/10.1016/j.wsif.2013.03.011

Rettig, E. M., Fick, S. E., & Hijmans, R. J. (2020). The Female Empowerment Index (FEMI): Spatial and temporal variation in women's empowerment in Nigeria. *Heliyon, 6*(5), e03829. https://doi.org/10.1016/j.heliyon.2020.e03829

Singh, R., Feroze, S. M., & Ray, L. I. (2013). Effects of drought on livelihoods and gender roles: A case study of Meghalaya. *Indian Journal of Gender Studies, 20*(3), 453–467. https://doi.org/10.1177/0971521513492012

Tanyanyiwa, V. I., & Mufunda, E. (2019). Gendered impacts of climate change: The Zimbabwe perspective. In W. L. Filho, A. M. Azul, L. Brandli, P. G. Özuyar, & T. Wall (Eds.), *Climate action* (pp. 1–12). Springer. https://doi.org/10.1007/978-3-319-71063-1_33-1

Tarif, K. (2022). *Climate change and violent conflict in West Africa: Assessing the evidence* [SIPRI Insights on Peace and Security No. 2022/3]. Stockholm International Peace Research Institute. https://www.sipri.org

Team Research Project. (2023). *Climate variability and resource conflicts in Nigeria*. Environment and Physical Infrastructure Policy Department, Nigerian Institute of Social and Economic Research (NISER).

Terry, G. (2009). No climate justice without gender justice: An overview of the issues. *Gender & Development, 17*(1), 5–18. https://doi.org/10.1080/13552070802696839

Tschakert, P., van Oort, B., St. Clair, A. L., & LaMadrid, A. (2013). Inequality and transformation analyses: A complementary lens for addressing vulnerability to climate change. *Climate and Development, 5*(4), 340–350. https://doi.org/10.1080/17565529.2013.828583

UNICEF. (2021). *The state of the world's children 2021: On my mind – Promoting, protecting and caring for children's mental health*. UNICEF. https://www.unicef.org/reports/state-worlds-children-2021

United Nations Development Programme (UNDP). (2020). *Haiti human development indicators*. http://hdr.undp.org/en/countries/profiles/HTI

United Nations Development Programme (UNDP). (2022). *Human development report 2021/2022: Uncertain times, unsettled lives*. http://hdr.undp.org

United Nations Office for the Coordination of Humanitarian Affairs (OCHA). (2022). *Nigeria: 2022 floods situation report*. https://reliefweb.int/report/nigeria/nigeria-2022-floods-situation-report

UN Women. (2010). *Gender assessment of the earthquake response in Haiti*. https://www.unwomen.org/en/digital-library/publications/2010/1/gender-assessment-of-the-earthquake-response-in-haiti

UN Women. (2017). *Women and girls in humanitarian action: Advancing gender equality in humanitarian action in Haiti*. https://www.unwomen.org

UN Women. (2021). *Participation of women in humanitarian coordination mechanisms in Haiti*. https://www.unwomen.org

USAID. (2018). *Climate change risk profile: West Africa (Sahel)*. United States Agency for International Development. https://www.climatelinks.org/

Wisner, B., Blaikie, P., Cannon, T., & Davis, I. (2004). *At risk: Natural hazards, people's vulnerability and disasters* (2nd ed.). Routledge.

World Bank. (2017). *Haiti – Risk and resilience assessment*. https://openknowledge.worldbank.org/handle/10986/28936

World Bank. (2021). *Climate change and gender equality in the Philippines*. https://documents.worldbank.org

World Bank. (2023a). *Nigeria economic update 2023*. https://www.worldbank.org/en/country/nigeria/publication/nigeria-economic-update

World Bank. (2023b). *Gender gaps in agriculture productivity and public spending in Nigeria*. GOV.UK. https://www.gov.uk/research-for-development-outputs/gender-gaps-in-agriculture-productivity-and-public-spending-in-nigeria

Chapter 6

Climate-induced Displacement and Migration in ECOWAS: The Gendered Dimension of Livelihood and Financial Resilience

Akeju Kemi Funlayo and Olalere Sunday Shina

Department of Economics, Faculty of the Social Sciences, Ekiti State University, Ado-Ekiti, Nigeria

Abstract

Climate-induced migration is an alternative for individuals who are incapable of coping with the environmental and social implications of climate change. Most individuals experience climate-induced displacement because of first-hand suffering from severe weather conditions as well as other consequences such as food shortages and competition over the earth's resources. This study investigates the livelihood and financial resilience of climate-induced displaced persons in Economic Community of West African States (ECOWAS) nations, focusing on Nigeria, Ghana, Niger, and Togo. The study shows a thorough grasp of how climate change exacerbates inequality and worsens pre-existing gender disparities, limiting women and girls' possession of resources and decision-making and impeding their capacity to cushion the effects of climate change and recover from disasters. It makes the case that there is variation by gender among people displaced by climate change; based on livelihood and financial resilience's adaptive and absorptive capacities, women have the fewest opportunities to obtain knowledge and resources related to climate resilience and adaptation. It offers practical advice for creating a more resilient and equitable future and concludes that the livelihood resilience of households that have been displaced by climate change may be improved through proper

Gender and Climate Finance in Africa: Addressing Inequalities and Bridging Gaps, 101–114

doi:10.1108/978-1-83742-085-820261006

governance in the financial transformation process. It advocates for a gender-transformative strategy that centres climate policy alternatives on women and girls.

Keywords: Climate change; migration; displacement; livelihood; financial resilience

Introduction

Climate change is one of today's most critical environmental challenges, which has far-reaching implications for human ecosystems and the economy (Raihan, 2023), with a profound impact on human migration and displacement (Poddar, 2024). The effects of climate change, such as extreme weather events like flooding, droughts, heatwaves, wildfires, and the shifts in weather trends that often result in loss of livelihood, are driving people to evacuate their places of residence frequently with disastrous implications on their pattern of living and leading to humanitarian emergencies (Ahmed et al., 2021; Kelman & Meriläinen, 2024). Migration and displacement brought on by climate change are complicated, multidimensional problems that are impacted by environmental, social, political, and economic variables (Bandh et al., 2021; Poddar, 2024). The effects have serious ramifications for economic growth, human rights, and worldwide security, especially in the less-developed nations of Africa and Asia, where the majority of the global population resides.

According to World Bank projections, up to 143 million people may likely face climate change displacement by 2050, mostly in South Asia, Latin America, and sub-Saharan Africa (Semenza & Ebi, 2019; Tripathy, 2024). Significant numbers of these people have been internally displaced by disasters, with an average of 25.4 million relocated earlier in the years between 2008 and 2015; however, the majority of these displacements were associated with weather events such as storms, flooding, and many more. Climate change is already having a major effect on human migration and displacement throughout Africa, as many nations are seeing an increase in the frequency and intensity of heat waves, droughts, and flooding (Maharaj, 2024; Mustak, 2022). These events are disrupting human settlements, agricultural output, and water availability. Rising temperatures are causing droughts in West African nations, including Burkina Faso, Niger, Gambia, Mali, Sudan, and Senegal (Eboreime et al., 2025; N'gobi et al., 2022).

Communities that are potentially at risk, many of whom are situated in areas where climate change is most prevalent, are disproportionately impacted by climate crises and frequently lack the resources to deal with a changing landscape (Smith et al., 2022). Most people relocate because they have no other choice than to abandon their homes in search of security and safety (Crawley, 2021), leading them into a life of lack and chronic poverty while also restricting options to escape it (DeLuca et al., 2019; Nash, 2024). As those who are forced to relocate frequently lose property and other possessions, the significance of safe, orderly, and responsible movement and migration is emphasised by the United Nations Sustainable Development Goal 10, which focuses on how to reduce disparities both within and between nations (Hammond et al., 2024; Klein Solomon & Sheldon, 2018). However, the accomplishment of this objective is hampered by climate-related extreme weather occurrences, such as food and water shortages.

As one of the most urgent problems of our day is climate change, with its profound effects on ecosystems and human society as rising temperatures, altered precipitation patterns, and an increase in the frequency and intensity of extreme weather events are just a few of the effects of climate change now being felt in West Africa (Adaawen, 2021; Sagna et al., 2021). At present, migration and displacement brought on by climate change are becoming more and more major issues, with enormous ramifications for human security, economic growth, and regional stability (Teye & Nikoi, 2022). The ECOWAS region has created several policies and initiatives to lessen communities' susceptibility to climate change because it understands how critical it is to combat migration and displacement brought on by climate change (Osei-Amponsah et al., 2023; Saber et al., 2025).

Few synthesis studies that thoroughly examine the gendered dimension and financial resilience of climate-induced displacement and migration outcomes exist in the ECOWAS region, even though a small number of studies have examined the connection between migration and climate change in the Global South. Therefore, with an emphasis on identifying important causes, trends, and consequences for policy and practice, this study seeks to further our understanding of the patterns of migration and displacement brought on by climate change in the ECOWAS area. It further investigates how gendered livelihood and financial resilience are affected by climate change-driven floods, drought, and rising temperatures in the ECOWAS area of Africa.

The Climate and Migration Nexus in ECOWAS

The ECOWAS Treaty, which was signed in May 1975, created the 15-member organisation with the main goal of advancing economic integration in all spheres of economic activity, with a focus on manufacturing, transportation, telecommunications, energy, agriculture, natural resources, trade, monetary and financial issues, and social and cultural issues (Nwangwu et al., 2019). The following countries are members of ECOWAS: Ghana, Guinea, Guinea Bissau, Liberia, Mali, Niger, Nigeria, Senegal, Sierra Leone, Togo, Burkina Faso, Cabo Verde, Cote d'Ivoire, Gambia, and Guinea. These countries comprise two Lusophone nations, five Anglophone countries, and eight Francophone countries.

Although West Africa's contribution to global climate change is very minimal, its geographical location and weak adaptive capacity make it highly vulnerable to the effects of climate change and variability (Ayodotun et al., 2019; Davies-Vollum et al., 2021). The number of people migrating due to climate change is expected to rise substantially in the coming years, and the livelihoods of people in the dry regions of West Africa, in particular, are adversely affected by increased temperature and fluctuating rainfall patterns because they depend on rain-fed agriculture and ecosystem services (Piguet, 2022). Flooding is also a common climate-induced hazard in some West African countries. In West Africa, earlier prediction shows that up to 32 million people will be on the move within their countries by 2050 due to climate change (Rigaud, de Sherbinin, Jones, Adamo, et al., 2021). Indeed, current evidence suggests that migration is considered to be a growing adaptation response in the face of severe climate change (Osei-Amponsah et al., 2023; Poddar, 2024).

According to IPCC (2022) report, at 2°C of global warming, West Africa is projected to experience a drier, more drought-prone, and arid climate, especially in the last decades of the 21st century. Climate-induced migration is projected to contribute significantly to the stock of global migrants, especially in regions that depend on natural resources, climate-vulnerable activities (e.g., agriculture) and have weak capacity to adapt to climate change impacts (Almulhim et al., 2024). West African agriculture, which largely involves the middle-age and aged group, is heavily dependent on rainfall, making it extremely susceptible to climate change. Despite that the modern ways of combating the adverse effects of climate change require educational knowledge, the youth often intend to neglect agricultural practices due to lower agricultural yields and inadequate access to agricultural support incentives (Osei-Amponsah et al., 2023). Although promoting climate-smart agriculture is a positive response, the increasing impacts of climate change, coupled with high population growth, make it difficult to achieve adequate food and livelihood security.

The West African region has a long tradition of migration linked to kinship and religious networks, but climate change is contributing more and more to migration decisions; migration has become a key adaptation option for most rural households (UN DESA, 2020). The high rate of mobility may also be associated with the ECOWAS Protocol on Free Movement of citizens of the 15 member-states. In many rural communities, both male and female youth migrate elsewhere within their country, to other West African nations, or even overseas to find alternative sources of livelihood (IOM, 2020). High levels of migration have characterised livelihoods in West Africa for centuries (Teye & Nikoi, 2022). In 2020, estimated data from the International Migration Stock indicated that there were 7,551,660 million immigrants in the 16 countries of West Africa (UN Population Division, 2020). The reasons for the movement of people include forced displacements and conflicts, transhumance, routine seasonal annual shifts in agriculture, search for employment and better economic opportunities, and impacts of climate change (Teye & Nikoi, 2022). The trend of migration within West Africa reveals that internal and cross-border displacement in the region has risen sharply in recent years, with climate change necessitating the recent movement across agricultural sectors (Leal Filho, Olaniyan, et al., 2022).

Consequences of Environmental Migration in ECOWAS

The impacts of extreme climatic events such as floods, drought, erosion, rising temperatures, and sea level rise are already significantly impacting people's livelihoods (Banu & Fazal, 2025; Jha & Dev, 2024). As some countries are concerned about desertification and drought, others are worried about hazards such as floods, coastal erosion, and sea-level rise. Rainfall variability and drought lead to severe food insecurity, causing people to move in search of food, just as sea-level rise combines with storms to create storm surges, leading to mass migration of people and livestock (Atanga & Tankpa, 2021; Hadley et al., 2023). As people migrate long distance, moves are likely to sever local ties and undermine social support systems (Faist, 2021).

There are also concerns about the effects of rapid urbanisation driven by migration on the sustainability of cities. For example, city planners are confronted with the issues of sustainable urban growth, pressure on urban services, and an increase in pollution and waste generation (Humbal et al., 2023). Recently, the increasing migration of Fulani herders and other vulnerable populations from the Sahel and their settlement in countries along the coast has also become a source of concern for regional governments (Olamide, 2024). This form of migration is triggered by climatic conditions and has also contributed to recurring conflict between herders and farmers or migrants and indigenous populations (Setrana & Kyei, 2021).

Climate change is now more than just an environmental problem in West Africa, especially in the Sahel region; it is also a major cause of political instability. Existing social and political conflicts are being exacerbated by climatic disruptions, especially in vulnerable regions like Burkina Faso, Mali, Guinea, Guinea-Bissau, and Niger. Prolonged droughts, erratic rainfall, and fast soil degradation are all problems in the Sahel, which cause displacement, tensions between communities, and a decline in confidence in governmental institutions. Also, climate change may intensify already-existing socioeconomic and ethnic tensions among displaced and host communities, causing internal conflicts over viable land and natural resources. According to a recent ECOWAS research reported by WASCAL, climate-related disturbances decreased agricultural productivity in the ECOWAS region by as much as 10% in 2024, raising pressure associated with inflation and food insecurity. The report further shows that if no mitigating measures are taken and global temperatures rise by the predicted 1.5°C between 2030 and 2052, the situation could worsen with adverse impact on households' survival. Climate change–related stresses have been triggering the movement of pastoralists from Niger, Mali, and Northern Nigeria to neighbouring countries in search of water and grassland for their animals (Leal Filho et al., 2022). The fishery sector in Senegal is highly hit by climate change as the ecosystems are affected by the rising of sea level with consequent coastal erosion and fish migration due to water climate variability and temperatures rising (Muringai et al., 2021; Rigaud, de Sherbinin, Jones, Abu-Ata, et al., 2021), which has led many Senegalese young fishermen out of job and to consider migration to Europe as a viable option.

Climate change has the capability to exacerbate the already-existing gender inequities by limiting women's access to financial support, health services, and educational opportunities. Displaced women living in internally displaced homes or within a host community may find it challenging to get viable economic resources, financial help, land for farming, and other legal support which hinder their ability to cope, re-strategise their lives, build resilience, and rebuild their lives. As the government and communities social support networks may break down as displacement induced by climate change take place, leaving women even more vulnerable and alone, it further retard their strength and empowerment. Women are disproportionately affected by climate-related psychological trauma and health risks, such as starvation and waterborne illnesses, particularly when they are not appropriately provided for in their new shelter homes. Women's health can also be severely impacted by heat stress and pollution exposure, especially during pregnancy, which may result in problems including low birth weight or early delivery, leading to high neonatal and infant mortality rates.

Regional Intervention and Strategies to Climate-induced Displacement and Migration in ECOWAS

The ECOWAS regional climate strategy and action plan was adopted at the Ordinary Session of the Conference of the Heads of State and Governments of the ECOWAS, held on 29 April 2022, in Accra, Ghana (Ichimi, 2024). It came as a result of a long consultation process with the institutions, departments, and specialist agencies of ECOWAS, Member States, and specialist regional institutions, and on the other hand, it is the culmination of several years of intervention and action by ECOWAS in the fight against climate change. Earlier the ECOWAS committee for drought control in the Sahel (CILSS), and the West African Economic and Monetary Union communique on COP26 and Climate Change of 2021 acknowledged the need to focus on regional climate finance (Canton, 2021; Onuoha et al., 2023).

The majority of the member nations of ECOWAS have established national mechanisms in place to lower the risk of natural disasters, though the degree of implementation and development varies across countries as the ability to prepare for sudden climate disasters varies according to geographical and institutional structures including regional national platforms for disaster management, national response plans that include disaster risk reduction strategies or policies, and legal provisions. Through its Humanitarian and Social Affairs Directorate, ECOWAS also created several actions, plans, and policies for handling and avoiding natural risks, involving climate and environmental risks. These include the Regional Strategy for the Management of Flood Risks and the Disasters Risks Reduction Policy and Action Plan for 2015–2030, which offer guidance to Member States, intergovernmental organisations, and their national services (Egbara et al., 2024; Kasimbazi, 2024; Saber et al., 2025).

Also, West African countries have ratified the Africa Union continental agreement for the Protection and Assistance of Internally Displaced Persons in Africa (also known as the Kampala Convention) which addresses internal displacement caused not only by armed conflict, but also by natural and man-made disasters, and focuses on the root causes of internal displacement to provide durable solutions (Bamidele & Pikirayi, 2024). Furthermore, in September 2020, the ECOWAS Commission adopted its Regional Migration Policy, which integrates the climate change dimension through its seventh pillar on addressing the impacts of climate change on migration (Kandilige & Yeboah, 2024). The ECOWAS regional climate strategy contributes towards a low-carbon development model by focusing on green and all resilient growth, strengthening the adaptive capacities of African economies, societies, and ecosystems (Nwaobi, 2025).

The vision of ECOWAS' regional climate strategy is drawn from the vision of the AU climate change strategy for the period 2022–2032 derives from that of Agenda 2063: The Africa we want, resilient to climate change. Its main objective is the achievement of the Agenda 2063 Vision by building the resilience and coping mechanism of the African continent to the impacts of climate change, thereby calling for a community that is resilient to the effects and impacts of climate change and that has managed to seize the associated economic opportunities in favour of long-term, low-carbon, sustainable development (Nwaobi, 2025). The strategy aims at providing Africa and its stakeholders with strategic orientations to tackle the challenges posed by climate change and liable to hinder the achievement of the Agenda 2063 objectives. More precisely, the strategy aims to contribute to the achievement of SDG 13 on urgent action to combat climate change and its impacts and of the objectives of the Paris Agreement, in particular to limit the increase in global temperatures to well below 2°C relative to pre-industrial levels and to strive for 1.5°C, but also to achieve the seven objectives of the Sendai Framework for reducing disaster risks.

However, despite these important efforts, the application of these protocols in national procedures remains limited and the scale of future displacement due to climate change impacts requires anticipatory measures within a limited transformative measures taken throughout the migration cycle to reduce the vulnerabilities of future environmental migrants. It becomes imperative that much more is needed across the ECOWAS region in providing scientific information for the preservation of biodiversity through stakeholders' contributions to climate change adaptation. With the region's low level of modelling and climate data prediction, adequate migration governance is essential for the implementation process to be successful.

Climate-induced Displaced and Migration: Countries Context

Nigeria

As temperatures rise, climate predictions constantly warn of increasing extreme precipitation and flood events throughout West Africa. Floods in Nigeria in 2022 alone damaged almost 80,000 homes, leading to the displacement of about 1.3 million people, and flooded large agricultural farms, severely impairing livelihoods and food production. Climate change is causing severe environmental degradation in Nigeria, as evidenced by rising temperatures, unpredictable rainfall patterns, and extreme weather. Excessive precipitation and frequent flood events in the Niger and Benue Rivers are attributed to erratic climate systems, warning of increased exposure to floods in the future. The situation of internally displaced people (IDPs) has increased in frequency as populations are forced to leave their homes due to environmental degradation and climate-related disasters (Olayinka & Okonkwo, 2020).

In Nigeria's flooding history, the 2022 floods made a large devastating impact with the over-flooding of the Niger and Benue Rivers, claiming over 3.2 million lives and resulting in the damage of billions of properties (Lenshie et al., 2022). The complicated relationship between the refugee situation in Benue State and climate change has presented difficulties for the Nigerian administration. Sufficient financial and infrastructural resources are needed to offer the impacted people long-term remedies. A similar scenario is that of the 2025 flooding in Mokwa, Niger state, where a large number of school children, and households' properties were swept away. People who are displaced frequently end up in overcrowded and underequipped IDP/camps, where they endure inadequate living circumstances with limited access to essential services, and increased susceptibility to health problems. The plight of IDPs, especially women and girls in flood-affected communities in Nigeria is one prominent example of how climate change-induced migration distorts women's daily living, health, and survival. Recent trends of displacement in Nigeria revealed that climate change has emerged as a critical driver of internal migration, particularly in Northern Nigeria, where environmental stressors such as drought, desertification, and flooding have led to a significant rise in displaced populations (IOM, 2020).

Ghana

Ghana represents a relevant case in the examination of household susceptibility to climate vulnerability through rising temperatures, floods, and sea-level rise (Dovie & Pabi, 2023). A large number of people have moved from rural to urban areas as a result of these climate-related stressors, and Accra's urbanisation pressures have increased (Damte et al., 2023). Migration in Ghana is not a recent phenomenon; it has always been determined by a combination of environmental, socioeconomic, political, and ethnic factors, but recently climate change has gradually become a key push factor propelling migration (Milán-García et al., 2021). Floods displaced about 259,000 people between 2008 and 2022, leading to economic and livelihood distortion and instability. Baffour (2024) reported that coastal communities in Ghana are impacted by sea-level rise, leading to environmental degradation, food insecurity and economic distortion, often these changes also exacerbates vulnerabilities among the poorest groups especially women who suffer from loss of farm lands, houses disruption and mental health challenges. Coastal communities in the Volta, Western, Central, and Greater Accra regions experience economic and non-economic losses every year due to sea-level rise and strong tidal waves. For example, the Keta municipality in the Volta region has experienced periodic tidal waves over the past few years, which have displaced people and put communities such as Kporkporgbor, Dzita, and Xorvi at risk of extinction. In November 2021, a tidal wave surge led to the displacement of about 4,000 people in Keta and its environs, destroying homes and properties. Placating the climate-induced displaced groups requires advanced health systems and well-funded national resilience measures in Ghana. Earlier studies have shown that Ghana, exposure to climate change is extreme, but national and local mitigation measures are either poorly funded or non-existent (Kila, 2023).

Niger

The Republic of Niger is located in West Africa, with three-quarters of its land covered by deserts due to the Sahel and the Sahara. In recent years, the nation has seen political unrest and security crises in the regions that border Mali, Burkina Faso, and Nigeria, where armed groups target both people and security troops. In recent decades, drought, illnesses, and floods have become more frequent and intense in Niger. With a few hot, semi-arid climate zones in the south, the majority of Niger is a hot desert. A significant section of the population suffers from chronic food insecurity as a result of Niger's vulnerability to natural calamities like droughts, floods, and locust infestations. Niger is particularly vulnerable to climate change and the risks that ensue with rising temperatures and the unpredictability of rainfall. The floods experienced in 2020 were an example of how the magnitude and rainfall unpredictability can impact Niger where thousands of hectares of cropland were destroyed, livestock perished, and more than 69,000 households lost their livelihoods (FAO, 2021). The temperature records in Niger show an increase, rising 1.5 times faster than in the rest of the world. By 2100, experts are predicting a 3–6°C rise in temperature, which will worsen food security, water scarcity, and further aggravate conflicts and humanitarian crises.

As more than 80% of Niger's population depends on agriculture, small-scale farmers are the most directly affected by climate variability, providing support for farmers becomes imperative and requires the formulation of an effective policy on a climate change mitigation framework in the country. Although Niger government has set the *National Policy on Climate Change* in motion, it requires financial resources for the implementation of the Nationally Determined Contribution (NDC) during the 2021–2030 period. Niger government counts on assistance from international cooperation to mobilise sufficient financial resources to achieve the objectives of its NDC, since the resources that can be mobilised at the national level are limited and insufficient, hence for Niger to make notable progress in advancing climate change support, it is important to build the capacity of actors to facilitate access to financial mechanisms and resources to promote the implementation of the NDC.

Togo

The Republic of Togo is located in West Africa, along the Gulf of Guinea, and borders with Ghana to the west, Benin to the east, Burkina Faso to the north (Kohnert, 2019). Togo's reliance on rain-fed agriculture and livestock increases its vulnerability to climate change and limits the capacity of poor households and communities to manage climate risk, increasing their vulnerability to climate-related shocks (Guerrera et al., 2021). Weather-related hazards, of which Togo is vulnerable, are likely to increase with climate change. Agriculture, energy, health, housing, water resources, and coastal areas will be particularly vulnerable to these climatic changes. Future climate change may worsen coastal erosion and lead to loss of goods and services, which is especially concerning as over 90% of the country's industrial units are located in coastal areas. In Togo, climate change is having a major effect on displacement, mostly due to a rise in the frequency and severity of extreme weather events like droughts and floods, which cause livelihood loss and relocation. The already precarious security situation in the Sahel region, which affects northern Togo, is made worse by rising temperatures and sea levels, especially in coastal areas. In Togo, women are disproportionately impacted by climate change, which increases their vulnerability and relocation. Women are displaced from their homes by environmental disasters like droughts and floods, which affect their safety, access to resources, and means of subsistence while also making them more vulnerable to gender-based violence (Sodokin & Nyatefe, 2021). Food insecurity results from climate-related calamities, including droughts and floods that destroy crops and cattle, affecting women's position as primary food providers. Many women are forced to migrate as a result of this loss of income, frequently to cities or informal settlements where they struggle to find safe homes and work.

Conclusion

This study indicates that climate change–induced relocation has a disproportionate impact on women's livelihood security and financial resilience across ECOWAS region. The core findings are that pre-existing gender inequalities, particularly those related to access to property ownership, formal financial services, and decision-making power, are not only persistent but also significantly exacerbated by relocation shocks. A large number of displaced women who frequently rely on climate-subsistence farming risk losing their jobs entirely. This is made worse by the gendered segregation of labour markets in host communities, which restricts their access to steady, well-paying jobs and pushes them into low-wage, exploitative, or precarious employment. Women's weak financial resilience becomes compromised by the displacement process, which restricts their ability to save, obtain credit, or take advantage of disaster assistance programmes. As a result, there is a greater chance of long-term poverty and a greater reliance on insufficient social safety nets.

Way Forward

This chapter explores climate-induced migration in ECOWAS with a focus on how it affects women's livelihood and their financial resilience across the region. The study discovered that most ECOWAS countries have experienced considerable induced displacement and movement patterns as a result of increasing floods in coastal areas and droughts in northern regions. Environmental hazards like erosion and flooding are common in most communities, causing homes, infrastructure, and livelihoods to be destroyed. In some cases, these disasters even result in fatalities, highlighting the communities' fragility. Families are under pressure from the environment to think about moving, yet there are limitations on their ability to do so to secure places and overcome the trauma of displacement. As primary caregivers and suppliers of food and fuel, women are more likely than men to be impacted by climate change, making them more susceptible to flooding and drought. To guarantee women's involvement in decision-making processes concerning climate change and disaster response, West African nations must create and execute climate adaptation and disaster risk reduction plans that particularly target the needs of women and girls.

Additionally, social protection services must be strengthened, and it is essential to give displaced women access to resources and chances for employment.

References

Adaawen, S. (2021). Understanding climate change and drought perceptions, impact and responses in the rural Savannah, West Africa. *Atmosphere*, *12*(5), 594.

Ahmed, A., Mohamed, N. S., Siddig, E. E., Algaily, T., Sulaiman, S., & Ali, Y. (2021). The impacts of climate change on displaced populations: A call for action. *The Journal of Climate Change and Health*, *3*, 100057.

Almulhim, A. I., Alverio, G. N., Sharifi, A., Shaw, R., Huq, S., Mahmud, M. J., & Abubakar, I. R. (2024). Climate-induced migration in the Global South: An in depth analysis. *npj Climate Action*, *3*(1), 47.

Atanga, R. A., & Tankpa, V. (2021). Climate change, flood disaster risk and food security nexus in Northern Ghana. *Frontiers in Sustainable Food Systems*, *5*, 706721.

Ayodotun, B., Bamba, S., & Adio, A. (2019). Vulnerability assessment of West African countries to climate change and variability. *Journal of Geoscience and Environment Protection*, *7*(06), 13.

Baffour, A. A. (2024). Climate change impacts and adaptation strategies for Ghana's coastal population: A qualitative inquiry. *Climate Change*, *10*, e6cc1033. https://doi.org/10.54905/disssi.v10i28.e6cc1033

Bamidele, S., & Pikirayi, I. (2024). African Union Kampala convention: The continuing dialogue on the protection of internally displaced persons in Sub-Saharan Africa. *Journal of Asian and African Studies*, 00219096231225944.

Bandh, S. A., Shafi, S., Peerzada, M., Rehman, T., Bashir, S., Wani, S. A., & Dar, R. (2021). Multidimensional analysis of global climate change: A review. *Environmental Science and Pollution Research*, *28*(20), 24872–24888.

Banu, N., & Fazal, S. (2025). Climate change, livelihood crisis and resilience: An introduction. In N. Banu & S. Fazal (Eds.), *Livelihoods and well-being in the era of climate change. Risk to resilience across India* (pp. 3–18). Springer Nature.

Canton, H. (2021). Economic Community of West African States—ECOWAS. In Europa Publications (Ed.), *The Europa directory of international organizations 2021* (23rd ed., pp. 534–542). Routledge.

Crawley, H. (2021). The politics of refugee protection in a (post) COVID-19 world. *Social Sciences*, *10*(3), 81.

Damte, E., Manteaw, B. O., & Wrigley-Asante, C. (2023). Urbanization, climate change and health vulnerabilities in slum communities in Ghana. *The Journal of Climate Change and Health*, *10*, 100189.

Davies-Vollum, K. S., Raha, D., & Koomson, D. (2021). Climate change impact and adaptation: Lagoonal fishing communities in West Africa. In W. Leal Filho, N. Oguge, D. Abbott, C. Iyala, & A. Q. Al-Amin (Eds.), *African handbook of climate change adaptation* (pp. 2221–2245). Springer International Publishing.

DeLuca, S., Wood, H., & Rosenblatt, P. (2019). Why poor families move (and where they go): Reactive mobility and residential decisions. *City & Community*, *18*(2), 556–593.

Dovie, D. B. K., & Pabi, O. (2023). Partial climatic risk screening, adaptation and livelihoods in a coastal urban area in Ghana. *Habitat International*, *138*, 102868.

Eboreime, E., Anjorin, O., Obi-Jeff, C., Ojo, T. M., & Hertelendy, A. (2025). From drought to displacement: Assessing the impacts of climate change on conflict and forced migration in West Africa's Sahel Region. *The Journal of Climate Change and Health, 23*, 100448.

Egbara, O., Chukwudi, C. E., Elumelu, C. S., & David, O. (2024). Comparative study of Southern Africa Development Commission (SADC) and Economic Community of West African States (ECOWAS) in conflict management: The case of Southern and Western Africa sub-regions. *Migration letters, 21*(5), 795–841.

Faist, T. (2021). The crucial meso-level. In T. Faist (Ed.), *International migration, immobility and development* (pp. 187–217). Routledge.

Food and Agriculture Organization of the United Nations. (2021). *Niger: Response to the 2020 floods – Emergency agricultural assistance*. FAO.

Guerrera, F., Martín-Martín, M., Tramontana, M., Nimon, B., & Essotina Kpémoua, K. (2021). Shoreline changes and coastal erosion: The case study of the coast of Togo (Bight of Benin, West Africa margin). *Geosciences, 11*(2), 40.

Hadley, K., Wheat, S., Rogers, H. H., Balakumar, A., Gonzales-Pacheco, D., Davis, S. S., Marwell, S. R., & Sorensen, C. (2023). Mechanisms underlying food insecurity in the aftermath of climate-related shocks: A systematic review. *The Lancet Planetary Health, 7*(3), e242–e250.

Hammond, L., Casentini, G., & Bakewell, O. (2024). Migration, inequalities and the Sustainable Development Goals. In A. Triandafyllidou & H. Akari (Eds.), *The Elgar companion to migration and the Sustainable Development Goals* (pp. 64–77). Edward Elgar Publishing.

Humbal, A., Chaudhary, N., & Pathak, B. (2023). Urbanization trends, climate change, and environmental sustainability. In B. Bakshi, C. B. Pande, & S. K. Singh (Eds.), *Climate change and urban environment sustainability* (pp. 151–166). Springer Nature.

Ichimi, G. S. (2024). The WTO, ECOWAS and the prospects for food security in West Africa. In G. S. Ichimi (Ed.), *The World Trade Organization and food security in West Africa: Prospects for the ECOWAS region* (pp. 107–162). Springer Nature.

Internal Displacement Monitoring Centre. (2016). *Global report on internal displacement 2016*. https://www.internal-displacement.org/global-report/grid2016/

IOM. (2020). *Migration and climate change nexus*. https://environmentalmigration.iom.int/migration-and-climate-change-nexus

IPCC. (2022). Summary for policymakers. In H. O. Pörtner, D. C. Roberts, M. Tignor, E. S. Poloczanska, K. Mintenbeck, A. Alegría, M. Nicolai, A. Okem, J. Petzold, B. Rama, & N. M. Weyer (Eds.), *Climate change 2022: Impacts, adaptation, and vulnerability. Contribution of Working Group II to the sixth assessment report of the Intergovernmental Panel on Climate Change* (pp. 3–33). Cambridge University Press.

Jha, M. K., & Dev, M. (2024). Impacts of climate change. In M. Azrour, J. Mabrouki, A. Alabdulatif, A. Guezzaz, & F. Amounas (Eds.), *Smart internet of things for environment and healthcare* (pp. 139–159). Springer Nature.

Kandilige, L., & Yeboah, T. (2024). West African migration regimes and the externalization of EU migration management policies. In G. Heck, E. Sevinin, E. Habersky, & C. Sandoval-García (Eds.), *Making routes: Mobility and the politics of migration in the Global South* (pp. 137–158). American University in Cairo Press.

Kandilige, L., & Yeboah, T. (2024). West African migration regimes and the externalization of EU migration management policies. In G. Heck, E. Sevinin, E. Habersky, & C. Sandoval-García (Eds.), *Making routes: Mobility and the politics of migration in the Global South* (pp. 137–158). American University in Cairo Press.

Kelman, I., & Meriläinen, E. (2024). Climate change, disasters and humanitarian action. In S. Roth, B. Purkayastha, & T. Denskus (Eds.), *Handbook on humanitarianism and inequality* (pp. 338–351). Edward Elgar Publishing.

Kila, K. O. (2023). Ghana and the global climate crisis: Rethinking the legal approach for climate change regulation of corporations in Ghana. *Environmental Law Review, 25*(4), 289–310.

Klein Solomon, M., & Sheldon, S. (2018). The global compact for migration: From the sustainable development goals to a comprehensive agreement on safe, orderly and regular migration. *International Journal of Refugee Law, 30*(4), 584–590.

Kohnert, D. (2019). Togo. In J. Abbink, S. Elischer, A. Mehler, & H. Melber (Eds.), *Africa yearbook. Volume 15: Politics, economy and society south of the Sahara in 2018* (pp. 179–186). Brill.

Leal Filho, W., Olaniyan, O. F., & Alverio, G. N. (2022). Where to go? Migration and climate change response in West Africa. *Geoforum, 137*, 83–87.

Leal Filho, W., Setti, A. F. F., Azeiteiro, U. M., Lokupitiya, E., Donkor, F. K., Etim, N. N., Matandirotya, N., Olooto, F. M., Sharifi, A., Nagy, G. J., & Djekic, I. (2022). An overview of the interactions between food production and climate change. *Science of The Total Environment, 838*, 156438.

Lenshie, N. E., Ojeh, V. N., Oruonye, E. D., Ezeibe, C., Ajaero, C., Nzeadibe, T. C., Celestine, U. U., & Osadebe, N. (2022). Geopolitics of climate change-induced conflict and population displacement in West Africa. *Local Environment, 27*(3), 287–308.

Maharaj, B. (2024). Climate change and human displacement: Some reflections from Africa. In M. Mishra, A. J. de Lucena, & B. Maharaj (Eds.), *Climate change and regional socio-economic systems in the Global South: Resilience strategies for sustainable development* (pp. 173–190). Springer Nature.

Milán-García, J., Caparrós-Martínez, J. L., Rueda-López, N., & de Pablo Valenciano, J. (2021). Climate change-induced migration: A bibliometric review. *Globalization and health, 17*(1), 74.

Muringai, R. T., Mafongoya, P. L., & Lottering, R. (2021). Climate change and variability impacts on sub-Saharan African fisheries: A review. *Reviews in Fisheries Science & Aquaculture, 29*(4), 706–720.

Mustak, S. (2022). Climate change and disaster-induced displacement in the Global South: A review. In P. Banik & A. Barman (Eds.), *Climate change, disaster and adaptations: Contextualising human responses to ecological change* (pp. 107–120). Springer Nature.

Nash, S. L. (2024). Climate protection for migration prevention: Comparison of policy discourses on climate change and migration in Austria, Germany, Denmark, and Sweden. *Journal of Comparative Policy Analysis: Research and Practice, 26*(3–4), 303–331.

N'gobi, G. M. L., Danani, K., & Soulé, M. (2022). Climate change and biodiversity in West Africa Sahel: A review. *Restoration Ecology, 4*, 20–29.

Nwangwu, C., Enyiazu, C., Nwagwu, E. J., & Ezeibe, C. C. (2019). Interrogating the relevance of the ECOWAS in global political economy. *Central European Journal of International & Security Studies, 13*(2), 64–87.

Nwaobi, G. C. (2025). Climate transition, decarbonization framework and energy sustainability in ECOWAS region. In G. C. Nwaobi (Ed.), *Decarbonization framework and energy sustainability in ECOWAS region* (pp. 1–134). Quantitative Economic Research Bureau (MPRA Paper 124215, University Library of Munich).

Olayinka, B. O., & Okonkwo, J. O. (2020). Climate change-induced displacements: Implications for internally displaced persons in Nigeria. *African Geographical Review, 39*(1), 61–78.

Onuoha, F. C., Ojewale, O., & Akogwu, C. J. (2023). Climate change and natural resource conflict in ECOW AS and ECCAS regions: Implications for state security forces. *African Journal on Conflict Resolution, 23*(2), 7–36.

Osei-Amponsah, C., Quarmine, W., & Okem, A. (2023). Understanding climate-induced migration in West Africa through the social transformation lens. *Frontiers in Sociology, 8*, 1173395.

Piguet, E. (2022). Linking climate change, environmental degradation, and migration: An update after 10 years. *Wiley Interdisciplinary Reviews: Climate Change*, *13*(1), e746.

Poddar, A. K. (2024). Climate change and migration: Developing policies to address the growing challenge of climate-induced displacement. *International Journal of Climate Change: Impacts & Responses*, *16*(1), 101–115.

Raihan, A. (2023). A review of the global climate change impacts, adaptation strategies, and mitigation options in the socio-economic and environmental sectors. *Journal of Environmental Science and Economics*, *2*(3), 36–58.

Rigaud, K. K., de Sherbinin, A., Jones, B., Abu-Ata, N. E., & Adamo, S. (2021). *Groundswell Africa: A deep dive into internal climate migration in Senegal*. World Bank.

Rigaud, K. K., de Sherbinin, A., Jones, B., Adamo, S., Maleki, D., Abu-Ata, N. E., Tall, A., & Tricaud, C. (2021). *Groundswell Africa: Internal climate migration in West African countries*. World Bank. https://openknowledge.worldbank.org/handle/10986/36404

Saber, M., Koroma, A., Posite, R. V., Ly, A., Tejan Bah, A. M., Abdulai, A., El-Rawy, M. A., & Mewafy, F. (2025). A comprehensive review of climate change adaptation and disaster risk reduction in Africa. *Journal of Water and Climate Change*, *16*(5), 1831–1862.

Sagna, P., Dipama, J. M., Vissin, E. W., Diomandé, B. I., Diop, C., Chabi, P. A. B., & Yade, M. (2021). Climate change and water resources in West Africa: A case study of Ivory Coast, Benin, Burkina Faso, and Senegal. In B. Njau, T. G. Ahmed, & N. E. M. A. Bakr (Eds.), *Climate change and water resources in Africa: Perspectives and solutions towards an imminent water crisis* (pp. 55–86). Springer Nature.

Semenza, J. C., & Ebi, K. L. (2019). Climate change impact on migration, travel, travel destinations, and the tourism industry. *Journal of Travel Medicine*, *26*, 5.

Setrana, M. B., & Kyei, J. R. K. O. (2021). Migration, farmer-herder conflict and the challenges of peace building in the Agogo traditional area, Ghana. *Ghana Journal of Geography*, *13*, 340–357. https://doi.org/10.4314/gjg.v13i2.13

Smith, G. S., Anjum, E., Francis, C., Deanes, L., & Acey, C. (2022). Climate change, environmental disasters, and health inequities: The underlying role of structural inequalities. *Current Environmental Health Reports*, *9*(1), 80–89.

Sodokin, K., & Nyatefe, V. (2021). Cash transfers, climate shocks vulnerability and households' resilience in Togo. *Discover Sustainability*, *2*(1), 3.

Sowale, O. A. (2025). Fulani herder-farmer identity conflict in West Africa with a particular focus on security implications for Nigeria. *African Identities*, *23*(2), 415–431.

Teye, J. K., & Nikoi, E. G. (2022). Climate-induced migration in West Africa. In J. K. Teye (Ed.), *Migration in West Africa: IMISCOE regional reader* (pp. 79–105). Springer International Publishing.

Tripathy, S. N. (2024). Climate change, migration, displacement in Asia and the Pacific: Role of UNDP. In S. N. Tripathy & A. K. Poddar (Eds.), *Climate change and migration: Challenges and adaptive strategies* (pp. 42–58). Kunal Books.

UN DESA. (2020). *International migration 2020: Highlights* (ST/ESA/SER.A/452). United Nations Department of Economic and Social Affairs, Population Division. https://www.un.org/en/desa/international-migration-2020-highlights

UN Population Division. (2020). *United Nations Population Division, Department of Economic and Social Affairs, Trends in International Migrant Stock*. https://www.un.org/development/desa/pd/content/international-migrant-stock

Chapter 7

Vulnerable Women's Participation in Climate Action and Alternative Financing for Livelihoods in the Northern Region of Ghana

Samson Sambian Konlan and Tanusha Raniga

Department of Social Work and Community Development, University of Johannesburg, South Africa

Abstract

The Kyoto Protocol and the Paris Agreement call for financial assistance, particularly climate financing from parties with more financial resources to those that are less endowed and vulnerable to prevent climate change and cope with its consequences. Given this context, women in Africa are more likely to be exposed to the impacts of climate change due to their roles and responsibilities, gender inequalities, and lack of access to resources for livelihoods. This chapter presents empirical evidence from the qualitative phase of a broader study. It explored vulnerable women's participation in climate action and the alternative financing they would need for livelihoods. The study involved 30 participants, of whom 15 were vulnerable women from the Northern Region of Ghana. The results showed women were involved in climate-sensitive activities such as slash-and-burn agricultural activities, excessive fuelwood harvest, and charcoal production, which contribute to greenhouse gas emissions. The women suggested that alternative climate financing should focus on climate-smart agriculture practices, providing electrical stoves and irrigation systems for livelihood diversification, and an adaptation strategy. The study will guide policymakers, social workers, and development practitioners on how to assist vulnerable women who depend on climate-sensitive activities to adapt to climate change, reduce emissions, and enhance livelihoods or include women in decision-making

Gender and Climate Finance in Africa: Addressing Inequalities and Bridging Gaps, 115–131

Published under exclusive licence by Emerald Publishing Limited
doi:10.1108/978-1-83742-085-820261007

regarding climate governance. In addition, the study is invaluable to policymakers in the implementation of ambitious climate action plans to meet Ghana's Nationally Determined Contributions (NDC).

Keywords: Climate change; emissions; financing; Ghana; livelihoods; vulnerable, women

Introduction

The Intergovernmental Panel on Climate Change (IPCC, 2018) called for an urgent global response from all segments of society to counter the impact of climate change. Thus, the Kyoto Protocol and the Paris Agreement call for financial assistance, particularly climate financing from parties with more financial resources to those that are less endowed and vulnerable to prevent climate change and cope with its consequences (UNFCCC, 2021). Climate finance refers to local, national or transnational financing, drawn from public, private, and alternative sources of financing, that seeks to support mitigation and adaptation actions that could address climate change (UNFCCC, 2021). In 2018, the IPCC shed light on how climate change contributes to the understanding of its causes and consequences and the options for risk management through adaptation and mitigation (IPCC, 2018). For many years, global warming has continued unabated, and we have witnessed an acceleration in sea-level rise (IPCC, 2018). Emissions of greenhouse gases due to human activities, the root cause of global warming, continue to increase, year after year (IPCC, 2018). Climate change is one of the most significant challenges facing humanity due to its detrimental effects (Koomson, 2023).

One of the United Nations' 2030 Sustainable Development Goals is to combat the global impacts of climate change (Dagnachew & Hof, 2023). Changing climatic conditions affect over 100 million people globally, exacerbating the gender poverty gap across nations and continents (Ray, 2021). Wright (2024) maintained that across the African continent, women bear an unequal burden when it comes to climate change impacts. Many women in the region rely primarily on climate-sensitive livelihoods, such as small-scale farming and manual labour (Babacan, 2021). Koomson (2023) added that climate change makes women highly exposed to the impacts of extreme weather events such as recurring droughts and floods, which damage crops and kill livestock upon which their livelihoods depend. Climate-smart agricultural practices have been adopted in African countries to address the problems of land degradation and desertification (Barasa et al., 2021). These projects aim to improve food security, enhance timber production, and lower crops and livestock vulnerability to climate change (Barasa et al., 2021). However, the role of women in the fight against climate change is not given much attention.

Ghana introduced the Livelihood Empowerment Against Poverty (LEAP) programme, a social protection initiative launched in 2008 (MoGCSP, 2023). It is a cash transfer programme designed to support extremely poor and vulnerable households by providing them with regular stipends (MoGCSP, 2023). However, female beneficiaries in the Northern Region of Ghana face greater challenges due to existing gender inequalities and their reliance on climate-sensitive resources for livelihoods, such as small-scale farming and manual labour (Glazebrook, 2017). In Ghana, women make up a large percentage of subsistence farmers who rely on rain-fed agriculture (Glazebrook, 2017).

The women engaged in slash-and-burn agriculture activities, excessive fuelwood harvest, and charcoal production, which degrade the forest (Glazebrook, 2017). Fuelwood and charcoal are widely used by Ghanaian households instead of electricity and other conventional energy sources (Acheampong et al., 2023). The impacts of these activities include extreme weather events such as recurring droughts and floods, which damage crops and kill livestock upon which their livelihoods depend (Acheampong et al., 2023). Although the vulnerable women receive cash from the state, it does not stop them from engaging in climate-sensitive activities for their livelihoods (MoGCSP, 2023).

According to UNFCCC (2021), climate finance flows in Ghana show that an annual average of USD 830 million was tracked in 2019 and 2020 but highlighting the pressing need to bolster climate finance to achieve Ghana's NDC. However, the agriculture, forestry, and land use sector receives the highest investment, with a significant focus on adaptation (UNFCCC, 2021). In addition, investments are also directed towards disaster risk management, policy support, and capacity building (World Bank, 2022). There was also nearly equal allocation of climate finance towards mitigation and adaptation in Ghana (World Bank, 2022). Climate change poses significant economic and environmental challenges to women (Opoku, 2019). The direction of the climate financing sources to the various sectors have proven insufficient to meet adaptation and mitigation needs of women (Acheampong et al., 2023). However, rural women in developing countries whose livelihoods largely depend on natural resources are among the most impacted by climate change (Koomson, 2023). For instance, women in Ghana are disproportionately impacted by climate change due to existing gender inequalities that limit their access to resources and place a heavier burden of climate-related tasks on them, such as water collection and smallholder farming (Assan et al., 2018). Koomson (2023) maintained that gender inequality and climate change lead to increased hardship, reduced economic opportunities, and negative health impacts, such as higher risks during pregnancy. As a result, attention has turned towards alternative financing mechanisms to women for mitigation and adaptation, but few empirical studies assess the alternative climate financing instruments to women (Acheampong et al., 2023). In Ghana, there are limited studies to understand their participation, needs and how to improve livelihoods through alternative climate financing (Acheampong et al., 2023). This study is situated within the sustainable livelihood framework for better understanding.

Hence, this chapter explored how women could participate in climate action and the alternative financing they would need to enhance livelihoods in the Northern Region of Ghana. The significance of the study is that it will guide policymakers, social workers, and development practitioners on how to assist vulnerable women who depend on climate-sensitive activities to adapt to climate change, reduce emissions, and enhance livelihoods. The alternative climate financing may not be cash for consumption, but initiatives such as microfinance, green entrepreneurship, or non-cash initiatives such as smart agriculture activities and conventional energy use to adapt to climate-related shocks and maintain livelihoods. This study will also enable climate-related stakeholders to include women in decision-making in climate governance. The chapter employs the sustainable livelihood framework as an interpretative tool to describe women's participation in climate action, their livelihoods, and alternative climate financing.

Conceptual Framework

A livelihood comprises the capabilities, assets (including both material and social resources), and activities required for a means of living. A livelihood is sustainable when it can cope with and recover from stresses and shocks and maintain or enhance its capabilities and assets both now and in the future, while not undermining the natural resource base (DFID, 2000, P1). In the sustainable livelihood framework, it is not impossible to utilise every element in a single study (Ellis, 2000). Thus, the study focuses on vulnerability and the interaction of the capitals for the outcome in the framework.

In the sustainable livelihood framework in Fig. 7.1, vulnerability context refers to the external environment that shapes people's livelihoods, encompassing factors like trends, shocks, and seasonality (Ashley, 2000). Devereux (2001) asserted

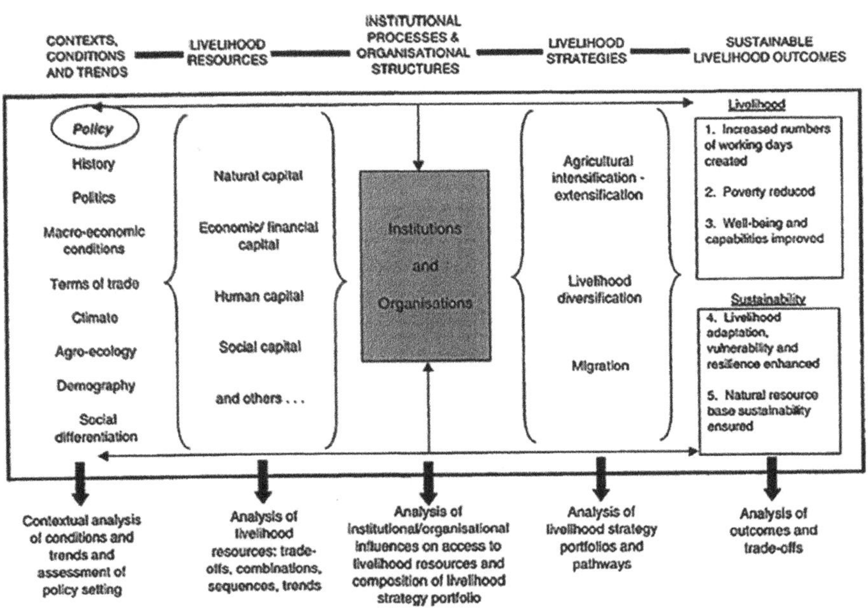

Fig. 7.1. The Sustainable Livelihoods Framework. *Source*: Scoones (1998, 2015, p. 36).

that these factors, over which people have limited or no control, directly impact their assets and livelihood options. Understanding the vulnerability context is crucial for designing effective interventions that support sustainable livelihoods (DFID, 2000).

The sustainable livelihood capitals in Fig. 7.1 are natural, human, social, physical, and financial, which are sometimes referred to as assets. These capitals interact in complex ways to shape individuals' and communities' ability to sustain their livelihoods (Ellis, 2000; Raniga, 2021). Scoones (2015) argued that interactions of the capitals can be both positive and negative, influencing access to resources, opportunities, and overall well-being. Serrat (2017) added that understanding these interactions is crucial for developing effective strategies to improve livelihoods, promote sustainable development, and use of resources. The key interactions are as follows:

Natural and human capital: Access to natural resources (like land or water) can be enhanced or constrained by human capabilities, such as knowledge, skills, and health classified as human capital (Morse & McNamara, 2013). Dube and Chatterjee (2022) explained that farmers with good agricultural knowledge (human capital) can better utilise land (natural capital) to improve crop yields. In relation to climate change and women's land use, climate-smart agriculture can be used to manage agricultural landscapes to sustainably increase productivity, enhance resilience to climate change, and reduce greenhouse gas emissions (Acheampong et al., 2023).

Social and financial capital: Strong social networks (social capital) can provide access to financial resources, such as loans or grants, or facilitate access to markets (Narula et al., 2021). Conversely, access to financial capital can strengthen social ties by enabling participation in community activities and building trust (Guo et al., 2022). In relation to women's access to financial capital, climate finance can come from local, national or transnational sources, drawn from public, private, and alternative sources of financing, that may support mitigation and adaptation actions that will address climate change and improve livelihoods (Glazebrook, 2017).

Physical and financial capital: Access to physical infrastructure, like transportation or irrigation systems (physical capital), can be facilitated by financial resources (Tabares et al., 2022). Conversely, financial capital can be used to maintain or improve physical assets (Dube & Chatterjee, 2022). For instance, women's access to irrigation may play a crucial role in climate change adaptation and mitigation by ensuring food security and improving water resource management (Morse & McNamara, 2013). It can help farmers adapt to water scarcity and extreme weather events, while also potentially reducing greenhouse gas emissions through improved water use efficiency (Scoones, 2015).

Natural and human: Natural capital, like forests, provides resources like fuelwood and charcoal, while human capital, like knowledge of foraging, influences access to those resources (Morse & McNamara, 2013). In relation to women's access to forest resources, as the forest is degrading, knowledge is needed to restore the degraded forests, implement sustainable forestry practices, and promote responsible consumption and production patterns (Guo et al., 2022). In addition to that knowledge for forest restoration, financial capital might be needed to purchase tools for planting trees or alternative options, including solar energy, biogas, electric stoves, and other forms of biomass (Scoones, 2015).

Climate financing could enable women's livelihood diversification (Scoones, 2015). For instance, a mix of livelihood capitals enables households to diversify their income sources (Guo et al., 2022). Access to land (natural capital), agricultural skills (human capital), and market connections (social capital) can allow farmers to engage in both smart agriculture activities and off-farm activities (Scoones, 2015).

Sustainable livelihood policies, institutions, and processes encompass the structures (like government agencies and NGOs), processes (like laws and cultural norms), and policies related to access to land and resource management that shape livelihoods (Krantz, 2001). These are crucial for enabling individuals and communities to achieve long-term well-being and resilience (Raniga, 2021). Livelihood strategies are the range and combination of activities and choices that people make in order to achieve their livelihood goals (Raniga et al., 2019). For instance, utilising the skills, knowledge, and resources that people already possess for income-generating activities to reduce vulnerability and shocks (Krantz, 2001). According to Scoones (2015), sustainable livelihood outcomes include more income, a strong voice, reduced vulnerability, improved food security, and more sustainable use of natural resources. The asterisks in the framework are just indicating individual livelihood outcomes. This sustainable livelihood framework guided how women could participate in climate action and the alternative financing they would need to enhance livelihoods in the Northern Region of Ghana.

Methodology

This study utilised a descriptive and interpretive research design in a qualitative methodology to gain an in-depth understanding of women's participation in climate action and alternative financing for livelihoods in the Northern Region of Ghana. The central premise of this chapter is that many women in the Northern part of Ghana rely primarily on climate-sensitive livelihood activities such as small-scale farming and manual labour, including fuelwood harvest and charcoal production, which contribute to climate change, which eventually exposes them to the impacts of extreme weather events such as recurring droughts and floods. Hence, participation in climate action and alternative financing could improve their livelihoods and reduce the impact of climate change. Qualitative research design allowed a surface and an in-depth understanding of the phenomenon (Creswell, 2014; Elliott & Timulak, 2005). The study was conducted in Sagnarigu Municipality, a suburb of Tamale, the Northern Regional Capital of Ghana. Sagnarigu Municipal Assembly (2020) reported that the municipality had high poverty rates, and many women participating in the LEAP cash transfer programme engage in climate-sensitive activities for their livelihoods.

Data Collection

The study employed a purposive sampling technique involving the selection of 30 LEAP cash beneficiary household heads, with a proportion of 15 males and 15 females as Sample I. The male is mentioned here because the data is part of a larger study but the information from the females is emphasised in this study. Purposive sampling was used based on predetermined selection criteria. The criteria included that a participant must have been receiving LEAP cash for a minimum of two years and must be the head of a household. The participants must have been involved in climate-sensitive activities for livelihoods. The participants in the study were drawn from the LEAP cash beneficiary register at the Sagnarigu Municipal Assembly, the Department of Social Welfare and Community Development. Sample II comprised six key informants, two each from the LEAP committee, social workers, and policymakers in the Northern Region of Ghana. The key informants were selected based on their knowledge of the LEAP cash transfer beneficiaries' livelihood activities.

However, Sample I involved two distinct methods for gathering data. In-depth interviews with the LEAP cash beneficiary household heads and a focus group discussion session with eight members who were willing to participate in a group setting. The study used interview guides with semi-structured and open-ended questions (Bryman, 2004). The individual in-depth interviews took approximately one hour with each participant and approximately two hours in the focus group discussion. The interview questions were designed to understand how women could participate in climate action and alternative financing to enhance their livelihoods in the Northern Region of Ghana. The interview and the focus group discussions with the LEAP cash beneficiaries were held in *Dagbani*, the local language, to allow the participants to express themselves freely, as they were not fluent in the English language.

Sample II involved face-to-face interviews with the key informants using an interview guide with semi-structured and open-ended questions. The interview was conducted entirely in English. The major themes were women's participation in climate action, sustainable livelihoods and alternative climate financing. Although notes were taken, all the interviews and the focus group discussion were recorded both in audio and video with the consent of the participants. Although the biographical components will not be discussed, pseudonyms were used to protect their identity and will be utilised in the chapter to support quotations. The key informants were denoted (K). Thus, (K1, K2) were for the two LEAP committee members, (K3, K4) for the two social workers, and (K5, K6) for the two policymakers.

Data Analysis

Braun and Clarke's (2006) six-step thematic analysis method for qualitative data analysis was used in this study. The first step involved familiarising oneself with the data by repeatedly listening to the audio recordings, transcribing the data, comparing it with field notes, and making initial notes on potential codes. In addition, reading through all the data several times to get a sense of overall ideas and tone. In the second step, the researcher coded key elements across the entire data set, organising information relevant to each code (Bryman, 2004). Coding means labelling chunks of text that represent certain ideas or themes (Bryman, 2004). For instance, highlighting key words, phrases, or sentences that seem meaningful such livelihood capitals, vulnerability, adaptation, and many more. The third step involved collating data into potential themes and gathering all relevant information for each theme (Lochmiller, 2021). This is known as axial coding which involved grouping related codes into broader categories or subthemes (Bryman, 2004). In the fourth step, the researcher reviewed the themes. In this study, it included climate-sensitive activities, livelihood capital, climate action, and alternative financing to ensure that they aligned with the coded extracts (Clarke & Braun, 2014). The fifth step focused on defining and naming the themes. Finally, the sixth step involved producing the report by selecting appropriate extracts, discussing the findings, interpreting the findings by relating the themes back to your research question or objectives, and ultimately addressing the research gap (Braun & Clarke, 2006).

Ethical Considerations

Ethical clearance for the study was obtained from the Senior Research Ethics Committee at the University of Johannesburg. In Ghana, approval was also granted by the Sagnarigu Municipal Assembly. Additionally, further permissions were secured from local community sub-chiefs and assemblymen, who acted as gatekeepers. At the participant level, an information letter was read aloud detailing the study's purpose, potential benefits, and risks. Participants were informed that confidentiality would be ensured in the face-to-face interviews but could not be fully guaranteed in a focus group discussion, as highlighted the complexity by Bryman (2004). Therefore, participants were encouraged to share information that could be discussed openly in a group setting. Following this, all participants willingly signed consent forms and participated in the study.

Findings

This section presents empirical evidence of the female LEAP cash beneficiary's climate-sensitive activities, access to livelihood capitals and interactions, and alternative climate financing from a broader study. These are put into two major themes: firstly, climate-sensitive activities, livelihood capital access and interactions, and secondly, participation in climate action and alternative financing for livelihoods. There are also subthemes under them for clarity. Thus, it presents the findings from the women, which is the main objective of this chapter, and excludes evidence from the men. However, information from the key informant will support the findings.

Theme 1: Climate-sensitive Activities, Livelihood Capital Access, and Interactions

The finding revealed that the female cash LEAP beneficiaries, even though they received cash from the state, it was too small to improve their livelihoods. They rather engaged in climate-sensitive livelihood activities. It was discovered that the women were aware that the climate was changing and threatened livelihoods drawn from agriculture, fishing, and other natural resources. In addition, they mentioned loss of crops, livestock, and damage to infrastructure, which eventually leads to decreased income, food insecurity, and displacement. However, they lacked human capital, such as knowledge and skills for sustainable land (natural capital) management practices, that could minimise the impact of climate variability. For instance, the lack of knowledge about planting trees in the right places, giving land back to nature and sustainable agricultural practices that could enhance food security, build resilience to climate impacts, and reduce greenhouse gas emissions was lacking. Two participants commented as:

> *F2*: Said: We engage in slash and burn, which involves cutting down trees and vegetation, which are then burned to clear land for agriculture. This is what we do every year to cultivate food crops. Our great-grandparents handed down this practice, and currently we use it.
>
> *F5*: Said: I do not want the slash and burn method, but I do not have another alternative. I can see that when we burn the vegetation, there is no protective cover of trees, and the soil is vulnerable to erosion. On my farmland, I can see erosion everywhere. The topsoil has been washed away.

Sub-theme 1.1: Interaction of Social and Financial Capital

The women revealed that they lacked social and financial capital. For instance, it was mentioned that financial capital can help them build resilience, participate in decision-making, and access resources and opportunities in the community rather than depending on climate-sensitive activities. It was also revealed that when it comes to decision making, they do not form part due to a lack of money. The men felt they had no money, and their contribution to decision-making was relevant. In addition, it was revealed that they lacked social capital, such as social interaction and cooperation, impacting how they function within society. Two participants said as follows:

> *P12*: said the network structure in this community is poor. I know social networks could facilitate access to information, opportunities, and support, but we do things individually. The quality of relationships between individuals and groups in the community could make us focus on trust, norms, and obligations to protect the environment. For instance, people destroy forests to make way for many things, including farming, charcoal production and fuelwood for commercial purposes.
>
> *P5*: Lack of financial support does not allow us to build networks and be involved in community participation, either to obtain knowledge or to share our knowledge. In addition, there is a link between financial capital and social capital. For instance, due to the lack of network and trust, access to savings, loans, and insurance is challenging.

Sub-theme 1.2: Interaction Between Physical and Financial Capital

In response to the interaction between physical and financial capital, the women revealed that they lacked irrigation systems and electrical stoves (physical capital) for energy. Hence, financial capital is needed to access these facilities. They added that financial capital can be used to maintain or improve physical assets. They need irrigation systems to help them improve their agricultural activities all year round. It was emphasised that they have a single season in a year, starting from May to November; the remaining months in the year are used for non-farm activities, including fuelwood harvest, charcoal production, and other forest resource extraction either for domestic use or commercial purposes. In addition, the lack of electrical stoves forces us to rely on fuel wood and charcoal in the community. Two participants commented:

> *P2*: It would have helped us a lot if we had irrigation systems in the community. For instance, in the dry season, we are forced to do climate-sensitive activities for our livelihoods. The irrigation systems could engage us during the dry season instead of destroying the forest for our livelihoods.
>
> *P13*: As for me, financial capital is needed to access these facilities, such as irrigation, farming tools and even electrical stoves, if they say harvesting and the use of fuelwood disturb the environment. Where can we get the money from? That is the challenge.

Sub-theme 1.3: Interaction Between Natural and Human

In response to the interaction between natural and human, the women mentioned that natural capital, like forests, provides resources like fuelwood and charcoal, while human capital, like knowledge, is needed to plant trees in areas vulnerable to extreme weather events. In relation to women's access to forest resources, as the forest is degrading, knowledge is needed to restore the degraded forests, implement sustainable forestry practices, and promote responsible consumption and production patterns. In addition to that knowledge for forest restoration, financial capital is required to purchase tools for planting trees. Two participants said:

> *P10*: We can only use alternative sources of energy, such as solar, biogas, electric stoves, and other forms of biomass, to avoid the destruction of the forest after the trees have been planted. We over-depend on natural resources for our livelihoods, thereby causing destruction to the environment.
>
> *P7*: If we could get financial assistance, it would enable women's livelihood diversification. For instance, a mix of livelihood capitals may enable women to diversify their income sources. Access to land (natural capital), agricultural skills (human capital), and market connections (social capital) can allow women to engage in both smart agriculture activities and off-farm activities.

Theme 2: Participation in Climate Action and Alternative Financing for Livelihoods

It was explained to women that climate finance refers to local, national or transnational financing, drawn from public, private and alternative sources of financing, that seeks to support mitigation and adaptation actions that will address climate change, and women could benefit from such projects. Hence, if they are to participate in such projects, what alternative financing will they prefer for livelihoods, considering their livelihood capital interactions with the environment? Two women responded that alternative climate financing for women should not be providing food for consumption but rather to improve human and natural capital for livelihood enhancement. The two female participants and a social worker commented as follows:

> *P5*: If we could get financial assistance from either national or international sources, we could be practising conservation tillage, water management, and crop diversification to help maintain or increase yields in the community. For instance, we lack the capacity to adopt drought-resistant crop varieties or knowledge of water harvesting techniques in this community.
>
> *P10*: We heard that by practising agroforestry, farmers can build resilience to climate variability and extreme weather events, but how can we do that when we practice slash and burn? We feel planting trees on your farm will prevent the growth of crops or lead to poor yields.
>
> *K4, social worker*: Alternative climate financing should focus on supporting women in alternative income-generating activities, such as handicrafts or small-scale businesses, which can reduce over-reliance on single, climate-sensitive livelihoods, such as excessive extraction of fuelwood or charcoal production. These are the major climate-sensitive activities apart from slash-and-burn agriculture activities in the community.

Sub-theme 2.1: Suggestions on Alternative Financing

In the interview, five women also emphasised that although cash is important for their livelihoods, alternative climate financing should focus on improving women's social networks in the community, such as cooperatives and local associations, which can facilitate the sharing of information about climate-resilient practices, like drought-resistant crops or water management techniques. In addition, they mentioned that climate financing projects should focus on enabling women's access to savings, loans and insurance. These will help them improve livelihoods, adapt to climate impacts and build resilience. They also revealed that there is an interaction between social and financial capital. For instance, climate financing should focus on improving networks among women and encourage entrepreneurship and small businesses that can enable access to capital, training, and technology for adaptation to climate change in the community. A key informant commented:

> *K3, social worker*: I feel that providing access to capital for women-led green enterprises, such as those focused on renewable energy or sustainable agriculture, can generate both economic and environmental benefits. If cash is given to the women and there is no training or guidance on how to use the funds, their role in the family will push them to divert.

In response to physical and financial capital, climate change financing should focus on providing irrigation systems because they can be a crucial adaptation strategy to mitigate the effects of climate change on agriculture, particularly in areas facing water scarcity. However, a key informant commented:

> *K6, policymaker*: The women are emphasising irrigation systems, but climate change can affect irrigation systems because rising temperatures and changed precipitation patterns lead to increased water demand for irrigation. We have seen frequent and severe droughts and floods in recent years, and these can disrupt water supplies and damage irrigation systems. I will support addressing the activities that cause climate change first, which will automatically lead to adaptation and livelihood enhancement.

On the contrary, another key informant supported the provision of irrigation systems, which will engage the women to farm all year round and avoid climate-sensitive activities during the dry season. The off-farm season is used to extract forest resources, leading to degradation. Two female participants and two social workers commented:

> *K3, social worker*: In my opinion, alternative climate financing should focus on women's access to irrigation systems, which may play a crucial role in climate change adaptation and mitigation by ensuring food security and improving water resource management. In addition, it may help farmers adapt to water scarcity and extreme weather events, while also potentially reducing greenhouse gas emissions through improved water use efficiency.
>
> *P8*: I would prefer alternative climate financing to focus on the development of infrastructure that can withstand climate-related disasters, such as flood defences or drought-resistant irrigation systems that improve water efficiency and crop production. The irrigation systems have the potential to improve the livelihood of the women in the community.
>
> *K4, social worker*: Climate change adaptation is more important. For instance, access to drought-resistant seeds (natural capital),

knowledge about climate-smart agriculture (human capital), and access to weather information (social capital) can help women adapt to climate change and enhance their livelihoods.

In the interview, five women said alternative climate change financing should focus on renewable energy, which may empower women to reduce greenhouse gas emissions and protect our forests by providing them with access to clean energy technologies. This will foster livelihood opportunities and enhance their role in climate action. For instance, it could be renewable energy for cooking and lighting. This may also create green jobs and improve women's participation in decision-making processes related to climate solutions.

Discussion

The findings suggest that the women wanted alternative climate financing to support agricultural activities. Khatri-Chhetri et al. (2020) support this view by asserting that climate-smart technologies are beneficial to women, specifically regarding their contribution to agricultural productivity and food security, which have been widely recognised in developing nations. They added that in recent years, research and development efforts in the global south have emphasised important issues affecting women in agriculture, such as increased access to land as a natural capital and financial capital, prominence in policymaking, and greater participation. The women mentioned sustainable agriculture practices that mitigate climate change effects. This resonates with Barasa et al.'s (2021) assertion that climate-smart agricultural practices have been adopted in African countries to address the problems of land degradation and desertification.

In addition, climate-smart agricultural practices have shown improvement in food security, enhanced timber production, and lower crops and livestock vulnerability to climate change (Barasa et al., 2021). The women mentioned that alternative climate financing should focus on the provision of irrigation systems (physical capital) to improve crop production and reduce greenhouse gas emissions. However, there was a concern that climate change can affect irrigation systems because rising temperatures and changed precipitation patterns can lead to increased water demand for irrigation. In addition, frequent and severe droughts and floods in recent years have disrupted water supplies and damaged irrigation systems. Abegunde et al. (2019) argued that certain manipulation of natural capital has been adopted by smallholder farmers in sub-Saharan Africa to address climate change variability. For instance, in areas with low precipitation, farmers substitute the farming of crops with high water requirements with the farming of crops with low water requirements to get maximum yield. Senyolo et al. (2018) argued that financial assistance is needed to support women in technology, including use of conservation agriculture, agroforestry, intercropping, agroecology, small-scale irrigation, livestock diversity, soil/water conservation and nutrient management, landscaping, mulching, minimising tillage and breeds, among others. Senyolo et al. (2018) added that with this recent climate change variability, the livelihood of women can only be enhanced if these areas are taken up by policymakers. Women alternative climate financial is crucial for mitigation, adaptation, resilience and livelihood enhancement.

The findings revealed women needed multiple livelihood capitals through climate financing for coping (livelihood outcome) and livelihood enhancements. Dube and Chatterjee (2022) explained that farmers with good agricultural knowledge (human capital) can better utilise land (natural capital) to improve crop yields. As the women were engaged in agriculture activities, climate change and women's land use, as well as climate-smart agriculture can be used to manage agricultural landscapes to sustainably increase productivity, enhance resilience to climate change, and reduce greenhouse gas emissions as the aim of the climate financing (Acheampong et al., 2023). These are regarded as positive livelihood outcomes that can reduce climate vulnerability. The findings also suggest that climate financing for adaptation is more important as there were frequent floods and droughts. For instance, access to drought-resistant seeds (natural capital), knowledge about climate-smart agriculture (human capital), and access to weather information though networks (social capital) can help women adapt to climate change and enhance their livelihoods.

Policy Implications

The study reveals that climate considerations need to be integrated into national development plans and policies to ensure that climate adaptation is mainstreamed so that climate finance reaches women who are most at risk in the Northern Region of Ghana. Policymakers should support vulnerable women in the Northern region in smart agriculture practices like optimised fertiliser use, reduced slash and burn, and reduced tillage to lower agriculture's contribution to greenhouse gas emissions, which are noted as a major driver of climate change. Climate finance should support women to integrate trees and shrubs into agricultural systems to enhance biodiversity, improve soil fertility, and provide shade for crops and livestock. With these smart agriculture practices, women can not only adapt to climate change but also contribute to a more sustainable and resilient food system. It was mentioned that knowledge and skills acquisition can be an alternative to climate financing.

Hence, vulnerable women need skills in utilising no-till farming, cover cropping, and crop rotation to improve soil health, increase water infiltration, and reduce erosion. Climate finance policies that will support local women with the knowledge and skills to adapt to climate change are crucial. For instance, implementing efficient irrigation systems, harvesting rainwater, and drought-tolerant crop varieties to optimise food production should be considered. Alternative climate finance projects should incorporate gender-responsive budgeting and decision-making frameworks that explicitly target women's multiple livelihood capitals. For instance, financing renewable energy cooperatives led by women can improve physical capital such as energy access, financial capital such as income from energy sales, and social capital such as collective organisation. Alternative climate financing should support livelihood diversification projects including agroforestry, eco-processing enterprises, and climate-smart agriculture that enhance women's natural, financial, and human capitals simultaneously.

Conclusion

This chapter explored how women could participate in climate action and the alternative financing they would need to enhance livelihoods in the Northern Region of Ghana. The responses were put into two major themes: Climate-sensitive activities, livelihood capital access, and interactions, and participation in climate action and alternative financing for livelihoods. The livelihood capitals interact in a complex way and enable vulnerable women to be involved in climate-sensitive activities such as slash-and-burn agricultural activities, excessive fuelwood harvest, and charcoal production, which contribute to greenhouse gas emissions. Alternative climate financing should focus on climate-smart agriculture practices, the provision of electrical stoves, access to credit for businesses, and the provision of irrigation systems for livelihood diversification, adapting to climate change and reducing greenhouse gas emissions.

Conflict of Interest

The authors have no conflicting interests to disclose.

Data Availability Statement

The data that support the findings of this study are available upon request from the authors. The data are not publicly available as they contain information that could compromise the ethical considerations or privacy of the research participants.

References

Abegunde, V. O., Sibanda, M., & Obi, A. (2019). The dynamics of climate change adaptation in Sub-Saharan Africa: A review of climate-smart agriculture among small-scale farmers. *Climate*, *7*(11), 132. https://doi.org/10.3390/cli7110132

Acheampong, P. P., Yeboah, S., Adabah, R., Asibuo, J. Y., Nchanji, E. B., Opoku, M., Toywa, J., & Lutomia, C. K. (2023). Gendered perceptions and adaptations to climate change in Ghana: What factors influence the choice of an adaptation strategy? *Frontiers in Sustainable Food Systems*, *7*, 1091812. https://doi.org/10.3389/fsufs.2023.1091812

Ashley, C. (2000). *Applying livelihood approaches to natural resource management initiatives: Experiences in Namibia and Kenya*. Overseas Development Institute.

Assan, E., Suvedi, M., Schmitt Olabisi, L., & Allen, A. (2018). Coping with and adapting to climate change: A gender perspective from smallholder farming in Ghana. *Environments*, *5*(8), 86. https://doi.org/10.3390/environments5080086

Babacan, H. (2021). Women and economic dimensions of climate change. *Economic Effects of Natural Disasters*, 77–95. https://doi.org/10.1016/b978-0-12-817465-4.00006-6

Barasa, P. M., Botai, C. M., Botai, J. O., & Mabhaudhi, T. (2021). A review of climate-smart agriculture research and applications in Africa. *Agronomy, 11*(6), 1255. https://doi.org/10.3390/agronomy11061255

Braun, V., & Clarke, V. (2006). Using thematic analysis in psychology, *Qualitative Research in Psychology, 3*(2), 77–101. https://doi.org/10.1191/1478088706qp063oa

Bryman, A. (2004). *Social research method.* Oxford University Press.

Clarke, V., & Braun, V. (2014). Thematic analysis. *Encyclopedia of Critical Psychology*, 1947–1952. https://doi.org/10.1007/978-1-4614-5583-7_311

Creswell, J. W. (2014). *Research design: Qualitative, quantitative and mixed method approaches.* Sage. https://doi.org/10.5539/elt.v12n5p40

Dagnachew, A., & Hof, A. (2023). *Climate change mitigation and SDGs: Modelling the regional potential of promising mitigation measures and assessing their impact on other SDGs.* https://doi.org/10.5194/egusphere-egu23-7411

Devereux, S. (2001). Livelihood insecurity and social protection: A re-emerging issue in rural development. *Development Policy Review, 19*(4), 507–519. https://onlinelibrary.wiley.com/doi/abs/10.1111/1467-7679.00148

DFID. (2000). *Sustainable livelihoods guidance sheets.* Department for International Development. www.livelihood.org/info/info_guidancesheets.htm

Dube, L. C., & Chatterjee, S. (2022). Assessing livelihood impact of forest carbon projects using sustainable livelihood framework. *Mitigation and Adaptation Strategies for Global Change, 27*(8). https://doi.org/10.1007/s11027-022-10022-9

Elliott, R., & Timulak, L. (2005). Descriptive and interpretive approaches to qualitative research. In J. Miles & P. Gilbert (Eds.), *A handbook of research methods for clinical and health psychology* (pp. 147–159). Oxford University Press.

Ellis, F. (2000). *Rural livelihoods and diversity in developing countries.* OUP.

Glazebrook, T. (2017). Women and climate change. In *Applied ethics* (pp. 545–557). Routledge. https://doi.org/10.4324/9781315097176-76

Guo, A., Wei, Y., Zhong, F., & Wang, P. (2022). How do climate change perception and value cognition affect farmers' sustainable livelihood capacity? An analysis based on an improved DFID sustainable livelihood framework. *Sustainable Production and Consumption, 33*, 636–650. https://doi.org/10.1016/j.spc.2022.08.002

IPCC. (2018). *Report responding to the invitation for IPCC.* Final Published Report. https://www.ipcc.ch/sr15/download/#chapter

Khatri-Chhetri, A., Regmi, P. P., Chanana, N., & Aggarwal, P. K. (2020). Potential of climate-smart agriculture in reducing women farmers' drudgery in high climatic risk areas. *Climatic Change, 158*, 29–42. https://doi.org/10.1007/s10584-018-2350-8

Koomson, P. (2023). Participating under constraints: Roles and limitations of rural women's involvement in climate change adaptation planning and implementation in Ghana. *Climate and Development, 16*(6), 459–470. https://doi.org/10.1080/17565529.2023.2236587

Krantz, L. (2001). *The sustainable livelihood approach to poverty reduction: An introduction. division for policy and socio-economic analysis.* Swedish International Development Cooperation Agency (SIDA). https://commdev.org/wp-content/uploads/pdf/publications/The-Sustainable-Livelihood-Approach-to-Poverty-Reduction-SIDA.pdf

Lochmiller, C. R. (2021). Conducting thematic analysis with qualitative data. *The Qualitative Report, 26*(6), 2029–2044. https://doi.org/10.46743/2160-3715/2021.5008

MoGCSP. (2023). *Livelihood empowerment against poverty.* https://leap.mogcsp.gov.gh/management/payments/

Morse, S., & McNamara, N. (2013). The sustainable livelihood approach in practice. *Sustainable Livelihood Approach*, 101–154. https://doi.org/10.1007/978-94-007-6268-8_4

Narula, S. A., Magray, M. A., & Desore, A. (2021). A sustainable livelihood framework to implement CSR project in coal mining sector. *Journal of Sustainable Mining*, *16*(3). https://doi.org/10.46873/2300-3960.1155

Opoku, E. A. (2019). *Gender in climate policy and climate finance in Ghana* [Doctoral dissertation, University of North Texas]. https://doi.org/10.12794/metadc1538740

Raniga, T. (2021). Role of economic development cooperatives in improving the livelihoods of women in Gauteng, South Africa. *Development Southern Africa*, *38*(4), 591–606. https://doi.org/10.1080/0376835X.2021.1906628

Raniga, T., Boecker, M., & Mthembu, M. (2019). Economic experiences and sustainable livelihoods of single mothers employed in the formal work sector in Germany and South Africa. *Social Work/Maatskaplike Werk*, *55*, *4*(2), 279–388. http://dx.doi.org/10.15270/52-2-758

Ray, C. A. (2021). *The impact of climate change on Africa's economies*. https://www.fpri.org/article/2021/10/the-impact-of-climate-change-on-africas-economies/#:~:text=Climate%20change%20threatens%20the%20lives,%2C%20poverty%2C%20and%20population%20displacement

Sagnarigu Municipal Assembly. (2020). *Annual progress report*. https://ndpc.gov.gh/media/NR_Sagnarigu_APR_2020.pdf

Scoones, I. (1998). Sustainable rural livelihoods: *A framework for analysis*. https://opendocs.ids.ac.uk/articles/report/Sustainable_Rural_Livelihoods_A_Framework_for_Analysis/26473384?file=48230770

Scoones, I. (2015). *Sustainable livelihoods and rural development* (p. xv). Practical Action Publishing. https://www.researchgate.net/publication/323103004_Scoones_Ian_2015_Sustainable_rural_livelihoods_and_rural_

Senyolo, M. P., Long, T. B., Blok, V., & Omta, O. (2018). How the characteristics of innovations impact their adoption: An exploration of climate-smart agricultural innovations in South Africa. *Journal of Cleaner Production*, *172*, 3825–3840. https://doi.org/10.1016/j.jclepro.2017.06.019

Serrat, O. (2017). The sustainable livelihoods approach In *Knowledge solutions* (pp. 21–26). Springer. https://doi.org/10.1007/978-981-10-0983-9_5

Serrat, O. (2017). The sustainable livelihoods approach. In *Knowledge solutions: Tools, methods, and approaches to drive organizational performance* (pp. 21–26). Springer Singapore. https://link.springer.com/chapter/10.1007/978-981-10-0983-9_5

Tabares, A., Londoño-Pineda, A., Cano, J. A., & Gómez-Montoya, R. (2022). Rural entrepreneurship: An analysis of current and emerging issues from the sustainable livelihood framework. *Economies*, *10*(6), 142. https://doi.org/10.3390/economies10060142

UNFCCC. (2021). *Updated nationally determined contribution under the Paris Agreement (2020-2030) – Ghana*. United Nations Framework Convention on Climate Change (UNFCCC). https://mesti.gov.gh/wp-content/uploads/2021/12/Ghanas-Updated-Nationally-DeterminedContribution-to-the-UNFCCC_2021.pdf

World Bank. (2022). *Country and climate development report – Ghana*. World Bank Group. https://openknowledge.worldbank.org/server/api/core/bitstreams/9c9764c1-076d-5dcc-8339-6e4f0de2b610/content

Wright, T. L. (2024).*Examining the role of cultural capital in access and equity for female C-STEM learners of color*. Pepperdine University. https://search.proquest.com/openview/a3959544f27417ca7f76ff2552e03a16/1?pq-origsite=gscholar&cbl=18750&diss=y

Chapter 8

Gender Responsive Climate Finance: Policy Frameworks, Barriers and Inclusive Strategies in East and North Africa

Joy Oluwatomi Folorunso

Nigerian Institute of Social and Economic Research (NISER), Ibadan, Nigeria

Abstract

Gender Responsive Climate Finance (GRCF) is vital for addressing the linked issues of climate change and gender inequality in East and North Africa. This chapter provides a comprehensive review of the policy frameworks, barriers, and inclusion strategies that influence GRCF in these regions. It covers international and regional climate agreements, such as the Paris Agreement and the United Nations Framework Convention on Climate Change (UNFCCC) Gender Action Plan (GAP). It highlights the importance of these agreements in promoting policy consistency for integrating gender into climate finance. Despite the existence of these frameworks, the chapter points out ongoing challenges, including the financial exclusion of women, institutional biases, deeply rooted socio-cultural customs, and gaps in gender-disaggregated data that impede accountability and targeted action. Inclusive strategies, such as gender-lens investing (GLI), gender budgeting, capacity building, participatory governance, and social protection mechanisms, are proposed as ways to advance gender equity and strengthen climate resilience. Evidence from both national and grassroots programmes demonstrates that increasing women's participation in climate finance management improves fairness and effectiveness. The chapter concludes with practical policy recommendations centred on institutionalising gender mainstreaming, enhancing gender-sensitive data systems, increasing innovative financing, and fostering multi-stakeholder collaboration. These actions are crucial to unlocking the transformative potential of climate finance and ensuring it is equitable, responsible, and

Gender and Climate Finance in Africa: Addressing Inequalities and Bridging Gaps, 133–153

doi:10.1108/978-1-83742-085-820261008

aligned with the Sustainable Development Goals (SDGs). By situating GRCF within broader socio-political contexts, this chapter contributes to the global debate on the transition to sustainable resilience in East and North Africa.

Keywords: Gender-responsive climate finance; East Africa; North Africa; policy frameworks; gender equity; climate resilience

Introduction

The concept of climate finance is an increasingly important tool in the fight against the complex nature of climate change, which has endangered weaker economies, such as those in East and North Africa. Another acute environmental stressor in the region is the frequency of droughts, desertification, and water shortages, which exacerbate socio-economic imbalances and jeopardise development (IPCC, 2022; World Bank, 2021). Although climate finance mechanisms are designed to direct resources towards mitigation and adaptation, their effects are significantly influenced by the extent to which they incorporate the social equity concept, particularly in terms of gender responsiveness.

GRCF involves the deliberate integration of gender insights into climate finance policies, plans, and implementation methods to address the unique vulnerabilities and adaptive capacities of women, men, and marginalised genders (Dazé et al., 2018). Climatic change affects women in East and North Africa disproportionately, not only because of biological differences but also because of deep-rooted social, economic, and political inequalities that limit their access to important resources, including land, credit, education, and access to decision-making platforms (Food and Agriculture Organization of the United Nations, 2019; United Nations Entity for Gender Equality and the Empowerment of Women, 2020). Indeed, in some cases, women make up a large proportion of the agricultural labour force but lack formal ownership of land and access to financial institutions, which reduces their vulnerability to climate shocks (Meinzen-Dick et al., 2019). Additionally, existing social standards systematically exclude women's roles in climate governance and restrict their participation in climate finance flows.

It is not only a social justice issue that requires the inclusion of gender equity in climate finance but also helps to make climate interventions more effective and sustainable. It has been empirically demonstrated that gender-responsive climate interventions lead to a more inclusive engagement process, address structural inequalities that are foundational to vulnerability, and enhance outcomes related to resilience (Agarwal, 2010; Meinzen-Dick et al., 2019). This is reflected in international policies, such as the UNFCCC GAP and the SDGs, specifically SDG 5 on gender equality and SDG 13 on climate action (UNFCCC, 2017; United Nations (UN), 2015).

Despite these commitments, the implementation of considering gender in climate finance practices in East and North Africa also faces long-term challenges. It is primarily dominated by structural barriers, including the inability of women to access formal financial systems, the insufficiency of disaggregated data on gender to monitor and hold accountable, bureaucratic barriers, and deep-rooted socio-cultural norms that limit women's agency (Terry, 2019). In addition, gender mainstreaming processes often tend to be trivialised, which diminishes gender equity to a mere checkbox, rather than leading to transformative change (Heikkinen & Pichler, 2020).

It is against this backdrop that this chapter critically examines the climate finance landscape in terms of gender responsiveness in East and North Africa, focusing on policy frameworks, barriers, and inclusive policies. It relies on a broad scope of academic literature, policy reviews, and case studies to explore the process of mainstreaming, or lack thereof, of gender considerations in climate finance mechanisms and policies. Other promising solutions to achieving gender equity and climate resilience, identified in the chapter, include GLI, participatory governance, and capacity-building initiatives. Through a combination of socio-political and economic analysis, it situates climate finance within a broader context of inequality and governance, advocating for a more equitable approach to climate justice and sustainable development.

Scope

This chapter's emphasis is on gender responsive climate finance in East and North Africa. The analysis focuses on Kenya, Ethiopia, Rwanda, and Uganda in East Africa since these countries have elaborated gender considerations in their Nationally Determined Contributions (NDCs), policies on climate finance, and gender and climate change policies. Also, countries of concern in North Africa for this study are Morocco and Egypt. This is because they have made some first steps in terms of integrating gender in national climate frameworks and renewable energy financing agendas. The review is based on policy developments as well as experiences of implementation since 2015, which is the period of adoption and operationalisation of the Paris Agreement as well as the increase in gender mainstreaming efforts in climate finance. Such a narrowing scope allows understanding the trends in each region, differences in institutions, and ongoing gender disparities in climate finance processes in a comparative manner.

Conceptual and Theoretical Foundations

GRCF is a novel yet essential area that combines climate finance policies with gender equity objectives, ensuring that climate intervention efforts do not perpetuate injustices but, on the contrary, contribute to justice and resilience (Dazé et al., 2018), as well as gender-informed financial flows. The conceptual definition of GRCF entails the proactive integration of gender considerations into the design, financing, implementation, and monitoring of climate-related financial flows, thereby supporting the diverse vulnerabilities and capacities of gendered social structures (Terry, 2019; UNFCCC, 2017). It goes beyond one-dimensional perspectives of considering climate and gender as distinct issues, promoting an intersectional perspective that considers the compounded identities of people, which comprise gender, class, ethnicity, and age (Crenshaw, 1991; Heikkinen & Pichler, 2020). The scope of GRCF encompasses both mitigation and adaptation financing flows, which intersect with international climate funds, national budgetary allocations, and local climate investments, based on the assumption that just transitions involve inclusive, gender-transformative financial investments (United Nations Entity for Gender Equality and the Empowerment of Women, 2020).

In theory, GRCF is overly relying on feminist political ecology, intersectionality theory, and gender justice ideas, offering strong models of power relations in climate finance governance (Rocheleau et al., 1996). Feminist political ecology critiques the tendency for environmental issues to disproportionately burden women due to asymmetric social relations and unequal access to resources, as well as how climate finance processes may perpetuate or exacerbate these inequalities (Agarwal, 1992). Intersectionality theory highlights the fact that gender is interacting with other identity markers, including ethnicity, socioeconomic status, and age, to create stratified vulnerabilities and unique exclusion patterns, which require differentiated responses to climate change (Crenshaw, 1991). Gender justice in climate finance emphasises balanced participation, identification, and reallocation of climate funds, which fosters responsibility towards marginalised genders as a sustainability objective (MacGregor, 2017). These overlapping theoretical foundations enable a comprehensive understanding of how climate finance mechanisms can either perpetuate or mitigate gendered injustices.

Gender-responsive practices have become increasingly integral to the climate response frameworks of internationally and regionally based climate governance. The UNFCCC formalised GRCF in its Lima Work Programme on Gender and the GAP, which requires greater gender integration in climate finance governance, capacity building, and climate finance implementation (UNFCCC, 2017). Such frameworks require parties to make their policies gender-sensitive, such as by NDCs and National Adaptation Plans (NAPs), which promote transparency and accountability of gender-equitable climate finance flows (Dazé et al., 2018). At the international finance architecture level, gender policies and action plans have been formulated in funds such as the Green Climate Fund (GCF) to mainstream gender in funding decision-making processes, project appraisal, and implementation monitoring. However, challenges persist in achieving meaningful and transformational gender outcomes (Heikkinen & Pichler, 2020).

These economic communities and climate initiatives in the East and North African regions also prioritise gender inclusion on a regional level. Gender mainstreaming in development and climate agendas is reflected in the African Union's (AU) Gender Policy and the African Climate Change Strategy, which encourage financial resources to be designed with a focus on empowering and adapting women (African Union, 2015; United Nations Economic Commission for Africa (UNECA), 2020). The East African Community (EAC) and the Intergovernmental Authority on Development (IGAD) consider gender-based issues in regional climate change interventions. However, implementation gaps remain due to funding, capability, and socio-cultural restrictions (Nyangena & Putzel, 2021). There is a relative lack of progress at the national level, and countries have varying degrees of gender integration in their climate finance approaches, which are typically influenced by the level of governance, institutional commitment, and civil society mobilisation (Le Masson et al., 2019).

Nevertheless, although these frameworks present formal undertakings, the implementation of gender responsiveness in climate finance is still a politico-technical issue. The lack of gender-disaggregated data, the insufficient incorporation of gender experience into project design, and normative biases persist as significant problems that impact investments and outcomes (Terry, 2019). Therefore, theoretical underpinnings should be combined with practical governance reforms and universalistic financing practices to turn promises into revolutionary effects in the field.

In short, the conceptual and theoretical bases of GRCF highlight a shift from an approach that treats gender as an add-on to one that identifies gender as central to the interpretation and reorganisation of climate finance governance. These foundations are based on feminist and intersectional analytical interpretations, which guide policy and practice in addressing structural inequalities and enhancing climate resilience. The existing systems of international and regional climate governance offer enabling policy spaces, but require amplified coherence, resources, and participatory processes to achieve gender justice in climate finance in East and North Africa.

Methodology

The chapter follows a qualitative and policy-based review approach. It compiles existing secondary data from peer-reviewed journal articles, national climate finance policies, NDC submissions, GAPs, and reports by international climate finance institutions, such as the United Nations Development Programme, UN Women, the Adaptation Fund and the GCF. The choice of the materials was based on the themes of gender integration, access to climate finance, institutional implementation mechanisms, and region-specific barriers.

No primary data collection was involved in the review, as the author analysed publicly available documents to determine trends, contradictions, and new practices in East and North Africa. This methodological exercise allows a comparative study of the policy directions and institutional voids of GRCF, which is consistent with the scope of the chapter.

Policy Frameworks Governing Gender and Climate Finance

GRCF is grounded in a complex network of international, regional, and national policy frameworks that should be utilised to facilitate equitable climate action and financing. Learning about this governance structure is a significant pillar to enhancing gender equity in climate finance in East and North Africa. This section will provide a scholarly reflection on the major international agreements, regional policy tools, the integration of gender into NDCs, and multilateral and bilateral climate funds in shaping the development of GRCF.

International Agreements and Gender Integration

Gender responsiveness has gradually taken root in the international climate governance system, primarily through the provisions of the UNFCCC. The Paris Agreement (2015) also explicitly recognises the importance of gender equality and women's empowerment in relation to climate outcomes, emphasising that gender-responsive strategies can enhance the effectiveness of climate policies and activities (UNFCCC, 2015). This is realised by the GAP, which was adopted in 2017 and improved in 2019 by the Lima Work Programme on Gender (UNFCCC, 2017). The GAP is a comprehensive roadmap for institutionalising gender equality in climate negotiations, capacity development, knowledge sharing, and financing.

According to the GAP, there are several priorities: building capacity on gender considerations for all stakeholders, creating and disseminating knowledge on the gender-climate nexus, ensuring coherence in gender mainstreaming throughout the UNFCCC processes, and empowering women to lead on climate action (UNFCCC, 2017). In addition, the plan also proposes gender-responsive financial flows as a measure to augment climate ambition, which interrelates gender equality with meeting the global climate targets. Nonetheless, there are still implementation issues. Despite these official promises, recent statistics suggest a significant discrepancy between policy and practice in Africa. Financial Sector Deepening (FSD) Africa (2023) observes that currently, gender-responsive budgeting is only present in 23% of African NDCs. Although 32% of the total climate finance was labelled as considering gender inequality, only 19% was found to be gender-responsive. This signifies that there is a continual underperformance of gender in climate finance mechanisms and their active operationalisation, which reflects the current issues faced by enforcement, capacity, and accountability on both national and multilateral fund levels.

As a supplement to the UNFCCC, the SDGs, including SDG 5 (Gender Equality) and SDG 13 (Climate Action), will provide a normative context that favours integrated principles (UN, 2015). The connections between these goals have encouraged countries and development partners to mainstream gender across climate finance mechanisms, embedding social inclusion as an imperative within sustainable development pathways.

Regional Climate Finance Policies in East and North Africa

Regional institutions have progressively aligned their climate agendas with global gender commitments and established mechanisms to promote gender-inclusive climate finance. Agenda 2063, as outlined by the AU, and the Gender Policy represent a continental perspective that promotes climate resilience, gender equality, and women's empowerment (African Union, 2015). The African Climate Change Strategy (2020–2030) by the AU also focuses on gender mainstreaming in climate adaptation and mitigation activities, including budgetary allocations that are likely to be gender-responsive (UNECA, 2020).

The East African Community (2022) has developed a policy on Climate Change in East Africa, which emphasises the need to promote gender equality as a cross-cutting priority. Gender mainstreaming to benefit vulnerable groups is also a priority of the IGAD Regional Climate Change Strategy, which emphasises the inclusion of women in accessing climate finance and in decision-making (Intergovernmental Authority on Development, 2021). Although it is formally acknowledged, the issues of uneven implementation are predominant, primarily due to capacity constraints, socio-cultural obstacles, and the lack of data disaggregated by gender to track the financial flows and effects in the area (Le Masson et al., 2019).

North African nations are members of the Arab League and Mediterranean programmes, which are relatively new in terms of integrating gender and climate finance. Examples include Egypt and Morocco, which have incorporated gender aspects into their national climate policies and adaptation plans. Many of these plans are typically supported by bilateral and multilateral donors (World Bank, 2022a). Nevertheless, institutional differences between regions and entrenched gender norms still hinder steady advancement in gender-responsive funding at scale.

Gender Mainstreaming in NDCs and National Climate Policies

NDC gender integration varies significantly in East and North Africa. Nations, such as Kenya, Ethiopia, and Rwanda, have incorporated gender goals into their mitigation and adaptation aspects of their NDCs, with objectives on women's participation, access to climate finance, and capacity building (United Nations Development Programme (UNDP), 2023). These undertakings are also further operationalised by NAPs, which offer guidelines on sectoral and local implementation, taking into account gender-sensitive measures. Nevertheless, not all countries have been able to convert gender-related promises into budgetary allocations and tangible programming, partly due to the poor coordination of climate and gender ministries, as well as ineffective monitoring systems (Dazé et al., 2018).

However, in comparison, even though some countries, like Morocco and Egypt, have already recognised gender in their climate plans, the NDPs tend to be more informative rather than operational, and concentration on measurable financing channels, which is a more pragmatic approach than that of East Africa (UNDP, 2023).

Moreover, several nations have come up with specific gender and climate change policies or strategies that are in addition to NDC gender mainstreaming. For example, the Gender and Climate Change Strategy of Uganda aims to increase women's access to climate financing and create gender-sensitive institutional capacity (Ministry of Gender, Labour and Social Development, Uganda, 2020). Nevertheless, the performance of these structures is greatly dependent on political goodwill, the availability of resources, and the integration of marginalised groups at the grassroots level.

Role and Influence of Multilateral and Bilateral Climate Funds

Multilateral climate funds are an important source of international finance for gender-responsive climate actions. Gender policy has been formalised, enabling the GCF, the largest dedicated global fund, to make gender policy commitments.

These commitments obligate the submission of gender-sensitive project proposals and project monitoring (Green Climate Fund, 2021). The GCF Gender Policy promotes gender mainstreaming in all its funding decisions, with a focus on participation, equitable outcomes, and gender-specific capacity building. Despite this improvement, independent assessment tests indicate a lack of sustainability, including disparities in gender knowledge in project design and inadequate sex-disaggregated data reporting in funded initiatives (GCF Independent Evaluation Unit, 2023).

Gender mainstreaming policies have also been implemented by other significant multilateral funds, such as the Adaptation Fund and the Global Environment Facility (GEF). However, their gendered budgets remain small in comparison to the overall funding volumes (World Resources Institute, 2022). Bilateral donors, including the UK's Foreign, Commonwealth and Development Office and Sweden's International Development Cooperation Agency, are giving GRCF a larger role in their programmes, with many having a specific aim of reinforcing women-led climate action and improving local adaptive capabilities (OECD, 2023a).

These funds have been used to support a range of projects exploring the nexus between gender and climate resilience in East and North Africa. However, there remains a challenge in accessing finance to grassroots women's organisations and marginalised communities. Obstacles such as complex accreditation processes, inadequate technical support regarding gender issues, and the unavailability of local information can be observed (Le Masson et al., 2019). Enhancing country ownership, creating gender-sensitive pipeline projects, and promoting community engagement have been identified as key channels through which climate finance flows are made more effective and inclusive.

Barriers to GRCF

There are various and overlapping obstacles to attaining GRCF in East and North Africa, including structural, institutional, socio-cultural, and data-based aspects. Besides causing inequalities in access to climate finance among women and marginalised gender groups, these barriers also compromise the effectiveness and sustainability of climate interventions. Here, the key barriers to gender inclusivity in climate finance are critically examined as structural (financial exclusions, institutional biases, socio-cultural forces), gender disparities in access and decision-making, and barriers in gender-disaggregated reporting and accountability systems. The effects of gender-blind financing on marginalised communities are reflected in case studies.

Structural Barriers: Financial Exclusion, Institutional Biases, and Socio-cultural Dynamics

Even though East and North Africa have structural barriers that are overriding, there is a great variation in nature and strength of those barriers between the two regions. One of the most significant obstacles that women face in enjoying the full benefits of climate finance is financial exclusion. In East and North Africa, as in most parts of the Global South, women are disproportionately underrepresented in accessing formal financial services. They often do not have any collateral, such as land titles or savings, upon which a loan or credit can be obtained, including financing related to climate change (GIZ, 2025). For example, although women make up between 60% and 80% of the agricultural labour force in certain East African nations, they receive less than 1 out of 10 agricultural credits, which restricts their ability to invest in climate-sensitive agriculture or recovery initiatives (United Nations Entity for Gender Equality and the Empowerment of Women, 2020). Additionally, there are still discriminatory national law systems that limit women's rights to own land, open bank accounts, and maintain fiscal independence (World Bank, 2022b). These financial and legal restraints strengthen economic marginalisation and limit women's direct access to climate finance.

On the institutional level, the governance of climate finance tends to reinforce gender biases that prevent the mainstreaming of gender. Gender policies are established in funding mechanisms such as the GCF, the GEF, and the Adaptation Fund. However, in reality, few funded projects are characterised by a significant level of gender integration. A GCF assessment conducted last year revealed a lack of gender competence in project development processes, with researchers determining that only 39% of projects involved gender specialists at the design stage (GCF Independent Evaluation Unit, 2023). Multifaceted and bureaucratic accreditation and application processes, with high technical and financial barriers, are also among the reasons why women-led organisations and grassroots actors are disproportionately sidelined due to their limited institutional capacity or formal registration status (GIZ, 2025). These institutional constraints are further exacerbated by the absence of specific capacity-building to assist women and marginalised groups in negotiating the climate finance systems.

Socio-cultural dynamics further entrench gender disparities in access to climate finance. Norms and practices often relegate women to domestic and reproductive roles, limiting their participation in formal economic activities and community decision-making forums where climate finance is allocated (Terry, 2019). This exclusion is particularly acute in rural and pastoral areas, where patriarchal structures restrict women's mobility, information access, and voice. Women are underrepresented in leadership positions within local climate governance bodies and financial institutions, thereby diminishing their influence on the distribution of climate finance and project priorities (Le Masson et al., 2019). The intersection of gender with poverty, ethnicity, and age amplifies these constraints, creating nuanced patterns of exclusion that require tailored policy responses.

Gendered Disparities in Climate Finance Access and Decision-making Power

In addition to access to funds, the imbalance in decision-making power is a crucial prerequisite for hindering women's access to climate finance. The underrepresentation of women in formal climate governance areas suggests that their concerns and expertise are often overlooked when developing projects and implementing them (UNFCCC, 2017). The majority of decisions regarding the design and distribution of climate finance often reflect the dominant interests and gender-blind strategies, thereby reinforcing the status quo (Heikkinen & Pichler, 2020).

Notably, adaptation projects that fail to incorporate women's views on water management or agricultural practices are at risk of being unsustainable and yielding suboptimal results. The omnibus of women in climate finance decision-making limits transformational adaptation and limits the distributive value of finance to men-dominated sectors and actors (Agarwal, 2010). This power inequity between the genders is also created in the family setup, as the women might not have control over the funds that are to be channelled by the climate projects, even though they are direct beneficiaries. These intra-household differences have consequences for the evaluation of project impacts and resilience over time (Meinzen-Dick et al., 2019).

Data Limitations and Challenges in Gender-disaggregated Climate Finance Monitoring

One of the essential obstacles to GRCF is the lack of gender-disaggregated data and monitoring systems. The lack of data makes it challenging to monitor the beneficiaries of climate finance and integrate mainstream gender considerations, as well as to empower policymakers, financiers, and practitioners (UNDP, 2023). Currently, climate finance reporting is more focused on financial amounts than on the gender effects of specific policies and women's agency (Gender Climate Tracker, 2024).

Gender data are not systematically collected at the national and project levels; therefore, it is challenging to understand what is being omitted, develop targeted interventions, and hold funders accountable for their gender commitments (Terry, 2019). As an illustration, some of the NDCs do not provide indicators of gender nor measurable targets related to the climate finance flows (Dazé et al., 2018). Moreover, the absence of sex-disaggregated beneficiary information in climate projects also means that it is not always possible to determine whether women themselves have fair access to and can shape climate finance investments. This divide continues to perpetuate gender-blind finance, in which funding can either support the status quo of inequality unintentionally.

Case Reflections on Consequences of Gender-blind Climate Finance

The negative impact of failing to consider gender sensitivity in the design and delivery of climate finance is evident in practice. Water resource management adaptation projects in East Africa often had poor take-up and sustainability when implemented without involving women (Le Masson et al., 2019). In documented situations, gender-blind irrigation infrastructure investments have reinforced the dominance of men over land and water, thereby excluding women farmers who previously managed small parcels of land (Meinzen-Dick et al., 2019). The above outcomes highlight that climate finance has the potential to focus on gender inequalities, but only if gender relations are not tackled.

Likewise, financing disaster recovery without a gender analysis will result in an unequal distribution of funds. Flood recovery investments in some areas of North Africa revealed that women, who tend to be the primary caregivers and food producers, did not receive any straightforward assistance, weakening the households' resilience in the aftermath of a disaster (United Nations Entity for Gender Equality and the Empowerment of Women, 2020). Climate finance that is gender-blind can increase vulnerabilities by distorting patriarchal systems thereby leaving women more vulnerable to adverse climate effects.

These demonstrations show that gender exclusion is not solely a social justice problem but a threat to the effectiveness and viability of the climate finance performance. Therefore, the gender gap can be bridged not only through rhetoric but also through fundamental changes in the structure and functioning of climate finance institutions, in resource allocation, and in interactions with beneficiaries.

Inclusive Strategies and Best Practices

To continue advancing gender-responsive climate financing in East and North Africa, it will be necessary to have conscious, creative initiatives and best practices that work to break the vice and increase the agency of women and marginalised groups. The chapter discusses some of the significant and effective inclusion strategies, including Gender lens investing (GLI)–can be ignored, because GLI is defined in abstract itself and gender budgeting in climate finance, capacity building and empowering women and marginalised groups, participatory governance and community-based climate finance processes, and tying social security systems to climate finance to limit vulnerabilities. The strategies are global and regional in nature and are realistic in integrating gender equity with climate resilience objectives.

GLI and Gender Budgeting in Climate Finance

GLI is a revolutionary approach that combines climate finance investments with gender equity objectives by incorporating gender factors into investment decisions, portfolio management, and impact evaluation (International Finance Corporation (IFC), 2024). GLI understands that women have been disproportionately affected by climate change and that incentivising women-led businesses and gender-neutral green technologies could yield better climate and socio-economic outcomes. The IFC announced that it has made nearly $11 billion in gender-focused investments, with approximately $5.5 billion invested directly in financial institutions that focus on women entrepreneurs and climate-smart projects (IFC, 2024). Some studies suggest that incorporating a gender lens into climate finance has the potential to accelerate green economic development, generating new employment opportunities and innovations, and reducing gender disparities in the labour force (Boston Consulting Group, 2023).

The concrete frameworks of GLI focus on identifying specific outcomes related to gender, aligning organisational policies with priorities, and monitoring the impact of gender on investment portfolios (WIFCAG et al., 2023). GI initiatives in East and North Africa have helped facilitate women-backed renewable energy projects, climate-resilient agribusiness initiatives, and rural women-driven financial inclusion initiatives, proving that it is indeed possible to mobilise capital towards gender-inclusive climate solutions (Women Organizing for Change in Agriculture and Natural Resource Management, 2023).

Gender budgeting is a supplement to GLI as it entrenches gender equity in government financial management in climatic sectors. It entails questioning government climate budgets and spending to ensure that resources are sufficiently directed to gender-differentiated areas of vulnerability and priority (United Nations Entity for Gender Equality and the Empowerment of Women, 2020). Some East African nations, including Kenya and Rwanda, have been experimenting with gender-responsive budgeting in their climate action plans, which have led to increased allocation of resources to women-oriented adaptation activities and capacity-building efforts (Le Masson & Codjoe, 2022).

Capacity Building and Empowerment

Capacity building is necessary to enable women and marginalised groups to participate in climate finance mechanisms in a meaningful manner. Women have been empowered by training programmes in climate adaptation skills, financial literacy, project management, and leadership, which enable them to own climate projects and negotiate better access to resources (Terry, 2019). As an example, organisations such as the African Women's Development Fund (AWDF, 2023) and local women's cooperatives have made significant contributions to climate resilience through skills development and peer learning in East and North African societies.

Empowerment is not just technical ability. It entails an increase in agency, leadership, and participation rights. Women can get a direct influence on the priorities of climate finance through gender-responsive climate projects that incorporate empowerment aspects (through governance training, advocacy skills, access to decision-making forums, etc.; United Nations Entity for Gender Equality and the Empowerment of Women, 2020). Pastoralist communities in Kenya and Ethiopia have demonstrated that a female-dominated community adaptation group has improved the performance of local governance and enhanced climate resilience by gaining access to both financial and natural resources (Le Masson et al., 2019).

Participatory Governance and Community-driven Finance Mechanisms

Models of inclusive governance, which enable community involvement, particularly that of women and the marginalised, are critical in ensuring that climate finance is translated into local and sustainable outcomes. Participatory budgeting and planning involve communities in the decision-making process concerning the allocation, implementation, and monitoring of climate finance, leading to increased transparency and ownership (OECD, 2023b). Community-based adaptation projects supported by decentralised climate finance schemes have also incorporated gender-sensitive consultations in parts of East Africa, enabling women to participate in prioritising water, reforestation, and disaster preparedness (Le Masson & Codjoe, 2022).

The structural access factors are also addressed through decentralising climate financing to communities, minimising bureaucratic twists and turns in national and international funding avenues (GIZ, 2025). For example, gender-sensitive climate funds in local government areas have mobilised financial resources to support women in engaging with small-scale renewable energy activities and agroforestry projects in Uganda and Tanzania, resulting in positive synergies between local governance and the effectiveness of climate finance (Independent Evaluation Group, 2023).

More inclusivity and responsiveness in climate finance can be further improved by interactive multi-stakeholder platforms that involve government, civil society, women's groups, and private sector actors. These platforms will facilitate the collective creation of knowledge and collaboration in a manner that other gendered experiences determine the design and evaluation of programmes (MacGregor, 2017).

Integrating Social Protection and Climate Finance

Unexplored opportunities of social protective systems combined with climate financing have the potential to alleviate the vulnerabilities and provide adaptive coping strategies to the marginalised gender groups. Insurance, livelihood support programmes, and cash transfers align with climate change mitigation and adaptation efforts, such as buffering against shocks and facilitating sustainable transitions (Premand & Stoeffler, 2022; World Bank, 2023). In East Africa, pilot projects that have integrated social safety nets with climate resilience initiatives, including asset-building transfers and climate-smart agriculture training for women, have been shown to improve food security and reduce poverty (UNDP, 2023).

Women-headed household climate risk insurance products mitigate the effects of climate shocks on women-headed households, thereby stabilising their incomes and facilitating reinvestment in resilience building (IFC, 2024). Social protection-oriented climate finance achieves a holistic approach by integrating financial protection with adaptive interventions, acknowledging the interplay between gender, poverty, and climate vulnerability.

Synthesis and Path Forward

These strategies of inclusion boil down to the fact that gender equity is not an add-on but a core part of adequate climate finance. GLI and budgeting mobilise resources in strategic ways to address gender discrepancies. Capacity building and empowerment enable marginalised groups to engage and lead. Participatory governance ensures accountability, local relevance, and integration with social protection, addressing systemic vulnerabilities.

Even with good examples, there exist difficulties in scaling and institutionalising such best practices. Sector coordination, political determination, and investment in robust monitoring and evaluation frameworks are crucial to entrench inclusivity in climate finance frameworks in East and North Africa. Additionally, socio-cultural resistance is a critical issue that warrants attention, and identifying allies within institutions is crucial for driving transformative change.

The way forward requires combined policy, practice, and financial innovations to acknowledge women and marginalised groups not as recipients but as actors and leaders of climate resilience. These strategies of inclusivity should be embraced, as they are the best chance to ensure fair, sustainable, and effective climate financing results in the region.

Regional Synthesis and Empirical Insights

To determine the feasibility of applying GRCF in East and North Africa, it is essential to consider the region's experience and the existing body of empirical data on interventions that have effectively incorporated gender factors into climate finance policies and projects. The section summarises the case studies of best practices, lessons from national and local implementations, and the critical role of civil society, women's organisations, and local actors in promoting gender equity in climate finance.

Case Studies Illustrating Successful GRCF Interventions

The practical examples of gender-responsible climate finance in East and North Africa demonstrate how applying a gender lens enhances climate resilience and social equality. Contributing examples of such case studies are the African Development Bank Inclusive Climate Action Initiative, supported by the Climate Investment Funds, and applied in co-operation with the International Union of Conservation of Nature. A notable example is a forest conservation and sustainable livelihoods initiative in Ghana, which utilised climate-specific finance to establish a mobilisation of women farmers. This initiative enabled them to access gender-specific training and resources, resulting in increased forest cover, enhanced food security, and improved income generation among the women participants (International Union for Conservation of Nature (IUCN), 2022). This intervention utilised the traditional knowledge of the women and their involvement in decision-making, which was crucial in ensuring the project's sustainability.

There was a renewable energy programme, a climate finance-funded initiative in Morocco, that specifically targeted women entrepreneurs in the solar energy sector, making it easier for them to access credit, training, and markets. Not only did this enhance women's economic participation, it was also utilised in national renewable energy ambitions, demonstrating how gender equity and climate objectives can intersect (IUCN, 2022). These case studies demonstrate that achieving more inclusive and effective climate outcomes is possible when climate finance actively addresses gender-specific constraints and opportunities.

Rwanda provides another good empirical point. The latest analysis of gender-transformative climate finance programmes highlighted the importance of analysing gender norms through project design and the role of enhancing women's leadership in climate governance at both local and national levels in improving access to climate finance for marginalised populations (Development Initiatives, 2024). An example is that women's rights organisations have been able to lobby for the adoption of gender indicators in Rwanda's national climate strategies and have been active in supervising projects to hold them accountable and responsive.

Kenya is also a good example of gender proactive integration into climate finance. The country's constitution guarantees gender equity in all development fields, including climate action, where policies encourage women to participate in climate action and control of resources. The GCF-supported Kenya Climate Change Adaptation Project prioritised women within community-driven ecosystem restoration programmes, resulting in enhanced resilience among vulnerable households and empowerment through microfinance linkages (UNFCCC, 2023). These programmes demonstrate that legal and policy frameworks supportive of gender equity are crucial, but they also require complementary financing mechanisms and technical support.

Lessons from National and Local Implementation in East and North Africa

Although these success stories indicate progress, the lessons from the broader experience in the region highlight enablers and ongoing challenges. Among the lessons is the need to incorporate gender goals throughout the entire climate finance cycle, from policy development to project monitoring. Nations and initiatives that incorporate gender factors exceptionally and systematically are more likely to achieve success in inclusivity and effectiveness (Le Masson et al., 2019). This entails multi-sectoral coordination among ministries of gender, environment, and finance, which is often lacking in most countries.

Gender equity has a higher chance of succeeding when implemented through local adaptation initiatives because they are closer to the beneficiaries, and they are also designed flexibly. Nevertheless, the expansion of effective local models presents a complication, especially within the institution of gender-responsive processes in national climate finance frameworks (UNDP, 2023). Sustained impact is limited by capacity gaps on the subnational level (such as insufficient knowledge on gender expertise among climate planners and inadequate data systems). Patterns in the allocation of funds also indicate a propensity to invest resources in either mitigation or large-scale infrastructure projects with fewer gender elements. In contrast, adaptation projects with a strong gender element are less likely to receive finance (GCF Independent Evaluation Unit, 2023).

Another key lesson is the importance of integrating local knowledge and addressing socio-cultural barriers. Other projects that directly address gender norms, develop female leadership, and make men gender-sensitive demonstrate more lasting outcomes in power relationships and better female involvement (MacGregor, 2017). On the other hand, failing to consider cultural contexts results in tokenistic inclusion rather than genuine empowerment.

Role of Civil Society, Women's Groups, and Local Actors

Civil society organisations, women's rights organisations, and local actors must not be left out in the promotion of GRCF in East and North Africa. Their activities include advocating for the gender mainstreaming of national and regional policies on climate change, capacity building in their communities, and the direct execution of gender-inclusive projects. Such groups are sometimes the missing link between the formal operations of the government and marginalised groups, ensuring that funding is available to the populations most affected by climatic factors.

Women's organisations have led the way in mobilising grassroots efforts for climate resilience activities. For example, the work of women's cooperatives supported by streams of climate financing donors in Tanzania, East Africa has led to improvements in agroecological processes, better management of water resources, and increased access to markets, resulting in enhanced environmental sustainability and economic self-reliance for women (Le Masson et al., 2019). These organisations often become pioneers in combining climate adaptation and gender equity, but they face structural obstacles, such as insufficient access to funds and capacity limitations.

At the regional level, networks such as the AWDF provide important platforms for sharing knowledge, advocacy, and technical support. They empower women's organisations in various countries to participate in policy discussions and exert greater pressure on governments and financial institutions to take gender-responsive climate action (AWDF, 2023). Such coalitions help elevate the voices of the marginalised and enhance intersectional climate finance.

Moreover, the role of local actors in participatory governance, as explained previously, makes governance more open and socially responsible. Climate finance is more responsive to a variety of gendered vulnerabilities and opportunities when their grassroots knowledge is involved in the project's design and implementation (OECD, 2023). Nevertheless, more governmental and financial support is essential to bolster the institutional capacity of these actors and break down barriers to formal climate finance programmes.

Synthesis

Together, both regional synthesis and empirical evidence indicate that, when climate finance is purposely mainstreamed with gender considerations, supported by policy frameworks, inclusive processes, and empowered local actors, the results will be fairer and more sustainable. Effective interventions leverage legal commitments, participatory governance, capacity-building efforts, and targeted funding to address gender-specific needs and support transformational change.

However, scaling up these achievements requires increased investment in institutional capacity and improved data infrastructure to track the effects of gender, as well as intensified partnerships between governments, donors, and civil society to establish inclusive climate finance systems. Breaking the socio-cultural limitations and achieving normative change is equally important for realising the full potential of gender-responsible climate finance in East and North Africa.

Conclusion

This chapter has demonstrated that the effectiveness of GRCF in East and North Africa is shaped not merely by the articulation of gender commitments in national policy frameworks but by the gendered power relations that mediate access to financial resources, institutional authority, and decision-making processes. Drawing on feminist political ecology, the chapter argued that climate finance operates within socio-political structures that determine whose knowledge is recognised, whose priorities are financed, and who ultimately benefits from adaptation and mitigation initiatives. Therefore, policy commitments alone are insufficient; without dismantling the power hierarchies embedded in climate governance, gender responsiveness risks remaining symbolic rather than transformative.

The cases examined reveal persistent implementation gaps despite notable progress in integrating gender language into climate policies. In East Africa, Kenya, Ethiopia, Rwanda, and Uganda have incorporated gender considerations in their NDCs and national climate legislation, yet women remain disproportionately excluded from climate finance mechanisms due to structural barriers such as restrictive land tenure systems, collateral requirements, and limited representation in financial institutions. While these countries have shown willingness to adopt gender-responsive frameworks, the institutional cultures that govern access to finance continue to privilege male-dominated networks, reinforcing the feminist political ecology claim that environmental and financial governance reproduce wider patriarchal relations. In North Africa, Morocco and Egypt demonstrate a different yet related dynamic. Both countries are advancing large-scale climate finance initiatives, particularly in renewable energy and mitigation infrastructure. However, these investments have been predominantly technocratic and state-led, with limited integration of gender as a strategic category of resource allocation. Women are largely absent from the design, ownership, and benefit structures of major climate projects, illustrating how national climate agendas, though well-financed, can consolidate existing hierarchies rather than redistribute power. These contrasts across regions affirm the chapter's central proposition: climate finance processes are not neutral instruments but socio-political arenas where gendered interests and capabilities shape outcomes.

Given these insights, the pursuit of GRCF must shift from inclusion as rhetoric to inclusion as practice. Policymakers across East and North Africa need to embed gender considerations at every stage of climate finance, from project conception to disbursement, monitoring, and evaluation. This requires strengthening gender budgeting mechanisms, ensuring that financial intermediaries adopt gender-lens investment criteria, and mandating the participation of women's organisations in climate governance platforms. Moreover, capacity-building initiatives must move beyond technical skills to address the structural and legal inequities that restrict women's access to land, technology, and credit. Without confronting these root causes, climate finance will continue to reflect rather than transform unequal gender relations.

This chapter contributes to the discourse on climate finance by highlighting that gender responsiveness is not solely a normative aspiration but a strategic necessity for equitable and effective climate action in Africa. The evidence presented underscores that transformative climate finance depends on recognising and restructuring the political and economic relations that shape gendered access to resources. For East and North Africa to realise the full potential of climate investments, the gendered dimensions of financial decision-making must be made visible, accountable, and structurally central to climate governance.

Policy Recommendations and Strategic Directions

Advancing GRCF in East and North Africa requires an integrated recalibration of policy, institutional practice, and financial architecture. The evidence presented in this chapter shows that existing gender commitments are undermined not by a lack of policy intent, but by entrenched structural asymmetries that mediate access to financial and political capital. Accordingly, policy reforms must go beyond the inclusion of gender language to directly intervene in the power relations that shape resource allocation and decision-making processes.

Institutionalise Gender-lens Financing Criteria: Climate finance facilities, particularly national designated authorities, commercial banks, and development finance institutions, must adopt mandatory gender-lens investment frameworks. This includes gender-disaggregated eligibility criteria, gender-responsive risk assessments, and incentives for private investors to integrate women-led enterprises into low-carbon and adaptation value chains. Without such requirements, women's participation remains peripheral and vulnerable to discretionary interpretation.

Strengthen Gender Budgeting and Compliance Mechanisms: Countries should incorporate gender-responsive budgeting within national climate programmes and require reporting on gender outcomes at all stages of the finance cycle. Establishing legally binding accountability systems, rather than optional policy annexes, ensures that gender integration shifts from rhetorical alignment to measurable performance.

Expand Women's Access to Collateral and Climate Credit Instruments: Financial exclusion remains a structural bottleneck. Governments should reform land tenure and asset ownership laws to enable women to leverage property as collateral while expanding climate-specific credit guarantees, blended finance schemes, and micro-finance instruments tailored to women-led adaptation initiatives. These reforms align with feminist political ecology by directly addressing the gendered control of resources.

Embed Women's Organisations in Climate Governance Platforms: Token consultation has not translated into transformative participation. National climate councils, NDC revision committees, and renewable energy investment boards must include grassroots and women's rights organisations as decision-making actors, not observers. This disrupts institutional path dependencies that centralise expertise within male-dominated bureaucratic cultures.

Prioritise Capacity Development for Gender-responsive Implementation: Technical capacity-building should focus on policy actors and financial intermediaries who design and administer climate finance, not solely on end beneficiaries. Training programmes must include gender-sensitive financial appraisal, participatory planning, and monitoring frameworks that capture socio-economic power dynamics rather than generic beneficiary counts.

Regional Harmonisation and Knowledge Exchange: East and North African regional bodies, such as COMESA, EAC, and the AU, should create harmonised standards for GRCF and support cross-country learning platforms. Countries like Rwanda and Kenya offer institutional models that can be adapted to North African contexts, where gender integration remains technocratic but under-socialised.

Strategic Direction

The future of climate finance in Africa hinges on a paradigm shift: from gender inclusion as an ancillary objective to gender equality as a determinant of climate resilience and economic transformation. Aligning climate finance with feminist political ecology enables policymakers to see gender not as a variable to be added, but as a structural condition that shapes who benefits from climate transitions. Only when financial systems, legal structures, and governance practices are reconfigured to recognise and redistribute power can climate finance catalyse equitable and sustainable adaptation and mitigation outcomes across the continent.

References

African Union. (2015). *African Union gender policy*. African Union Commission.

African Women's Development Fund (AWDF). (2023). *African Women's Development Fund annual report*. African Women's Development Fund.

Agarwal, B. (1992). The gender and environment debate: Lessons from India. *Feminist Studies*, *18*(1), 119–158. https://doi.org/10.2307/3178217

Agarwal, B. (2010). *Gender and green governance: The political economy of women's presence within and beyond community forestry*. Oxford University Press.

Boston Consulting Group. (2023). *The economic case for closing the gender gap in the green economy*. Boston Consulting Group.

Crenshaw, K. (1991). Mapping the margins: Intersectionality, identity politics, and violence against women of color. *Stanford Law Review*, *43*(6), 1241–1299. https://doi.org/10.2307/1229039

Dazé, A., Kolerus, C., & Le Masson, V. (2018). Gender-responsive national climate policies: A critical analysis of the nationally determined contributions. *Climate and Development*, *10*(1), 50–60. https://doi.org/10.1080/17565529.2017.1300086

Development Initiatives. (2024). *From gender-relevant to gender-transformative climate finance: Rwanda case study*. Development Initiatives.

East African Community. (2022). *East African Community climate change policy*. East African Community.
Food and Agriculture Organization of the United Nations. (2019). *The state of food and agriculture 2019: Moving forward on food loss and waste reduction*. Food and Agriculture Organization of the United Nations.
FSD Africa. (2023). *FSD Africa impact report – 2023*. https://fsdafrica.org/wp-content/uploads/2025/05/FSD-Africa-Impact-Report-11.12.23.pdf
Gender Climate Tracker. (2024). *Gender Climate Tracker database*. https://genderclimatetracker.org/
GCF Independent Evaluation Unit. (2023). *Gender mainstreaming evaluation report*. Green Climate Fund.
Green Climate Fund. (2021). *Green Climate Fund gender policy*. Green Climate Fund.
GIZ. (2025). *Gender and access to climate finance: Policy brief*. Deutsche Gesellschaft für Internationale Zusammenarbeit.
Heikkinen, S., & Pichler, M. (2020). Gender and climate finance: A critical reflection on norms and practices. *Climate Policy*, *20*(5), 573–585. https://doi.org/10.1080/14693062.2020.1745742
Independent Evaluation Group. (2023). *Decentralised climate finance: Best practices for gender inclusion*. Independent Evaluation Group.
Intergovernmental Authority on Development. (2021). *Regional climate change strategy*. Intergovernmental Authority on Development.
International Finance Corporation (IFC). (2024). *Pursuing gender-inclusive climate investments*. International Finance Corporation.
International Union for Conservation of Nature (IUCN). (2022). *Strengthening gender-responsive climate action: African Development Bank/CIF inclusive climate action initiative*. International Union for Conservation of Nature.
IPCC. (2022). Climate change 2022: Impacts, adaptation and vulnerability. *Contribution of Working Group II to the sixth assessment report of the Intergovernmental Panel on Climate Change*. Cambridge University Press.
Le Masson, V., & Codjoe, S. (2022). Gender-responsive climate finance in Africa: Emerging lessons. *Climate and Development*, *14*(7), 649–660. https://doi.org/10.1080/17565529.2021.1976609
Le Masson, V., Forino, G., Kaijage, E., & Odhiambo, H. (2019). The gendered politics of local climate adaptation funding in East Africa: Why donors and politics matter. *Climate and Development*, *11*(4), 301–311. https://doi.org/10.1080/17565529.2018.1481419
MacGregor, S. (2017). Gender and climate change in the global South: A critical overview. *Gender & Development*, *25*(2), 185–204. https://doi.org/10.1080/13552074.2017.1348526
Meinzen-Dick, R., Quisumbing, A., Doss, C., & Theis, S. (2019). Women's land rights as a pathway to poverty reduction: Framework and review of available evidence. *Agricultural Systems*, *172*, 72–82. https://doi.org/10.1016/j.agsy.2018.10.009
Ministry of Gender, Labour and Social Development, Uganda. (2020). *Uganda gender and climate change strategy*. Ministry of Gender, Labour and Social Development.
Nyangena, W., & Putzel, L. (2021). Climate change adaptation governance in the Horn of Africa: The role of regional institutions. *Climate Policy*, *21*(3), 350–364. https://doi.org/10.1080/14693062.2020.1823539
Organisation for Economic Co-operation and Development (OECD). (2023a). *Multi-stakeholder partnerships for climate finance*. Organisation for Economic Co-operation and Development.
Organisation for Economic Co-operation and Development (OECD). (2023b). *Participatory budgeting for climate finance*. Organisation for Economic Co-operation and Development.

Premand, P., & Stoeffler, Q. (2022). Cash transfers, climatic shocks and resilience in the Sahel. *Journal of Environmental Economics and Management, 116,* 102744.
Rocheleau, D., Thomas-Slayter, B., & Wangari, E. (1996). *Feminist political ecology: Global issues and local experiences.* Routledge.
Terry, G. (2019). *Gender, climate change, and finance: Accountability for gender-responsive climate finance.* Routledge.
United Nations (UN). (2015). *Transforming our world: The 2030 Agenda for Sustainable Development.* United Nations. https://sdgs.un.org/2030agenda
United Nations Development Programme (UNDP). (2023). *Gender and climate finance in Africa.* United Nations Development Programme.
United Nations Economic Commission for Africa (UNECA). (2020). *African Climate Change Strategy 2020–2030.* United Nations Economic Commission for Africa.
United Nations Entity for Gender Equality and the Empowerment of Women. (2020). *Gender equality and climate change: The role of women in climate resilience and sustainable development.* UN Women.
United Nations Framework Convention on Climate Change (UNFCCC). (2015). *Paris Agreement.* United Nations Framework Convention on Climate Change. https://unfccc.int/process-and-meetings/the-paris-agreement
United Nations Framework Convention on Climate Change (UNFCCC). (2017). *Gender action plan.* United Nations Framework Convention on Climate Change. https://unfccc.int/topics/gender/workstreams/the-gender-action-plan
United Nations Framework Convention on Climate Change (UNFCCC). (2023). *Kenya: Green Climate Fund-funded climate change adaptation project.* United Nations Framework Convention on Climate Change.
WIFCAG, 2X Global, Aviva, & Oliver Wyman Forum. (2023). *Guidance for applying a gender lens to climate investing.* WIFCAG; 2X Global; Aviva; Oliver Wyman Forum.
Women Organizing for Change in Agriculture and Natural Resource Management. (2023). *Inclusive gender and climate finance: Reports and case studies.* Women Organizing for Change in Agriculture and Natural Resource Management.
World Bank. (2021). *Climate change overview: Sub-Saharan Africa.* The World Bank Group.
World Bank. (2022a). *Climate finance overview: North Africa.* The World Bank Group.
World Bank. (2022b). *Women, business, and the law 2022: A decade of reform.* The World Bank Group.
World Bank. (2023). *Sahel adaptive social protection program (SASPP).* The World Bank Group.
World Resources Institute. (2022). *Gender and climate.* World Resources Institute.

Chapter 9

Climate Finance and Gender Inclusivity in Africa: Lessons from South Africa, Ethiopia, and Senegal

Modinat Mosunmola Adekunle

Environment and Physical Infrastructure Policy Department, Nigerian Institute of Social and Economic Research (NISER), Nigeria

Abstract

Climate finance has emerged as a critical mechanism for addressing the impacts of climate change by supporting adaptation and mitigation initiatives. Yet, questions of inclusivity persist, as women, particularly in rural and marginalised communities of the Global South, experience climate risks differently due to entrenched cultural, social, and economic inequalities. This chapter undertakes a comparative analysis of South Africa (Southern Africa), Ethiopia (Eastern Africa), and Senegal (West Africa) to examine how national climate policies, financing structures, and project outcomes integrate gender considerations and support women's participation.

Findings indicate important regional variations. South Africa demonstrates relatively advanced institutional frameworks for gender-responsive climate finance, but benefits remain unevenly distributed across sectors and social groups. Ethiopia, by contrast, faces severe climate risks alongside limited institutional and financial capacity, with women's access to climate resources often constrained by systemic barriers. Senegal presents a more progressive case, where policy reforms and donor-driven initiatives have foregrounded women's roles in adaptation, yet structural financial inequalities continue to limit transformative impact.

The analysis highlights that while progress has been made, gender gaps in access, participation, and benefit-sharing remain significant across all three contexts. Bridging these gaps requires more robust gender

Gender and Climate Finance in Africa: Addressing Inequalities and Bridging Gaps, 155–171

doi:10.1108/978-1-83742-085-820261009

mainstreaming in climate finance policies, targeted capacity building for women, and inclusive monitoring and evaluation mechanisms to ensure accountability. Advancing such measures is essential for promoting gender equity, enhancing resilience, and fostering inclusive climate finance across Africa's diverse regions.

Keywords: Africa; climate finance; gender inequality; inclusivity, women's participation

1. Introduction

Africa contributes minimally to climate change yet saddled with the effects, which leave it vulnerable due to the lack of adaptive capacity. One of the most persistent developmental challenges in Africa today is climate change, and this has great implications for Africa's economies, ecosystems and societies. Relying majorly on climate-sensitive sectors such as fishery, rain-fed agriculture and forestry, coupled with inadequate infrastructure and institutional weaknesses, further reduces Africa's resilience (Parmesan et al., 2022). Climate finance is therefore crucial. Global adaptation needs between 2020 and 2030 are estimated at up to USD 1 trillion, and developing countries alone may require more than USD 600 billion annually by 2030 (Isah et al., 2025; Lüdemann & Ruppel, 2013). Despite these urgent needs, climate finance remains inadequate and unevenly distributed, often reinforcing existing gender inequalities. To address the negative impacts of climate change, African countries rely heavily on mechanisms such as the Green Climate Fund (GCF), bilateral aid, and multilateral development banks (Lüdemann & Ruppel, 2013; Timilsina, 2021).

Across much of Africa, patrilineal norms continue to influence households and community structures, limiting women's decision-making authority and economic autonomy, particularly those in rural areas. These socio-cultural dynamics raise questions about equity and inclusivity in the deployment of climate finance. Evidence shows that women in rural and low-income communities face disproportionate exposure to climate change risks due to their dependence on nature-based economic activities and reliance on fossil fuels for energy, as well as their restricted access to credit, among other factors.[1] In the same vein, women play important roles as environmental stewards and contribute significantly to the management of natural resources, informal financial practices, and community-based adaptation when given the wherewithal and space to participate (Rao et al., 2019). These realities underscore the importance of integrating gender consideration into climate finance policies and programmes.

To reflect varying governance traditions, donor engagement, and instructional frameworks in climate finance, this chapter provides a comparative analysis

[1]https://www.un.org/womenwatch/feature/climate_change/downloads/Women_and_Climate_Change_Factsheet.pdf

of South Africa, Ethiopia, and Senegal, representing Southern, Eastern, and Western Africa, respectively. These countries were selected because they display diverse financial structures and governance structure that offer insights for advancing gender-inclusive climate finance in Africa. South Africa possesses relatively stronger institutional frameworks and policy integration but continues to face challenges of implementation and monitoring. Ethiopia exhibits fragmented gender inclusion and donor-dependent financing despite its ambitious climate policies. Senegal is characterised by donor-promising outcomes through donor supported community initiatives, yet systemic issues such as entrenched patriarchy and unequal land access continue to pose barriers.

A comparative approach is appropriate as it highlights recurrent challenges that recur in different contexts, such as institutional inertia and poor gender-disaggregated data. Also, it draws attention to differences shaped by resource endowments, external funding, and past governance structures. This analysis draws on secondary data sources, empirical research, policy assessments, and recent literature from the three countries, situating these cases within broader discussions on gender and climate justice. The chapter also aligns with the Sustainable Development Goals (SDGs), particularly SDG 5, which emphasises eliminating structural barriers and SDG 13, which calls for climate action that prioritises equity and resilience (United Nations, 2015). Linking national and regional efforts to these global frameworks reinforces the argument that gender responsive climate finance is not only a matter of policy preference but a shared global obligation.

The chapter proceeds by outlining the conceptual and analytical framework, followed by a regional contextualisation of Southern, Eastern, and Western Africa and an examination of specific situations in South Africa, Ethiopia, and Senegal. It then presents the three case studies, synthesises cross-cutting insights, policy implications and concludes by underscoring the importance of inclusive finance for equitable and sustainable development in Africa.

2. Conceptual and Analytical Framework

2.1. Gender and Climate Justice Nexus

This chapter is hinged on the climate and gender justice nexus. As Schlosberg and Collins (2014), contend, those who contribute least to climate change often bear its heaviest consequences. Women, especially in low-income areas, lack access to resources, are generally excluded from decision-making, etc., which further compounds their vulnerability to the vagaries of climate change (Jerneck, 2018). Although climate change affects entire communities, its effects are uneven. Women and children, particularly in Africa, experience disproportionate burdens due to underlying factors such as existing workloads and increased time required to fetch fuelwood, water, and other essential resources (Flatø et al., 2017).

The climate and gender justice nexus aims to not only take care of environmental factors but also the social inequalities that have long existed in societies, particularly in Africa. Infusing gender considerations into climate finance is crucial for achieving distributive and procedural justice. Viewing climate change from the angle of justice emphasises the need to address structural inequalities and strengthen women's agency as a central component of effective and inclusive climate responses.

2.2. Defining Gender-responsive Climate Finance

While no single, universally agreed-upon definition exists, gender-responsive climate finance generally incorporates the elements of intentionality, accountability, participation, and empowerment outcomes cut across policy frameworks and literature (United Nations Framework Convention on Climate Change (UNFCCC), 2019). Gender-responsive climate finance refers to the deliberate integration of gender analysis into financial instruments, resource allocation and project design in ways that support women's social and economic empowerment and address power imbalances that worsens climate vulnerability. Despite these aspirations, gender consideration in climate finance remains rhetorical rather than substantive, with limited gender disaggregated data available to demonstrate real impact (Cohen, 2018). It is therefore vital to strengthen evidence and accountability mechanisms to advance genuine gender responsiveness.

2.3. Analytical Framework for Cross-country Comparison

For comparative analysis, the conceptual framework (Fig. 9.1) used in this chapter is built around the dimensions of policies, institutions, finance flows, and implementation capacity. These four dimensions are conceptualised as fundamental drives that collectively shape gender outcomes. Each dimension is represented as an individual component with a direct, converging impact on gender related outcomes.

The policy environment aspect deals with the presence of a gender lens in national climate and finance polices, shaping the regulatory and strategic

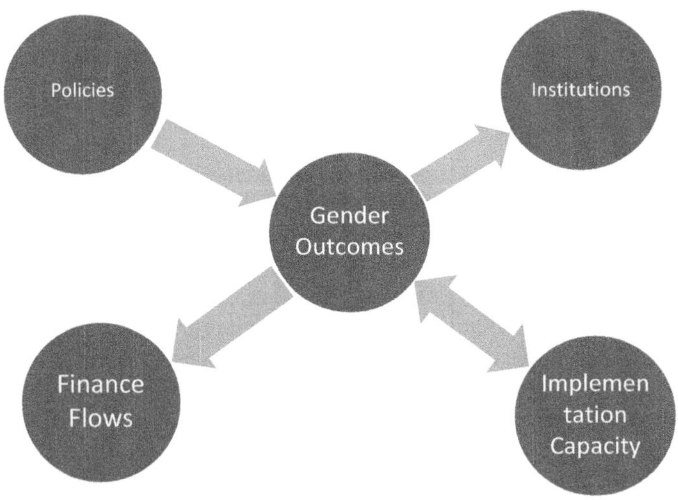

Fig. 9.1. Analytical Framework Illustrating the Four Dimensions of Gender-responsive Climate Finance. *Source*: Author's elaboration, 2025.

environment. The institutional capacity captures the mechanisms, available expertise, and organisational norms that support gender mainstreaming, reflecting formal and informal cultural norms. Finance flows focus on the accessibility of climate finance for women and other marginalised groups as well as the targeting and distribution of resources. The effectiveness of the implementation of climate finance is crucial, as it highlights the ability to operationalise, deliver, and monitor climate finance programmes, ensuring accountability and assessment of programme outcomes.

The framework illustrates these four dimensions as converging towards gender related outcomes such as participation, empowerment, resilience, justice, and implementation effectiveness. The framework depicts that gender equity in climate finance is the product of interacting policy, institutional, financial, and operational factors. The framework draws on insights from feminist institutionalism to examine how formal policies interact with organisational culture and informal norms to influence gender mainstreaming. As such, the framework serves as a conceptual tool for carrying out cross-country comparative analyses, helping identify strengths, gaps, and areas of improvement for advancing gender-responsive climate finance intervention.

3. Regional and Country Contexts

As diverse as the continent is in terms of regions so it reflects in its climate finance landscape. Southern Africa combines relatively advanced institutional frameworks with persistent inequality. Eastern Africa, on the other hand, is more reliant on external donations, armed with ambitious strategies, but lacks institutional depth. West Africa promotes community-driven initiatives but also faces entrenched structural barriers.

The basis of selecting South Africa, Ethiopia, and Senegal therefore allows for a comparative examination of a middle-income country with strong institutions but persistent inequality (South Africa); a low-income, aid-dependent state with ambitious but fragmented gender integration (Ethiopia); and a country that is donor-influenced and where inclusive projects coexist with structural barriers (Senegal).

3.1. Southern Africa

South Africa, characterised by relatively higher institutional and financial capacity, is one of the African countries at the forefront of developing national climate strategies that integrate adaptation and mitigation into development planning compared to other countries in the south and sub-regions in Africa. South Africa boasts of relatively mature institutional structures for gender and climate finance integration. The National Climate Change Response White Paper and subsequent Nationally Determined Contributions (NDCs) of South Africa set ambitious strategies for low-carbon transitions (Republic of South Africa, 2021). Regional organisations such as the Southern African Development Community (SADC) have made committed efforts to ensure gender equality in climate action (SADC & SARDC, 2022).

Despite these advances, the region remains highly vulnerable to climate shocks, most especially drought and heat extremes, with women in rural households often shouldering disproportionate burdens in subsistence or rainfed agriculture and resource collection. Female-headed households exhibit higher economic vulnerability to rainfall shocks (Flatø et al., 2017). The gender wage gaps and labour market segmentation, among others, constrain women's adaptive capacity as temperature increases and sectoral exposure reduces working hours mostly for low-skilled female labour in outdoor economic activities, with implications for wages and labour supply (Shayegh & Dasgupta, 2024). The case of South Africa reflects both the potential of institutionalised climate finance frameworks and persistent barriers to effective gender mainstreaming.

3.2. Eastern Africa

East Africa faces with climate vagaries of prolonged droughts and erratic rainfall, and is considered the hardest hit region. The challenges of having lofty, ambitious climate policies and the inability to balance the same resource constraints can be gleaned from Ethiopia. Launched in year 2011, the Climate Resilient Green Economy (CRGE) strategy was lauded widely for its ambitious nature, but implementation has been largely dependent on donor finance (World Bank, 2020). Ethiopia is a recipient of significant international funding for climate finance, but its domestic financial commitment remained constrained.

When it comes to smallholder farmers, Ethiopian women face systematic barriers to climate change adaptation, especially in having access to credit, the existence of insecure land tenure, and limited participation in extension services (Teklewold et al., 2022). While climate-smart agricultural initiatives have demonstrated positive gender outcomes, they are often marred by issues of being short-term and fragmented in nature (Abegaz et al., 2024; Tesfaye et al., 2023). Consequently, despite policy recognition of gender issues, Ethiopia struggles with effective implementation due to capacity constraints and coordination challenges at the various levels of government.

3.3. West Africa

West Africa faces multitude problems which impact climate change more. These vulnerabilities include rapidly growing population, food insecurity, and political unrest. Senegal is widely cited for its leadership in championing community-driven adaptation initiatives, through programmes such as the Decentralised Climate Fund (DCF). The country has received a huge amount of funding for adaptation, particularly in agriculture, coastal protection, and waste management (Patnaik, 2021).

As in many African contexts, Senegalese women play crucial roles in agriculture and informal finance systems, yet remain largely excluded from land ownership, credit, and key decision-making spaces (Guérin, 2006). Klug et al. (2024) note that despite incorporating gender, the national climate lacks systematic operationalisation. Thus, projecting Senegal as a potential for inclusivity in terms of planning community-based projects, but these are limited due to the absence of structural restructuring.

4. Case Study Analysis

4.1. South Africa

4.1.1. Policies

Through the National Climate Change Response Policy of 2011, the 2018 draft Climate Change Bill and the latest NDC, South Africa boasts one of the most advanced climate policy frameworks on the continent, positioning climate action at the centre of national development planning (Republic of South Africa, 2021). While these policies acknowledge gender disparities and identify vulnerable groups, the policies lack robust gender-responsive budgeting mechanisms. This gap is also evident in sectoral policies, such as the Renewable Energy Independent Power Producer Procurement Programme, which incorporates gender criteria within its local development component, but have not met with consistent enforcement (Baker, 2015).

4.1.2. Institutions

Institutional adoption of gender strategies is often influenced by external requirements particularly from international financial institutions. Evidence suggests that financial intermediaries linked to the GCF and the Development Bank of Southern Africa are trying to incorporate gender frameworks, yet focal point remains weakly integrated (Gerhard et al., 2023). Gender is frequently treated as a compliance requirement rather than a transformative priority.

4.1.3. Financial Flow and Implementation Capacity

South Africa attracts significant domestic and international climate finance, including Just Energy Transition Partnership (JETP). Launched in 2021, the JETP pledged USD 8.5 billion, although only a fraction had been expended by 2024. While the initiative is laudable, concerns remain regarding the extent to which gender considerations are integrated into transition projects (Gürtler, 2025).

For long now, women, particularly in marginalised areas continue to face heightened vulnerability to climate shocks and have limited access to insurance or adaptation finance (Baker, 2015; Flatø et al., 2017). When it comes to economic activities, climate change also disproportionately affects female employment and wages, with women significantly underrepresented in green economic sector (Shayegh & Dasgupta, 2024). Thus, mobilised finance has yet to translate to measurable gender-equitable outcomes.

South Africa clearly demonstrates strong policy resolve and institutional structure, but this is marred by weak monitoring, limited gender-disaggregated finance tracking, and insufficient accountability mechanisms.

4.2. Ethiopia

4.2.1. Policies

Gender and climate finance in Ethiopia is characterised by heavy dependence on international climate funding, fragmented gender integration, and limited domestic financial commitment. While Ethiopia's 2011 CRGE is ambitious, aiming for a climate-resilient middle-income status by 2025 and factoring in gender equality but lacks greatly in operational details (Assefa & Gebrehiwot, 2023).

The World Bank report (2020) highlights the CRGE as an ambitious guiding framework that has driven substantial mitigation and adaptation efforts since inception. Nonetheless, the strategy lacks clear gender sensitive budgeting, indicators, and monitoring systems (Mersha & van Laerhoven, 2016). Ethiopia's National Adaptation Programmes of Action (NAPA), designed under the UNFCCC, to identify priority adaptation needs for least developed countries, were intended to be gender-responsive. Yet earlier NAPAs prioritised technical objectives rather than gender inclusion (Wredström, 2024).

4.2.2. Institutions

The Ethiopian Ministry of Finance is where the CRGE facility is domiciled and channels donor climate finance. Although it has guidelines on social inclusion, gender mainstreaming is clearly inconsistent across the different projects (World Bank, 2020). In other words, besides coordinating finance, they do not monitor gender outcomes. Although the Ministries of Water and Agriculture have units dedicated to gender, they lack adequate funding and legal backing linked to weak institutional coordination (Mersha & van Laerhoven, 2016).

At the grassroots levels, women's participation in community-based adaptation committees remains limited by social norms and workloads (Tesfaye et al., 2023). This overall picture is one of strong policy ambition largely constrained by limited institutional leverage.

4.2.3. Financial Flow and Implementation Capacity

Ethiopia relies heavily on international donors such as the World Bank, GCF, and bilateral partners in financing most climate programmes. Based on recent climate-finance landscape assessments, approximately USD 944 million is committed to adaptation in the Ethiopian national landscape (Climate Policy Initiative (CPI), 2022). Climate-smart agriculture initiatives are also tied to donor-funded projects (Abegaz et al., 2024).

Studies reveal that women adopt fewer and less diverse adaptation measures, often constrained by insecure land tenure and limited access to extension services (Teklewold et al., 2022). Even when women participate, the benefits remain temporary. Tesfaye et al. (2023) find that empowerment opportunities in decision-making diminishes once projects end, thus depicting short-term gains.

Women face barriers to land and credit, making them disadvantaged, thus limiting the adoption of climate-smart adaptation practices (Teklewold et al., 2022). Local adaptation efforts often insufficiently reflect gendered vulnerabilities, with women frequently marginalised in decision-making and benefit sharing.

4.3. Senegal

4.3.1. Policies

Senegal has made notable progress in formal gender commitments, from ratifying international conventions to adopting a constitution that guarantees gender equality and equity and the prohibition of all discrimination based on sex, to the National Gender Equity Strategy introduced in 2003 and updated in 2016, provides an overaching framework (Direction de l'Environnement et des Etablissements Classes (DEEK), n.d.). The DCFs initiative further supports communities in Mali and Senegal to become more resilient to climate change through locally controlled adaptation funds.

Despite these advances, significant disparity persists particularly in agriculture, as reforms have not adequately dealt with women's lack of access to land and the fact that markets remain restricted. Although Senegal integrates women-centred adaptation projects into national climate strategies, gender-responsive budgeting remains weak (Maisonnave & Mamboundou, 2022). This gives the impression of the presence of aspirational strategies with little or no implementation. Besides the agricultural sector, gender mainstreaming policies are also present in the energy sector, but also face weak enforcement, reflecting broader challenges of poor political will and accountability (Klug et al., 2024).

4.3.2. Institutions

Through a partnership with the Accelerating Impacts of CGIAR Climate Research for Africa AICCRA, Senegal's Ministry of Agriculture is coordinating the development of a Gender and Climate Action Plan for the agriculture sector. This is essential to inform the national cross-sectoral Gender and Climate Action, which is being led by the Ministry of Environment, the National Designated Authority.[2] These funds help local committees to allocate adaptation resources. According to Patnaik (2021), when inclusive design measures such as quotas and training were introduced. Women's participation and leadership increased in energy policy processes. Also the influence of donor institutes has driven some progress when it comes to gender audit, but it is hardly sustainable and lacks local ownership (Clancy & Mohlakoana, 2020). Although DCFs have quotas to improve women's participation, ministries still lack the capacity to achieve this. Even though donor-driven initiatives try to compensate for this weakness, they are hardly sustainable (Klug et al., 2024; Patnaik, 2021).

4.3.3. Financial Flow and Implementation Capacity

Senegal's climate financing is largely dependent on international donor organisations. The DCF, for instance, is approximately $30,000 per investment, though small, such donor-funded projects have encouraged women's participation in

---

[2]https://aiccra.cgiar.org/news/senegal-launching-gender-and-climate-action-plan-agriculture-sector-informed-aiccra-engagement

specific communities but not sufficient to drive desired national change (Quevedo et al., 2019). In other words, gains are not systemic but rather project-bound.

According to Patnaik (2021), women tend to benefit more when they actively participate in the decision-making process. However, access to climate information, credit, and leadership opportunities by women remains constrained, highlighting the need for culturally sensitive and contextually relevant interventions. Inequality is further deepened at the macrolevel as agricultural and economic reforms are funded under structural adjustment and liberalisation (Maisonnave & Mamboundou, 2022). Hence, financial flow often fails to connect to reforms at the national level.

Senegal depends on donor-driven projects that enhance inclusivity but yet remains fragmented as a result of existing structural inequality in land, finance and the issue of institutional capacity. If there are no systemic reforms, gender inclusive finance risks remaining project-bound rather than being transformative.

All three countries show significant gaps in monitoring systems. National gender-disaggregated finance datasets do not exist, and available participation figures are mainly drawn from individual project evaluations, as opined by Patnaik (2021) in the case of Senegal.

5. Comparative Insights

5.1. Cross-cutting Barriers

Despite regional differences between the countries under review, common barriers to female inclusivity in climate finance are three. These barriers that consistently hinder gender inclusive climate finance are a lack of gender-disaggregated data, institutional weakness, and women's financial exclusion.

5.1.1. Lack of Gender-disaggregated Data

Insufficient gender-disaggregated finance data is a common challenge to all three countries. Despite having advanced monitoring systems through its Treasury, South Africa rarely tracks beneficiaries based on gender (Gerhard et al., 2023). In Ethiopia, the CRGE facility reporting gives an idea of total finance disbursement but omits gender-specific outcomes, thus making it difficult to bring to light gender issues through proper evaluation (World Bank, 2020). The DCF in Senegal monitors women's participation but not the long-term empowerment process (Patnaik, 2021). All these lack of appropriate gender data makes it difficult to paint the real impact of finance based on gender.

5.1.2. Institutional Weakness

Despite similar barriers and the existence of gender focal points across ministries in all three regions, institutions are weak as a result of being under-resourced and lacking the required authority. South Africa struggles with coordination as the inter-ministerial organisation is weak, leading to fragmented integration

(Republic of South Africa, 2021). In Ethiopia, the struggle is basically about coordination; gender units exist but are merely symbolic without budgets (Mersha & van Laerhoven, 2016). Senegal has donor-driven projects which promote quotas and training but struggle with sustainability (Klug et al., 2024).

5.1.3. Women's Exclusion from Finance

Challenges of access to credit facilities, land, and insurance are common with all three countries, as is common almost everywhere, particularly in developing countries like in Africa. Women are marginalised both in formal and informal financial settings when they try to access funds, land, as well as decision-making. Women are, for instance, highly underrepresented in green jobs in the renewable energy sector in South Africa (Baker, 2015). Ethiopian women adopt fewer adaptation practices because of poor access to extension services and insecure tenure (Teklewold et al., 2022). Most women in Senegal are dependent on the informal financial networks that are largely invisible to formal climate finance flows (Guérin, 2006). These constraints collectively restrict women's ability to benefit from finance programmes.

5.2. Divergent Pathways

Despite shared barriers among these countries, each reflects a distinct trajectory. The different pathways of gender and climate finance in the study areas are largely shaped by governance traditions, policy priorities, and external donor influence.

While South Africa is characterised by strong frameworks, it is poor in implementation. Sophisticated gender inclusive climate policies and financial intermediaries, yet pre-existing inequality and inadequate monitoring imply that gendered vulnerabilities are still on the rise (Flatø et al., 2017). The disparity between policy ambition and the gap in implementation in South Africa can be attributed to the fact that energy and financial institutions are technically oriented and have largely long dominated by males (Gerhard et al., 2023). Despite the existence of gender strategies, women have limited authority in budgeting, project governance and face restrictions in the green space (Alexander et al., 2024), thus, narrowing the scope for gendered responsive programming despite advanced national frameworks.

In the Eastern part of Africa, Ethiopia has great donor dependency but is saddled with fragmented results. The presence of international financial aid enables ambitious strategies, but national ownership and institutionalisation of gender remains weak. As donations are withdrawn, so do the gains from climate-smart agriculture projects fade, lacking sustainability (Tesfaye et al., 2023). This is not far-fetched as long-standing social norms and customs interact with donor donor-driven finance model and thus cause gaps in implementation. In many parts of Africa, participation of women in local adaptation programmes is marred by customary land rights, limited mobility and household labour expectations.

Senegal has donor-driven community projects; if inclusive, they can enhance women's participation benefits (Patnaik, 2021). However, existing structural exclusion due to inequality in land, access to finance, etc., leads to further gendered disparities (Maisonnave & Mamboundou, 2022).

Women's participation in climate finance depends not only on policy provision but also a cultural and organisational transformation that remains inadequate. Besides, intersectional factors such as marital status, socio-economic status complicate the gender narrative, which calls for more appropriate methods as these barriers affect women in different spheres of life differently. Many women in rural areas who depend on livelihoods such as rain-fed agriculture, natural resources-based occupations, and depend on informal financial systems, experience far greater barriers in accessing climate finance benefits. Whenever they participate in project committees, this is often influenced by customs and traditions as regards power, little or no access to lands, and being overburdened with taking care of the home front. Women in urban centres, on the other hand, have access to better opportunities than rural women. Despite having better access to information, markets and formal institutions, urban women remain underrepresented in decision-making spheres that define priorities of climate-finance and are mostly found in service jobs that are not related to emerging green-economy opportunities.

Disparities further occur when the socio-economic status comes to play, as poorer women have very little or no access to finances or collateral to even get a loan, while wealthier women have better opportunities and readily benefit from trainings and funding channels. All these differences illuminate the reason why gender-responsive climate finance remains difficult to institutionalise. It also points to the need for interventions that move beyond formal policy inclusion to address the social hierarchies and political-economy incentives that shape the needs that are prioritised, who participate, and who ultimately benefits.

Overall, institutional and socio-cultural barriers persist across the three countries. Gender provisions remain largely symbolic, as gender units lack authority, resources, and monitoring systems, while organisational cultures continue to favour established hierarchies. These institutional weaknesses interact with long-standing cultural norms around land rights, gender roles and decision-making, which further lead to gendered exclusion even when policies appear progressive. It is also important to note that outcomes are not consistent, such that when compared to urban women, women in rural areas face greater obstacles because of their limited and mostly nature-based livelihoods and less access to formal governance systems, finance, and information. Women in urban centres, on the other hand, have stronger networks and job opportunities but are still under-represented in financial and climate-related workspaces.

These distinctions underscore the need for climate finance initiatives that address both structural norms and the diverse social positions women occupy across socio-economic and geographic contexts. Effective gender-responsive climate finance requires interventions that go beyond formal policy commitments to confront social levels and political-economy dynamics that influence whose needs are prioritised and who ultimately benefits.

6. Policy Implications and Recommendations

Addressing the multidimensional problems identified in this chapter requires an integrated set of policy actions. The following recommendations are suggested.

6.1. Strengthening Gender-inclusive Budgeting

Gender consideration should be systematically embedded across all stages of climate finance programmes, from the design, approval, implementation, and evaluation to ensure the equitable distribution of resources. And such inclusion should be one beyond mere mentions in climate finance policy documents.

On an individual basis, South Africa could do more to expand the focus of gender by building on its existing Treasury's climate budgeting to introduce gender tagging. Also, Ethiopia should do the same by embedding gender in the CRGE facility's financial reporting. While Senegal, on the other hand, could extend quotas and inclusive design principles beyond present community projects into national budgetary processes to ensure sustainability.

6.2. Regional Harmonisation

The different unions in existence in the continent of Africa such as the African Union (AU) and the Regional Economic Communities (RECs) such as Economic Community of West African States (ECOWAS), SADC, and the Intergovernmental Authority on Development (IGAD) should come together to develop standardised gender inclusive climate finance policies geared towards facilitating cross-border cooperation, and learn from one another. SADC could institutionalise gender audit across climate programmes, building on South Africa's frameworks. IGAD could create the regional guideline through strengthening Ethiopia's integration, while ECOWAS could replicate Senegal's DCF model across West Africa, with the AU Agenda 2063 proving the overarching guide for leveraging gender climate integration.

6.3. Enhancing Monitoring and Accountability

Countries should develop robust gender sensitive mechanisms as a capable system to indicate and properly track and evaluate gender outcomes and ensure accountability among all stakeholders. It is very crucial to have regular gender audits as suggested in the works of Clancy and Mohlakoana (2020), who investigated Senegal's energy sector. Credible disaggregated reporting and independent monitoring by independent monitoring bodies like civil society or regional watchdogs at different stages of climate programmes is also crucial to increase transparency.

6.4. Ensuring Financial Inclusion and Leadership

All hands must be on deck towards supporting women's access to financial services, credit, and risk management tools. The fostering of women's participation in leadership at all levels of climate governance should be encouraged to achieve gender inclusivity. This could be achieved in South Africa by focusing on women entrepreneurs in the renewable energy sector, improving land rights should be made available to Ethiopian women and linking informal savings groups to formal finance settings will go a long way for women in Senegal.

6.5. Addressing Structural Barriers

Interventions should be put in place to tackle socio-cultural norms which hinder women's access to finance and leadership roles to help lessen the greater vulnerability they have to bear and institutional apathy that undermines gender inclusion in climate finance.

7. Conclusion

This chapter presented a comparative analysis of South Africa, Ethiopia, and Senegal by examining the extent of gender inclusivity within climate finance across Africa's subregions. Lessons from South Africa reveal the presence of more advanced policy frameworks and institutional sophistication but lack adequate implementation. The flow of climate finance seems substantial, like the JETP but is marred by weak gender budgeting and limited monitoring, which further excludes women.

Ethiopia is characterised by ambitious national climate strategies like the CRGE but is undermined by dependency on international donors and fragmented gender integration. Most of the short-term programmes fail to translate to sustainable positive outcomes due to inadequate structural reforms. There is a need for national ownership, sustained budgetary allocation, and the presence of strong institutions to ensure gender inclusivity.

The DCF donor initiatives in Senegal reveal that inclusive design through quotas, outreach, and capacity building can significantly enhance women's participation and benefits. However, structural issues such as unequal access to land, finances, and institutional capacity limit transformative outcomes. Senegal's experience shows promise of inclusive project design as well as the danger of over-reliance on externally driven interventions in the absence of systemic reform.

Despite these cases, cross-cutting barriers have emerged and include the persistent lack of gender-disaggregated data, which obfuscate outcomes, weak institutions where gender units lack authority or resources and the exclusion of women from formal financial institutions. Thus, confirming the feminist critiques that climate finance often reproduces existing inequalities rather than leads to desired transformation. In the same vein, divergent pathways illustrate the importance of context. How gender is integrated in climate finance is shaped by government policies, donor influence, and tradition. Key policy implications and recommendations include strengthening gender-responsive financing and tracking, harmonised regional approaches by various bodies such as the AU and RECs and improving women's access to land, credit, and financial services.

Inclusive gender-responsive climate finance is essential for advancing equity and sustainable development in Africa. Having inclusive climate financing can both redress historical injustices and enhance the resilience of African countries to climate shocks. Without such integration, climate finance would rather further exacerbate existing inequalities and undermine its effectiveness. This comparative insights from South Africa, Ethiopia, and Senegal point to the need for a more transformative, gender inclusive approach to climate finance across the continent.

References

Abegaz, A., Abera, W., Jaquet, S., & Tamene, L. (2024). Adoption of climate-smart agricultural practices (CSAPs) in Ethiopia. *Climate Risk Management*, *45*, 100628. https://doi.org/10.1016/j.crm.2024.100628

Alexander, N-R., Cazzaniga, M., Fabrizio, S., Jaumotte, F., Li, L., Mondragon, J., Priano, S., & Tavares, M. M. (2024). *Green jobs and the future of work for women and men* [IMF Staff Discussion Note 2024/003, International Monetary Fund].

Assefa, E., & Gebrehiwot, G. (2023). Gender dimensions of climate change adaptation in Tigray, Ethiopia. *Global Environmental Change*, *82*, 102737. https://doi.org/10.1016/j.gloenvcha.2023.102737

Baker, L. (2015). The evolving role of finance in South Africa's renewable energy sector. *Geoforum*, *64*, 146–156. https://doi.org/10.1016/j.geoforum.2015.06.017

Clancy, J. S., & Mohlakoana, N. (2020). Gender audits: An approach to engendering energy policy in Nepal, Kenya and Senegal. *Energy Research & Social Science*, *62*, 101378. https://doi.org/101016/j.erss.2019.101378

Climate Policy Initiative (CPI). (2022) *Landscape of climate finance in Ethiopia*. Climate Policy Initiative. https://www.climatepolicyinitiative.org/wp-content/uploads/2022/11/Landscape-of-Climate-Finance-in-Ethiopia.pdf

Cohen, M. (2018). Gender and climate change financing: Coming out of the margin. *Feminist Economics*, *24*, 188–190. https://doi.org/10.1080/13545701.2017.1421319

Direction de l'Environnement et des Etablissements Classes (DEEC). (n.d.). *Gender mainstreaming in nation climate action in Sub-Saharan Africa: The case of Senegal*. https://unfccc.int/sites/default/files/resource/SENEGAl%20Therese%20Fay%20English.pdf

Flatø, M., Muttarak, R., & Pelser, A. (2017). Women, weather, and woes: The triangular dynamics of female-headed households, economic vulnerability, and climate variability in South Africa. *World Development*, *90*, 41–62. https://doi.org/10.1016/j.worlddev.2016.08.015

Gerhard, M., Jones-Phillipson, E., & Ndeleni, X. (2023). Strategies for gender mainstreaming in climate finance mobilisation in Southern Africa. *PLOS Climate*, *2*(11), e0000254. https://doi.org/10.1371/journal.pclm.0000254

Guérin, I. (2006). Women and money: Lessons from Senegal. *Development and Change*, *37*(3), 549–570. https://doi.org/10.1111/j.0012-155X.2006.00490.x

Gürtler, K. (2025). What space for justice? The just energy transition partnership with South Africa. *Earth System Governance*, *26*, 100285. https://doi.org/10.1016/j.esg.2025.100285

Isah, A., Egli, F., Schmidt, T., & Stünzi, A. (2025). Quantifying climate finance needs in the nationally determined contributions of developing countries. *Climate Policy*, *25*(9), 1442–1459. https://doi.org/10.1080/14693062.2025.2460607

Jerneck, A. (2018). Taking gender seriously in climate change adaptation and sustainability science research: views from feminist debates and sub-Saharan small-scale agriculture. *Sustainability Science*, *13*(2), 403–416. https://doi.org/10.1007/s11625-017-0464-y

Klug, T. W., Saparapa, R., Plutshack, V., Agradi, M., Appiah, S., & Nunoo, I. (2024). The political economy of gender mainstreaming in energy access in Senegal. *Environmental Research: Climate*, *3*(4), 045011. https://iopscience.iop.org/article/10.1088/2752-5295/ad6bb5/pdf

Lüdemann, C., & Ruppel, O. C. (2013). International climate finance: Policies, structures and challenges. In O. C. Ruppel, C. Roschmann, & K. Ruppel-Schlichting (Eds.), *Climate change: International law and global governance: Volume II: Policy, diplomacy and governance in a changing environment* (pp. 375–408). Nomos Verlagsgesellschaft mbH & Co. KG. https://doi.org/10.5771/9783845242774_375

Maisonnave, H., & Mamboundou, P. N. (2022). Agricultural economic reforms, gender inequality and poverty in Senegal. *Journal of Policy Modeling*, *44*(2), 361–374. https://doi.org/10.1016/j.jpolmod.2022.03.006

Mersha, A. A., & Van Laerhoven, F. (2016). A gender approach to understanding the differentiated impact of barriers to adaptation: Responses to climate change in rural Ethiopia. *Regional Environmental Change*, *16*(6), 1701–1713. https://doi.org/10.1016/j.jpolmod.2022.03.006

Parmesan, C., Morecroft, M. D., Trisurat, Y., & Mezzi, D. (2022). *Climate change 2022: Impacts, adaptation and vulnerability* [Research Report, GIEC; IPCC]. ffhal-03774939f. https://hal.science/hal-03774939v1

Patnaik, H. A. (2021). Gender and participation in community based adaptation: Evidence from the decentralized climate funds project in Senegal. *World Development*, *142*, 105448. https://doi.org/10.1016/j.worlddev.2021.105448

Quevedo, A., Bird, N., Amsalu, A., Crick, F., Gargule, A., & Suji, O. (2019). *Country experiences with decentralised climate finance: Early outcomes* [Working Paper, Braced Knowledge Manager. Overseas Development Institute]. https://odi.org/documents/6056/12901.pdf

Rao, N., Lawson, E. T., Raditloaneng, W. N., Solomon, D., & Angula, M. N. (2019). Gendered vulnerabilities to climate change: Insights from the semi-arid regions of Africa and Asia. *Climate and Development*, *11*(1), 14–26. https://doi.org/10.1080/17565529.2017.1372266

Republic of South Africa. (2021). *South Africa's updated nationally determined contribution*. Department of Forestry, Fisheries and the Environment. South Africa updated first NDC September 2021.pdf

Schlosberg, D., & Collins, L. B. (2014). From environmental to climate justice: Climate change and the discourse of environmental justice. *Wiley Interdisciplinary Reviews: Climate Change*, *5*(3), 359–374. https://doi.org/10.1002/wcc.275

Shayegh, S., & Dasgupta, S. (2024). Climate change, labour availability and the future of gender inequality in South Africa. *Climate and Development*, *16*(3), 209–226.

Southern African Development Community (SADC), Southern African Research and Documentation Centre (SARDC). (2022). *SADC gender and development monitor 2022*. SADC.

Teklewold, H., Bezabih, M., & Gebrehiwot, T. (2022). Gender differences on the choices of a portfolio of climate change adaptation strategies in Ethiopia. *Climate Risk Management*, *38*, 100467. https://doi.org/10.1016/j.crm.2022.100467

Tesfaye, A., Radeny, M., Ogada, M. J., Recha, J. W., Ambaw, G., Chanana, N., Huyer, S., Demeke, G., & Solomon, D. (2023). Gender empowerment and parity in East Africa: Evidence from climate-smart agriculture in Ethiopia and Kenya. *Climate and Development*, *15*(9), 768–778. https://doi.org/10.1080/17565529.2022.2154124

Timilsina, G. R. (2021). Financing climate change adaptation: International initiatives. *Sustainability*, *13*(12), 6515. https://doi.org/10.3390/su13126515

United Nations (UN). (2015). *Transforming our world: The 2030 agenda for sustainable development*. United Nations. https://sdgs.un.org/2030agendaUnited Nations.

United Nations Framework Convention on Climate Change (UNFCCC). (2019). *Enhanced Lima work programme on gender and its gender action plan*. Conference of the Parties (COP). https://unfcc.int/decision?f%5BO%=conference%3A4252

World Bank. (2020). *Ethiopia Climate Resilient Green Economy Facility annual report 2019/20*. World Bank. https://documents1.worldbank.org/curated/en/099431406152240521/pdf/P1711160560c540d50a1ae0261b2c6c4de3.pdf

Wredström, E. (2024). *How do climate change adaptation plans consider gender?: An analysis of national adaptation plans in Sub-Saharan Africa* [Dissertation]. https://urn.kb.se/resolve?urn=urn:nbn:se:lnu:diva-127214

Chapter 10

Climate Change, Financial Development, and Structural Factors: Gendered Impacts on Women's Agricultural Employment in Nigeria and Kenya

Kafilah Lola Gold

College of Business and Economics, University of Johannesburg, Johannesburg, South Africa

Abstract

Climate change disproportionately affects women, especially in sectors like agriculture, where exposure to environmental stressors interacts with persistent gender gaps. This study quantifies the gendered impacts of climate change and financial development on women's agricultural employment in Nigeria and Kenya, using annual secondary data from 1991 to 2022. Anchored in theories of gendered institutions, capabilities, and structural transformation, the analysis employs Ordinary Least Squares (OLS) and Newey–West heteroskedasticity- and autocorrelation-consistent estimates using harmonised secondary data obtained from the World Bank, World Development Indicators (WDI), FAOSTAT, and the Global Economy. Climate exposure is captured through land temperature change, while financial development, urbanisation, and education proxy structural and human capital dynamics. The results reveal country-specific pathways. In Nigeria, women's participation in agriculture declined steadily with rising urbanisation and financial deepening, indicating that finance-led and structural transformation displaced women towards non-farm activities. In Kenya, higher temperatures, financial development, and education have all significantly and negatively influenced women's agricultural employment, reflecting climate stress compounded by finance-driven exclusion and human capital-induced sectoral shifts. The interaction between temperature

Gender and Climate Finance in Africa: Addressing Inequalities and Bridging Gaps, 173–203

Published under exclusive licence by Emerald Publishing Limited
doi:10.1108/978-1-83742-085-820261010

and finance was insignificant, suggesting that existing financial systems have yet to buffer women against climate shocks. These findings confirm that climate stress and financial systems jointly shape women's economic opportunities, consistent with the theoretical expectation that institutional design determines gender outcomes. The study provides evidence to inform policies that integrate Gender Action Plans (GAPs), devolved small-grant facilities, and climate-smart investments that reduce women's time burdens and enhance resilience.

Keywords: Climate change; financial development; agriculture; urbanisation; education; employment

Introduction

Climate change is a defining development and equity challenge whose impacts disproportionately affect women due to structural inequalities in assets, information, and decision-making power across households, markets, and institutions (Angula et al., 2021; Elwell et al., 2023). In Sub-Saharan Africa (SSA), where women's livelihoods are closely tied to climate-sensitive sectors such as rain-fed agriculture, climate variability and extremes amplify pre-existing gender gaps in productivity, income stability, and control over resources (Elwell et al., 2023; Gerhard et al., 2023). The Intergovernmental Panel on Climate Change (IPCC) concludes with high confidence that the frequency and intensity of heavy rainfall events will increase across most of Africa as global warming rises, alongside substantial increases in heat extremes, with significant implications for food security and rural labour dynamics (Gold, 2024; Trisos et al., 2022). Of the countries in the SSA region, Nigeria and Kenya exemplify these dynamics, as recent observational records document persistent warming, recurrent drought-flood cycles, and heightened rainfall variability that disrupt agricultural labour and income (IPCC, 2021).

In Nigeria, the Nigerian Meteorological Agency reports that 2023 was nearly as warm as the national record (2021) (NiMet, 2024), continuing a persistent warming trend since 1981, accompanied by intense rainfall and recurrent flooding, with major socioeconomic impacts (Keyamo, 2024). In Kenya, long-term records from the Kenya Meteorological Department show rising temperatures, recurrent drought-flood cycles, and large rainfall variability, with 2024 the hottest year on record (KMD, 2023, 2024). These trends mirror IPCC findings for East and West Africa, rising heat extremes, irregular precipitation, and intensifying water stress that undermine agricultural productivity, labour allocation, and women's time burdens (IPCC, 2021; Ranasinghe et al., 2021). Fig. 10.1 shows persistent increases in land-surface temperature and agricultural water stress, particularly in Kenya. Women in rural areas bear the heaviest burden as primary food producers and water collectors, yet gender-specific climate impacts on agricultural livelihoods remain underexplored.

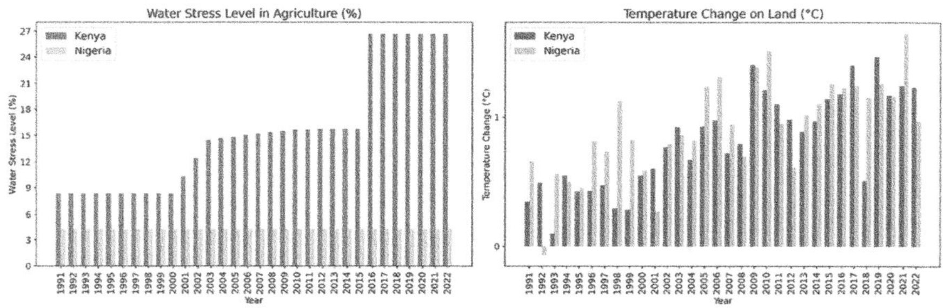

Fig. 10.1. Water Stress Level in Agriculture and Temperature Change on Land in Nigeria and Kenya, 1991–2022. *Source*: Author's compilation from FAOSTAT (2024).

To address the gendered climate agriculture challenges nexus, climate finance becomes the primary policy instrument through which governments and financial intermediaries reduce climate risk by funding adaptive assets and services. The expanding gender-and-climate finance literature identifies design features that can improve women's access, voice, and resilience. At the institutional level, the Green Climate Fund (GCF) has catalysed reforms within African financial institutions, including mandatory gender analyses, project-level GAPs, dedicated gender staff, and sex-disaggregated monitoring (Gerhard et al., 2023). Yet, implementation remains uneven, with under-budgeted GAPs and weak expenditure tracking (Elwell et al., 2023). Evidence also shows that direct or enhanced direct access (EDA) and devolved small-grant facilities reach women more effectively than large centralised projects, provided procedures are simplified (Caldwell & Larsen, 2021; Manuamorn & Biesbroek, 2020; Price, 2021). Enterprise-level research shows persistent credit barriers for women-led firms, high collateral, short tenors, and costly capital (Sesan et al., 2019). Fig. 10.2 illustrates these structural constraints between Nigeria and Kenya. Nigeria's financial development is consistently higher but volatile (Sonja, 2022), while Kenya's trajectory is steadier, driven by mobile money and microfinance innovations that reflect broader women's basic digital financial inclusion (World Bank, 2024a). These platforms do not yet operate with explicit climate-finance mandates, but their widespread use demonstrates a viable pathway through which decentralised, gender-responsive climate finance could be channelled. This contrast justifies the comparative design of the study by showing how differing financial architectures condition women's resilience in the agricultural sector to climate stress.

Despite this progress, two critical gaps remain for Nigeria and Kenya. First, limited country-specific, empirical work traces how climate variability and extremes translate into measurable changes in women's agricultural outcomes (productivity, labour force participation) in these two economies using comparable, harmonised indicators over time. Much of the existing evidence is either regional, single-country but outside Nigeria/Kenya, design-stage or institutional (rather than outcome-level), or it lacks sex-disaggregated agricultural measures

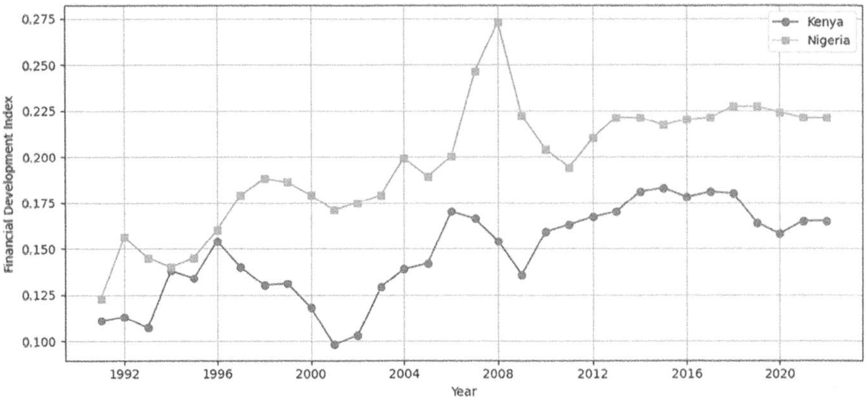

Fig. 10.2. Financial Development Index in Kenya and Nigeria (1991–2022). *Source*: Author's compilation from TheGlobalEconomy.com (2025).

(Angula et al., 2021; Caldwell & Larsen, 2021; Elwell et al., 2023; Omukuti et al., 2022; Price, 2021). Second, a dearth of quantitative studies connects gender-responsive climate finance, including instrument design and implementation features such as costed GAPs, small-grant windows, and simplified procedures, to women's agricultural resilience outcomes in Nigeria and Kenya. Most analyses stop at documenting barriers and promising mechanisms rather than estimating their associations with women's agricultural productivity or labour participation at the country level (Elwell et al., 2023; Gerhard et al., 2023; Omukuti et al., 2022).

This study advances the literature in three ways. First, it provides a comparative, country-level analysis of Nigeria and Kenya, focusing on women's agricultural employment using harmonised annual secondary data for 1991–2022. These datasets were sourced from the World Bank, WDI, FAOSTAT, and the Global Economy. Second, it introduces an empirically transparent specification that captures climate exposure through FAOSTAT's annual temperature change on land and water stress indicators, variables directly linked to heat burdens and freshwater constraints women face in agriculture. Third, it examines the role of financial development and urbanisation as structural factors shaping women's agricultural employment and conditioning the relationship between climate stressors and gendered outcomes. It is worth mentioning that structural force also affects men; however, extensive evidence (Graham et al., 2016; Gray & Thiede, 2024; World Bank, 2024b) shows that women experience these shifts differently because they face more binding constraints. This includes unequal land and collateral rights, higher unpaid care and water collection burdens, and limited access to credit and extension services, hence, the concentrates on women's employment in agriculture. In doing so, the study moves beyond purely descriptive accounts to offer an accessible, OLS-based comparative assessment of how climate exposure, financial development, and structural transformation influence women's employment in agriculture, with estimates interpreted as associations rather than causal effects.

Specifically, the primary objective of this study is to examine gendered impacts of climate change on women in agriculture in Nigeria and Kenya and the role of finance. While the study aims to:

(i) Estimate the impact of rising land temperatures and increasing water stress on women's agricultural employment in Nigeria and Kenya.
(ii) Analyse whether financial development and urbanisation affect climate stressors and women's agricultural employment.
(iii) Compare patterns across Nigeria and Kenya, identifying policy-relevant differences in exposure, financial systems, and structural drivers of gendered labour outcomes.

The empirical evidence is intended to inform policies that prioritise adaptive assets such as irrigation infrastructure and climate-smart technologies, while ensuring climate finance mechanisms are accessible to women farmers through simplified procedures, devoted small-grant facilities, and cost-simplifying procedures, decentralised small-grant facilities, and costed GAPs. Strengthening women's access to financial systems and embedding gender considerations into the national climate finance frameworks will be vital for mitigating employment risks associated with climate stressors. The study contributes comparative evidence that inclusive climate finance is essential for equitable adaptation and sustainable livelihoods in SSA. The chapter proceeds with a theoretical literature review, followed by empirical literature, methodology, results and discussion, and concludes with key insights and policy recommendations.

Literature Review

Theoretical Framework

The framework integrates three interconnected theoretical perspectives to explain how climate stressors and financial systems shape women's opportunities in agriculture in Kenya and Nigeria: (i) gendered institutions and bargaining power, (ii) capabilities and constraints, and (iii) structural transformation mediated by finance and governance. Together, these theories show that climate change is not gender-neutral and that financial development benefits women only when finance is explicitly designed to be gender-responsive. First, gendered institutions and intra-household bargaining emphasise how access to assets, fallback positions, and time burdens jointly determine women's participation in market work (Agarwal, 1997; Kabeer, 1999; Sen, 1987). In many rural African settings, unequal land and collateral rights, unpaid care, and water collection responsibilities constrain women's ability to engage in paid agricultural employment. In time-allocation models, shocks that raise domestic time reduce women's market labour supply (Becker, 1965). Rising water stress lengthens collection time, while higher temperatures depress crop productivity and increase production risk, lowering female employment in agriculture. Institutional features of climate and development finance can either ease or reinforce these constraints, depending on whether gender commitments are backed by adequate resources and accountability (Elwell et al., 2023; Gerhard et al., 2023).

Second, the capability approach conceptualises development as the expansion of substantive freedoms (Nussbaum, 2000; Sen, 1999). Climate stress erodes these freedoms through yield losses, time burdens, and credit rationing mechanisms (Stiglitz & Weiss, 1981). Evidence from East African clean-energy value chains shows that collateral and interest rate barriers limit women's participation, whereas group-based and simplified financial arrangements ease exclusion by offering alternative pathways to credit that women are more likely to access (Sesan et al., 2019). At the macrolevel, financial deepening can fund adaptation and diversification, but its overall effect on women's agricultural employment is ambiguous, as finance may also accelerate capital deepening that displaces female labour. "More finance" benefits women only when accompanied by gender-responsive rules, direct-access modalities, devolved grants, and budgeted GAPs (Caldwell & Larsen, 2021; Manuamorn & Biesbroek, 2020; Omukuti et al., 2022; Price, 2021).

Third, structural transformation theories explain the reallocation of labour from agriculture to higher-productivity sectors as urbanisation proceeds and human capital accumulates (Herrendorf et al., 2014). Urbanisation enlarges non-farm opportunities, reducing the share of women's jobs in agriculture. Higher primary enrolment reduces youth farm labour and builds capabilities for later transitions to services and industry. Whether these shifts enhance women's agencies depends on the financial and governance architectures available. Weak transparency and accountability hinder women's control over local resources (Manuamorn & Biesbroek, 2020; Omukuti et al., 2022). These insights guide the variable selection (as shown in Fig. 10.3), where female agricultural employment is examined in relation to temperature change, water stress, financial development, and urbanisation.

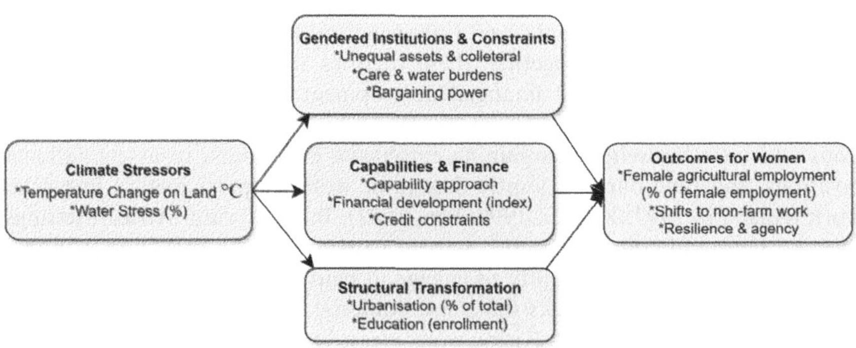

Fig. 10.3. Conceptual Framework. *Source*: Author's.

Empirical Review

Climate Stress, Gender, and Agricultural Employment

A growing empirical literature links hotter conditions and hydrological stress to lower agricultural productivity and reallocating labour out of farming, with particularly strong effects in low- and middle-income countries. In emerging economies, a 1°C increase in seasonal temperatures reduces agricultural value-added growth contemporaneously and in subsequent seasons, implying persistent contraction in farm labour demand during heat-exposed periods (Nguyen & Pienknagura, 2024). Long-run panel evidence for SSA similarly finds sizeable adverse effects of temperature on agricultural growth, consistent with a reduction in employment demand and earnings in agriculture (Talib et al., 2021). Climate stress interacts with existing gender gaps to shape women's economic roles. In rural areas, women's responsibilities for food production and resource management heighten exposure to climate variability, while limited asset ownership, restricted access to finance and extension, and underrepresentation in decision forums constrain their adaptation choices (Gerhard et al., 2023; Price, 2021). Qualitative evidence from Namibia's ecosystem-based adaptation programme highlights leadership imbalances, unequal opportunities for livelihood, and uneven participation in public fora, motivating early gender analysis, capacity building, and sex-disaggregated indicators (Angula et al., 2021). At the enterprise level, East African value chain research finds women-led firms face tighter credit constraints, higher collateral requirements, and shorter loan tenors, concentrating women in lower-value nodes with thinner margins (Sesan et al., 2019).

Temperature Change, Water Stress, and Women's Employment Link

Higher temperature anomalies raise heat stress and depress crop productivity, increasing production risk. In settings where women are concentrated in lower-paid, casual, or seasonal roles, declining productivity and higher variance reduce demand for female agricultural labour or shift women's time towards household coping (e.g., safeguarding food and water) rather than market work. Although most climate-labour studies are not sex-disaggregated, rather, adjacent work shows that hotter-than-usual conditions increase temporary migration and undermine women's well-being, suggesting channels (health, mobility, and coping) through which heat can depress women's paid agricultural participation (Gray & Thiede, 2024). In Kenya and Nigeria, literature consistently links climate variability and warming with depressed yields and increased exposure, reinforcing the plausibility of reduced female agricultural employment through both demand-side (lower labour demand) and supply-side (time and health burdens) mechanisms (Bryan et al., 2013). Greater water stress interfaces with women's labour through the time use and health channels. Multi-country studies across 24 SSA countries show that when collection times exceed 30 minutes, adult women are the primary collectors in the majority of households, with millions of women and girls devoting substantial time to water fetching (Graham et al., 2016), which reduces participation in schooling and market work. World Bank (2024b) dashboards reinforce this pattern, confirming that in roughly 80% of households without on-premises water, women and girls are responsible, implying sizable opportunity costs for paid work. Likewise, Angula et al. (2021) and Demie et al. (2016) noted that increased domestic burdens reduced participation in paid activities and training, lowering women's measured employment in agriculture, even if unpaid subsistence work rises. Water scarcity can depress irrigation productivity and increase volatility, reducing the returns to women's paid farm work. In climate-finance practice, the risk that water stress exacerbates exclusion is explicitly targeted by design guidance calling for early gender analysis, sex-disaggregated indicators, and devolved small-grant facilities supporting women's groups. In short, temperature and water stress are expected to be negatively associated with women's employment in agriculture, recognising that short-run, subsistence-driven labour intensification could locally offset these effects (Angula et al., 2021).

Financial Development, Urbanisation, and Education as Drivers of Sectoral Reallocation

Macroeconomic and sectoral evidence indicates that deeper financial systems alleviate capital allocation frictions, expand scale-intensive tradable sectors and hasten labour reallocation out of agriculture (Buera et al., 2011; Gold & Tregenna, 2025). In developing economies, broad structural and financial sector reforms raise productivity, with modest short-term effects but longer-term support for shifts towards non-farm activities (Konte et al., 2022). Therefore, deeper finance can both (a) enable adaptation investments (irrigation, climate-smart inputs) and (b) accelerate structural change towards capital-intensive, non-farm sectors. Whether this lowers women's agricultural employment in ways that expand women's opportunities or displaces them from paid work depends on their effective access to finance. Sectoral studies in East Africa show women face binding collateral and tenor constraints that limit entry into higher return, climate-relevant value chain nodes, and through group-based and simplified finance, can partially offset these barriers (Sesan et al., 2019). Secondly, institutional analyses across southern Africa find that GCF-accreditation and gender policy requirements have catalysed reforms, mandatory gender analyses, costed GAPs, embedded gender staff, and sex-disaggregated monitoring systems, which are preconditions for building gender-responsive financial pipelines (Gerhard et al., 2023). Thirdly, cross portfolio reviews highlight persistent implementation gaps, as many projects and credible expenditure tracking, weakening delivery to women despite formal commitments (Elwell et al., 2023).

Regarding urbanisation, cross-country evidence shows that as economies urbanise, employment shifts from agriculture to services and industry. Urbanisation expands non-farm opportunities for women, while higher primary enrolment reduces youth labour participation in farm activities and builds capabilities for later transitions (Angula et al., 2021; Gerhard et al., 2023). These structural forces in climate-affected settings may condition how women respond to shocks such as migration, human capital, and labour determinants. From the review evidence and summary matrix (Table 10.1), most studies focus on design features rather than providing sex disaggregated country-panel estimates linking temperature and water stress to women's agricultural employment. Few quantify how macrolevel financial development interacts with climate stress to shape women's sectoral allocation. This study directly addresses these gaps using nationally representative, sex disaggregated employment data, climate indicators, and structural variables (financial development, urbanisation, education), while testing theoretically motivated interactions (finance × climate; urbanisation × climate).

Table 10.1. Summary of Empirical Review.

Authors	**Scope/Method/ Period**	**Main Findings**	**Study Gap**
Earsom (2024)	Africa/Transition finance/Policy analysis (2020–2023)	Transition finance compacts need ex-ante gender accountability	No demonstration of impacts on women's access or resilience
Gerhard et al. (2023)	Southern Africa/ Institutional analysis (post-2015)	GCF reforms (GAPs, gender staff, disaggregated monitoring) improved institutional capacity	No evidence of whether reforms translate into women's resilience or economic outcomes
Angula et al. (2021)	Namibia/ Qualitative case study (2015–2020)	Ecosystem-based adaptation exposed gendered climate impacts, leadership gaps; early gender analysis recommended	No empirical link to finance delivery or measurable women's outcomes
Price (2021)	Global/Africa/ Synthesis review (2010s)	Accreditation complexity, large-project bias; advocates EDA and small grants	No statistical evidence on how access barriers affect women beneficiaries
Caldwell and Larsen (2021)	Global/GCF/ Operational diagnostic (2010–2020)	Recommend tranche funding, small-grant templates, and clearer guidance	Gender impacts of operational reforms are untested

(*Continued*)

Table 10.1. (*Continued*)

Authors	Scope/Method/ Period	Main Findings	Study Gap
Omukuti et al. (2022)	GCF portfolio/ Portfolio analysis (2010–2020)	Local delivery is inconsistently defined; one project required GAP-linked women's grants	Weak traceability; limited outcome measurement for women
Elwell et al. (2023)	GCF portfolio/ Portfolio analysis (2015–2022)	GAPs are often underfunded (<0.02% budgets allocated)	Implementation failures; little effect on access, agency, or resilience
Manuamorn and Biesbroek (2020)	Global/ Adaptation Fund systematic review (63 projects) up to 2017	Direct-access projects are more participatory, gender-focused	No sex-disaggregated outcome data
Sesan et al. (2019)	East Africa/ Qualitative value chain case study (2010s)	Women in the cookstoves sector are concentrated in low-value roles; group finance eased barriers	Not situated in public climate finance; limited link to resilience or empowerment

Source: Author's.

Methodology

Data and Variables Description

Using annual secondary data from 1991 to 2022, the study employs a parsimonious set of variables aligned with theory and data availability. It is worth mentioning that variables such as precipitation are excluded due to severe data gaps for Nigeria and Kenya; instead, water stress is used as a proxy for hydrological pressure. Also, female secondary school enrolment was replaced with primary school enrolment. The dependent variable is female employment in agriculture, while the key explanatory climate stressors variables are temperature and water stress indicators, and structural factors include financial development, urban population, and primary education enrolment. These variables reflect broader processes of structural transformation influencing women's labour allocation. Table 10.2

Table 10.2. Variables, Descriptions, Sources, and Expected Signs.

Variable/Code	Definition and Description	Source	Expected Sign
Female employment in agriculture (% of female employment) – ***FEA***	Share of female employment in agriculture relative to total female employment in a country and year	WDI	Dependent variable
Temperature change on land (°C) – ***TEMP***	Measures as annual mean temperature change on land relative to the 1951–1980 baseline. It is expected that heat stress crops yield and raise production risk, time burdens, and reduce labour demand in agriculture by pushing women out of the sector (Angula et al., 2021)	FAOSTAT	Negative (higher heat reduces women's agricultural employment)
Water stress (%) – ***WSTRESS***	Freshwater withdrawals as percentage of available renewable water resources for agriculture-focused. Based on SDG 6.4.2, increase time for water collection, reduce women's participation in paid farm work and training (Angula et al., 2021). This pattern reflects the broader gendered vulnerability to resource scarcity (Trisos et al., 2022)	FAOSTAT	Negative (greater stress reduces women's agricultural employment)
Financial development index – ***FINDEV***	Composite index of financial institutions and markets development (Svirydzenka, 2016); proxy for financial depth (Gold & Tregenna, 2025). It is expected that deeper finance can ease women's constraints if access and accountability exist; without them, benefits may bypass women or reinforce gaps (Gerhard et al., 2023)	The global economy	Positive (if finance is accessible; otherwise, neutral/weak)
Urban population (% of total population) – ***URBAN***	Urbanisation is a proxy for structural control for rural–urban transitions that shape women's participation in agriculture (Herrendorf et al., 2014)	WDI	Negative (urbanisation shifts women out of agriculture)
Education Gross primary school enrolment (%) – ***EDU_scaled***	Education as human capital accumulation affects women's sectoral employment. Schooling raises non-farm employability and earnings potential, especially for younger females (Psacharopoulos & Patrinos, 2018)	WDI	Negative

Source: Author's.

summarises the variables, definitions, descriptions, sources, and the expected signs of association based on theory and prior evidence.

Model and Estimation

Empirical Model

Following the theoretical link between finance, structural change, and labour allocation (Buera et al., 2011; Herrendorf et al., 2014; Konte et al., 2022) and gender-responsive climate-finance frameworks that highlight how institutional rules shape women's access and agency (Gerhard et al., 2023; Omukuti et al., 2022), agricultural employment is modelled as a function of climate stress, financial development, and structural factors. Evidence from Namibia and Southern African implementing entities motivates the gendered channels through which climate exposure and the financial system interact (Angula et al., 2021; Becker, 1965; Gerhard et al., 2023; Omukuti et al., 2022).

Hence, the following baseline functional model is estimated for Nigeria and Kenya separately:

$$FEA_t = f(TEMP_t, WSTRESS_t, FINDEV_t, URBAN_t, EDU_t) \tag{1}$$

where:

FEA_t = Female employment in agriculture (% of female employment).

$TEMP_t$ = Temperature change on land (°C).

$WSTRESS_t$ = Water stress (%); included for Kenya because it varies; no variation in Nigeria.

$FINDEV_t$ = Financial development index (proxy for financial depth).

$URBAN_t$ = Urban population (% of total population).

EDU_t = Primary school enrolment (% gross); proxy for human capital development (scaled).

The estimable baseline model is given as:

$$FEA_t = \alpha_0 + \alpha_1 TEMP_t + \alpha_2 WSTRESS_t + \alpha_3 FINDEV_t + \alpha_4 URBAN_t + \alpha_5 EDU_t + \mu_t) \tag{2}$$

Expected signs (priors): $\alpha_1 < 0$: Rising temperature reduces women's agricultural employment through heat stress and productivity loss. $\alpha_2 < 0$: Increasing water stress reduces women's paid farm work by raising time burdens and lowering irrigated productivity. α_3 *ambiguous*: Finance can either support adaptation (positive) or accelerate structural existence (negative). $\alpha_4 < 0$: Urbanisation typically shifts women from agriculture to services or trade. $\alpha_0 < 0$: Higher education enrolment lowers women's agricultural employment by keeping young women in school and facilitating non-farm transitions. To test whether finance and structural conditions moderate the impact of climate stress, the model is extended as:

$$FEA_t = \alpha_0 + \alpha_1 TEMP_t + \alpha_2 WSTRESS_t + \alpha_3 FINDEV_t + \alpha_4 URBAN_t + \alpha_5 EDU_t + \gamma_1(TEMP_t \times FINDEV_t) \gamma_2(TEMP_t \times URBAN_t) + \mu_t \quad (3)$$

Priors: $\gamma_1 > 0$: Finance mitigates the negative impact of temperature on women's employment; $\gamma_2 < 0$: Urbanisation may amplify climate-induced exist from agriculture.

Given adjustment lags, a one year of climate exposure is also estimated:

$$FEA_t = \alpha_0 + \alpha_1 TEMP_{t-1} + \alpha_2 WSTRESS_{t-1} + \alpha_3 FINDEV_t + \alpha_4 URBAN_t + \alpha_5 EDU_t + \mu_t \quad (4)$$

Estimation Method

The study employs OLS, estimated separately for Nigeria and Kenya over the period of 1991–2022, consistent with the practices for small-sample, transparent, and policy-relevant analysis (Angrist & Pischke, 2009; Gujarati & Porter, 2009). OLS is preferred for its interpretability and suitability for evaluating associations rather than strict causality, a priority in gender-focused climate research. Heteroskedasticity and autocorrelation are addressed using Newey–West standard errors (SEs). The Newey–West specification applies a lag length of 1, which corrects for first-order serial correlation in the error term, as indicated by the Breusch–Godfrey test, without lagging any of the explanatory variables. Diagnostics performed include: (i) heteroskedasticity (White/Breusch–Pagan) (Breusch & Pagan, 1979; White, 1980), (ii) autocorrelation (Durbin–Watson or Breusch–Godfrey), (iii) multicollinearity, VIF < 5 threshold (Gold, 2024), and (iv) functional-form validation (Ramsey RESET test). A linear time trend (gt) is included only where residual drift is observed. Given that the data represent bounded shares or annual changes, variables are expected to be weakly trending but not explosive, making OLS with HAC corrections an appropriate choice.

Result and Discussion

This section presents the empirical results and interprets the estimated coefficients as associations rather than causal effects. Findings are cross-referenced with descriptive trend patterns for each country (FEA, TEMP, WSTRESS, FINDEV, URBAN, EDU) and discussed within a gender-responsive finance framework that links climate exposure, financial development, and women's labour outcomes.

Nigeria: Empirical Results and Discussion

Descriptive Statistics and Correlation Analysis

Table 10.3(A and B) reports the descriptive statistics and correlation matrix for Nigeria. On average, about 37% of Nigerian women were employed in agriculture between 1991 and 2022, declining steadily as urbanisation (mean = 41%) and financial development (index = 0.19) increased. Average land-surface temperature rose by nearly 1°C above the 1981–2010 baseline, confirming a warming trend. The correlation matrix reveals a strong inverse relationship between female agricultural employment and urbanisation ($r = -0.98$) and financial development ($r = -0.81$), indicating that structural and financial transformation jointly reduce women's participation in agriculture. Temperature also correlates negatively with female employment ($r = -0.67$), consistent with climate stress effects, while education shows only a weak association. These results highlight the combined influence of climate dynamics and structural change on gendered labour outcomes in Nigeria, providing the context for the regression analyses that follow.

Table 10.3. Descriptive Statistics and Correlation Matrix for Nigeria.

Descriptive Statistics

Variable	**Mean**	**Std. Dev.**	**Min**	**Max**	**Interpretation**
FEA	37.37	7.26	25.61	47.53	Women form roughly one-third of the agricultural labour force; steady decline mirrors structural change
TEMP	0.93	0.37	−0.07	1.65	Land temperature rose steadily, indicating gradual warming
FINDEV	0.196	0.034	0.123	0.273	Financial depth improved modestly but remains low overall
URBAN	40.90	7.42	30.18	53.52	Urbanisation increased, reflecting Nigeria's demographic transition
EDU_ scaled	3.73	21.11	0.00	119.43	High dispersion due to scale

Correlation Matrix

Variables	**TEMP**	**FINDEV**	**URBAN**	**EDU_ scaled**	**Interpretation**
FEA	−0.666	−0.807	−0.978	−0.296	Female agricultural employment strongly declines with urbanisation and finance; it is moderately linked to temperature

Table 10.3. (*Continued*)

Variables	TEMP	FINDEV	URBAN	EDU_ scaled	Interpretation
TEMP	1.000	0.580	0.686	0.021	Temperature correlates positively with structural variables, showing concurrent global warming and development trends
FINDEV		1.000	0.793	0.134	Finance and urbanisation expand together; there is a limited short-term link with education
URBAN			1.000	0.311	Urbanisation dominates the structural correlation pattern and absorbs the long-run trend
EDU_ scaled				1.000	Weak correlations reflect slow-moving education progress relative to structural change

Source: Author's.

Note: Correlations above 0.7 or below –0.7 indicate strong relationships.

Baseline OLS Model with Robust SEs

The OLS estimates, presented in Table 10.4, establish the baseline relationships among the variables. However, because annual macroeconomic and climate data often exhibit autocorrelation and heteroskedasticity, the OLS estimator may yield biased SEs. To address these issues, the Newey–West heteroskedasticity-and autocorrelation-consistent (HAC) estimator was adopted. Hence, the discussion focuses on the Newey–West estimates, which provide a more reliable inference.

Newey–West Models

Table 10.5 reports the Newey–West estimated models, where specifications incorporating the interaction between temperature and urbanisation (Model 4) were retained as the preferred model. This serves as robustness checks as it captures both the direct effects of climate stress and the moderating role of structural transformation, while satisfying standard diagnostic criteria.

Table 10.4. Baseline OLS Estimates of Female Agricultural Employment in Nigeria.

Variable	Coefficient (p-Value)	Expected Sign	Interpretation
TEMP	0.323 (0.747)	–	Temperature change has no significant effect on women's agricultural employment; limited inter-annual variability may explain the weak coefficient
FINDEV	–18.980 (0.027)**	±	Financial development significantly reduces female agricultural employment, indicating that finance-led structural transformation may initially displace women from farm work
URBAN	–0.900 (0.000)***	–	Urbanisation exerts a strong negative effect, confirming that as Nigeria urbanises, women transition out of agriculture towards non-farm activities
*EDU_*	0.001 (0.962)	–	Education is insignificant, suggesting that slow-moving human capital gains likely manifest in later structural changes
Constant	77.588 (0.000)***	–	Baseline female agricultural employment level when explanatory variables are zero (not directly interpretable)
Model Statistics:			
No. of observations	32		R-squared = 0.9589; Root MSE = 1.5758
Diagnostic Tests:			
Breusch–Pagan	χ^2 = 10.79 (0.00)		Heteroskedasticity detected → corrected using robust/Newey–West SEs
White	χ^2 = 18.50 (0.047)		Confirms heteroskedasticity
Breusch–Godfrey	χ^2 = 25.84 (0.000)		Serial correlation is present
Mean VIF	2.55		Multicollinearity is within an acceptable range (<5)
RESET	F = 34.57 (0.000)		Functional-form misspecification is addressed in later interaction models

Source: Author's.

Notes: Dependent variable: Female employment in agriculture (% of female employment). Robust (Huber-White) SEs are reported. All variables are in levels except education, which is scaled for comparability.

*** $p<0.01$, ** $p<0.05$, * $p<0.1$.

Table 10.5. Comparative Newey–West Regression for Nigeria.

Variable	Model 1 TEMP × URBAN	Model 2 TEMP × FINDEV	Model 3 (All Controls)	Model 4 (Baseline)	Significance Trend
TEMP	–13.42 (0.013)**	–10.78 (0.19)	0.34 (0.78)	0.33 (0.75)	Becomes significant only when interacted with urbanisation, confirming moderating role
FINDEV	–9.89 (0.284)	–61.17 (0.103)*	–18.57 (0.07)*	–18.68 (0.04)**	Consistently negative; significant at 5–10% in simpler models, reflecting finance-led reallocation
URBAN	−1.92 (0.001)***	−1.34 (0.007)**	−0.87 (0.020)**	−0.87 (0.02)**	Strong, stable adverse effect across all models; confirms structural transition
EDU_scaled	0.011 (0.437)	0.006 (0.695)	0.001 (0.970)	–	Always insignificant; education effects are long-term
Interaction	TEMP×URBAN 0.355 (0.013)**	TEMP×FINDEV 58.43 (0.217)	–	–	Only TEMP×URBAN significant ($p =$ 0.013); urbanisation mitigates climate impacts
T (trend)	0.501 (0.058)*	0.320 (0.31)	–0.021 (0.94)	–0.020 (0.91)	Marginally positive only in Model 1
Constant	–889.63 (0.081)*	–538.74 (0.373)	119.10 (0.82)	117.16 (0.82)	Intercepts vary and are not economically interpretable

Source: Author's.

Note: Dependent variable: Female employment in agriculture (% of female employment).

***$p < 0.01$, **$p < 0.05$, *$p < 0.10$.

Discussion of Findings: Nigeria

Across the four models, the coefficient for urbanisation (URBAN) is consistently negative and highly significant, confirming that as Nigeria urbanises, women exit agriculture for non-farm activities. The descriptive and econometric findings are reinforced by Fig. 10.4, which depicts the inverse relationship between female agricultural employment and rising urbanisation over 1991–2022. This is consistent with the theoretical expectation that urban expansion and structural transformation reduce women's agricultural employment share (Herrendorf et al., 2014).

Financial development (FINDEV) remains negative, occasionally significant, supporting the view that finance-driven modernisation initially disadvantages women unless explicitly inclusive. As illustrated in Fig. 10.5, agricultural employment among women, measured in %, has declined, while the financial development index shows a gradual increase, suggesting improved access to financial services over time. This aligns with Elwell et al. (2023) and Omukuti et al. (2022), who find that nominal financial deepening yields limited gender benefits unless paired with targeted, cost GAPs and devolved financial delivery mechanisms.

Temperature is significant only in Model 1, where its interaction with urbanisation (TEMP×URBAN) mitigates the adverse effects of climate stress. This indicates that women in more urbanised areas are better positioned to diversify their livelihoods and access climate-finance mechanisms. The findings align with the IPCC (Trisos et al., 2022) evidence that higher mean temperatures constrain agricultural output and disproportionately affect women in smallholder farming systems. Education remains insignificant, highlighting that human capital improvements take longer to affect sectoral employment structures. Model 1 is therefore the most robust and theoretically consistent specification, integrating

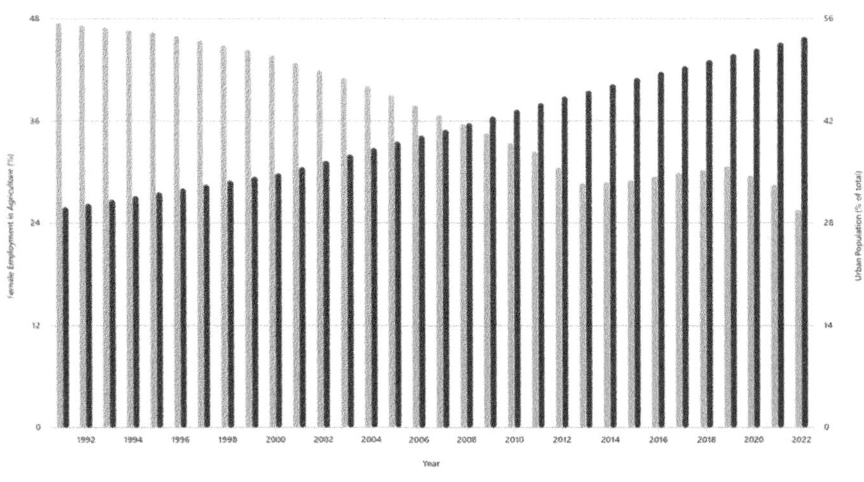

Fig. 10.4. Trends in Female Agricultural Employment and Urbanisation in Nigeria (1991–2022). *Source*: Author's computation from WDI (2024).

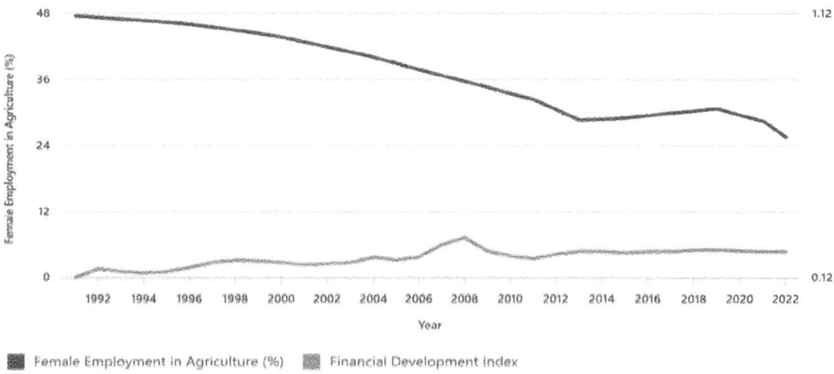

Fig. 10.5. Trends in Female Agricultural Employment and Financial Development Index in Nigeria (1991–2022). *Source*: Author's computation from WDI (2024) and TheGlobalEconomy.com (2025).

direct climate effects and structural moderators. Furthermore, to assess whether these dynamics are context-specific or generalisable within SSA, the same model specification is estimated for Kenya, where climate variability and decentralised fiancé systems differ markedly from those in Nigeria.

Kenya: Empirical Results and Discussion

Descriptive Statistics and Correlation Analysis

Table 10.6 presents the summary statistics and correlation results for Kenya. On average, about 48% of Kenyan women were employed in agriculture between 1991 and 2022, indicating a gradual structural shift from farming as the economy diversified. The mean temperature increased by nearly 0.82°C, confirming a steady warming trend. The correlation matrix reveals a strong negative association between female agricultural employment and both temperature ($r = -0.82$) and financial development ($r = -0.79$), suggesting that rising climate stress and structural transformation reduce women's participation in agriculture. Education exhibits a weaker negative relationship ($r = -0.046$), implying that human capital improvements take longer to translate into sectoral reallocation. These results are consistent with expectations that climate variability and financial deepening jointly shape gendered employment outcomes in Kenya's agricultural sector.

Baseline OLS Model with Robust SEs

The OLS estimates for Kenya, presented in Table 10.7, establish the baseline associations between climate stressors, financial development, and women's agricultural employment. As with Nigeria, annual macroeconomic and environmental data for Kenya are prone to serial correlation and heteroskedasticity, which can bias the conventional OLS SEs. To correct for these issues, the Newey–West HAC

Table 10.6. Descriptive Statistics and Correlation Matrix for Kenya.

A. Descriptive Statistics

Variable	Mean	Std. Dev.	Min	Max	Interpretation
FEA	47.62	8.07	34.80	58.69	Women's agricultural employment remains relatively high but shows a gradual decline, reflecting early stages of structural transformation
TEMP	0.82	0.37	0.10	1.47	Mean land temperature increased steadily, consistent with Kenya's long-term warming trend
FINDEV	0.15	0.03	0.10	0.18	Financial development deepened moderately, though access disparities persist between men and women
EDU_ scaled	0.98	3.38	0.00	15.73	Education enrolment expanded slowly, with fluctuations reflecting reforms and varying data coverage

B. Correlation Matrix

Variables	FEA	TEMP	FINDEV	EDU_scaled	Interpretation
FEA	1.000				Baseline variable (female agricultural employment)
TEMP	−0.818	1.000			Higher temperatures correlate negatively with female agricultural employment, consistent with climate stress effects
FINDEV	−0.791	0.611	1.000		Financial development is positively correlated with temperature and negatively correlated with female agricultural employment, suggesting structural change
EDU_ scaled	−0.461	0.327	0.192	1.000	Education is weakly associated with other variables, reflecting its long-run rather than short-term influence

Source: Author's.

Note: Correlations above 0.7 or below –0.7 indicate strong relationships.

Table 10.7. Baseline OLS Estimates of Female Agricultural Employment in Kenya.

Variable	Coefficient (p-Value)	Expected Sign	Interpretation
TEMP	−9.918 (0.002)***	–	Rising land temperatures significantly reduce women's agricultural employment, consistent with climate-induced productivity losses and labour withdrawal from heat-stressed sectors
FINDEV	−150.479 (0.003)***	±	Financial development has a strong negative effect, suggesting that as financial systems deepen, capital-intensive growth displaces women from low-productivity agricultural roles unless finance is gender-responsive
EDU_scaled	−0.529 (0.000)***	–	Higher educational attainment reduces the share of women in agriculture, reflecting human capital-driven transitions towards non-farm and service-sector employment
Constant	78.490 (0.000)***	–	Represents baseline female agricultural employment when explanatory variables are zero (not directly interpretable)
Model Statistics:			
No. of observations	32		R-squared = 0.846; Root MSE = 3.34
Diagnostic Tests:			
Breusch–Pagan	$\chi^2 = 0.14$ (0.709)		Fail to reject H_0 – No heteroskedasticity detected
White	$\chi^2 = 20.24$ (0.009)		Reject H_0 – some heteroskedasticity present; robust SEs applied

(Continued)

Table 10.7. *(Continued)*

Variable	**Coefficient (*p*-Value)**	**Expected Sign**	**Interpretation**
Breusch–Godfrey	$\chi^2 = 6.13$ (0.013)		Serial correlation present: Newey–West correction recommended
Mean VIF	1.48		No multicollinearity concern (<5)
RESET	$F = 1.81$ (0.172)		No evidence of functional-form misspecification

Source: Author's.

Notes: Dependent variable: Female employment in agriculture (% of female employment). Robust (Huber–White) SEs are reported. All variables are in levels except education, which is scaled for comparability.

*** $p<0.01$, ** $p<0.05$, * $p<0.10$.

estimator was employed. Consequently, the discussion emphasises the Newey–West results, which yield more robust and efficient inference for Kenya's time-series data.

Newey–West Models

Table 10.8 reports the Newey–West estimated models for Kenya, where specifications incorporating the interaction between temperature (Model 3) were retained as the preferred model. This serves as robustness checks as it captures both the direct effects of climate stress and the moderating role of structural transformation, while satisfying standard diagnostic criteria. Furthermore, the interaction effect result is presented in Appendix.

Discussion of Findings: Kenya

Across all models, temperature (TEMP) and financial development (FINDEV) exhibit strong, significant, and negative effects on women's agricultural employment in Kenya (Fig. 10.6A and B). A 1°C increase in land temperature reduces female agricultural participation by roughly 3–4% points. These findings align with the capability approach (Nussbaum, 2000; Sen, 1999), which posits that climate stress constrains women's substantive freedoms by increasing time burdens and reducing agricultural productivity. These results reinforce Trisos et al.'s (2022) assessments that intensifying heat and hydrological variability disproportionately constrain women's productive and adaptive capacities in East Africa.

Similarly, highly developed financial systems are associated with a decline in women's agricultural employment, as shown in Fig. 10.7. A plausible reason is that finance enables structural transformation towards non-farm sectors, especially in the absence of explicitly gender-responsive intermediation. Those shifts may not translate into commensurate opportunities for women leaving agriculture. This

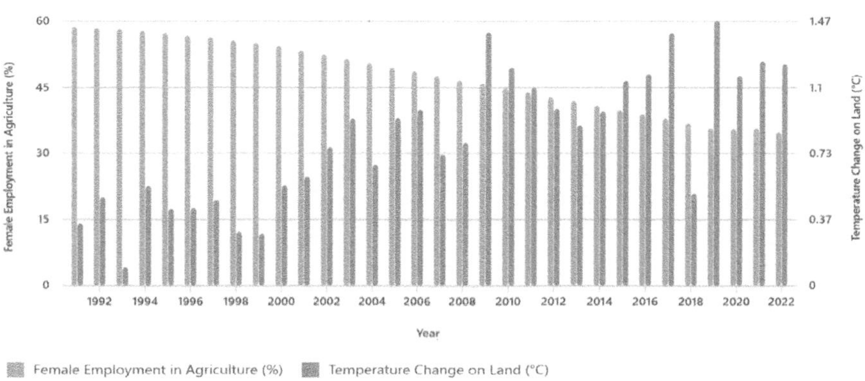

Fig. 10.6. Trends in Female Agricultural Employment and Urbanisation in Nigeria (1991–2022). *Source*: Author's computation from WDI (2024) and FAOSTAT (2024).

Table 10.8. Comparative Newey–West Regression for Kenya.

Variable	Model TEMP×FINDEV	Model 2 (All Controls)	Model 3 (Baseline)	Significance Trend
TEMP	−3.70 (0.003)***	−3.69 (0.002)***	−4.29 (0.001)***	Consistently negative and highly significant, confirming that rising land temperatures depress women's agricultural employment through productivity and time-burden channels
FINDEV	−3.85 (0.001)***	−3.79 (0.003)***	−3.77 (0.003)***	Stable and significant; finance-led structural change is associated with declining female agricultural production
EDU_scaled	−0.52 (0.000)***	−0.53 (0.000)***	–	Highly significant and negative, showing that as education improves, women transition from agriculture to higher-return non-farm sectors
Interaction	TEMP×FINDEV 0.33 (0.733)	–	–	Insignificant; financial depth does not moderate climate impacts on women's employment in Kenya
Constant	48.33 (0.000)***	48.14 (0.000)***	47.62 (0.000)***	Positive and stable across models; represents baseline female agricultural employment level

Source: Author's

Note: Dependent variable: Female employment in agriculture (% of female employment).

***$p < 0.01$, **$p < 0.05$, *$p < 0.10$.

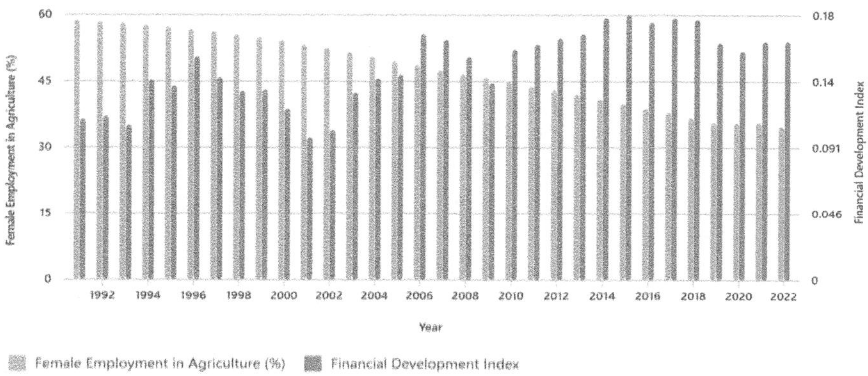

Fig. 10.7. Trends in Female Agricultural Employment and Urbanisation in Nigeria (1991–2022). *Source*: Author's computation from WDI (2024) and TheGlobalEconomy.com (2025).

finding aligns with evidence that generic finance often misses women-led agriculture/SMEs unless paired with targeted instruments and devolved windows (Elwell et al., 2023; Price, 2021). Theoretically, it is consistent with the gendered-institution and bargaining perspective (Agarwal, 1997; Kabeer, 1999), which emphasises that structural and institutional biases determine who benefits from finance.

Education (EDU_Scaled) is consistently negative and highly significant, implying that more schooling, that is, human capital, facilitates women's transition out of agriculture and into services and non-farm livelihoods (see Fig. 10.8). This aligns with structural transformation theory (Herrendorf et al., 2014) and mirrors the result of Angula et al. (2021), who observed that women's participation in formal adaptation and capacity-building programmes expands their non-farm opportunities.

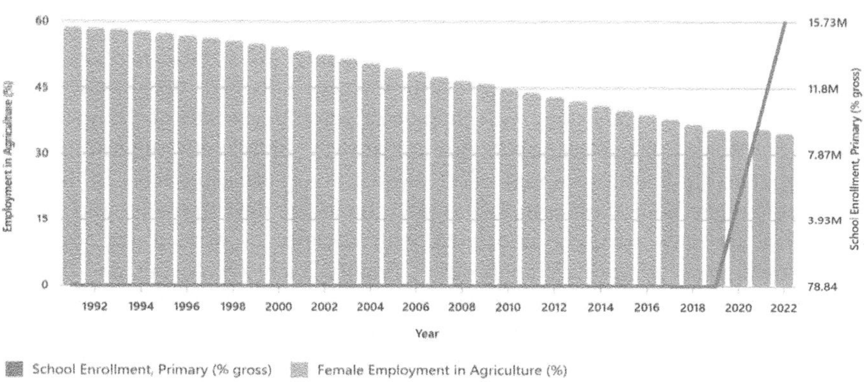

Fig. 10.8. Trends in Female Agricultural Employment and Urbanisation in Nigeria (1991–2022). *Source*: Author's computation from WDI (2024).

The interaction term between temperature and financial development is insignificant, suggesting that aggregate financial depth does not yet buffer climate shocks for women. Two possibilities remain: (i) there is no moderation at the aggregate level, or (ii) moderation operates through more proximate forms of finance (e.g., agricultural credit, guarantees, women's inclusion metrics, or small-grant facilities) that are not captured by the FINDEV index used in this study. Overall, Kenya's results confirm that both climate stress and finance-driven modernisation reduce women's agricultural participation over the sample period, underscoring the importance of targeted, gender-responsive climate finance mechanisms.

Comparative Insights: Nigeria and Kenya

In comparative terms, the results for Nigeria and Kenya reveal a shared structural pattern but distinct transmission mechanisms. In Nigeria, women's declining participation in agriculture is primarily driven by urbanisation and finance-led modernisation, consistent with the structural transformation hypothesis (Herrendorf et al., 2014). In contrast, Kenya's outcomes highlight a stronger climate-finance nexus, where temperature increases and non-inclusive financial deepening jointly constrain women's agricultural engagement, validating the capability approach and gendered institutional theory. While both countries demonstrate that financial development without gender-responsive safeguards can exacerbate exclusion (Elwell et al., 2023; Gerhard et al., 2023), Kenya's more pronounced climate sensitivity underscores the urgency of integrating gender-focused adaptation within financial governance. Thus, the findings collectively affirm that equitable climate finance and institutional design are essential to transforming women's climate vulnerability into sustainable economic opportunity across SSA.

Conclusion and Policy Implications

This study examined how climate stress and structural transformation influence women's agricultural employment in Nigeria and Kenya (1991–2022), using Newey–West estimates to address serial correlation and heteroskedasticity and ensure robust inference. Results indicate contrasting, yet complementary pathways. In Nigeria, women's agricultural employment falls with urbanisation and financial deepening, consistent with finance-driven modernisation. Temperature effects are weak, and education is not statistically significant, suggesting that improvements in human capital exert slower, long-term impacts. In Kenya, however, higher land temperatures, greater financial development, and rising education are each strongly associated with declines in women's agricultural employment, indicating that climate stress, finance-led restructuring, and human capital expansion collectively drive women's exit from agriculture. Although the temperature-finance interaction is insignificant in both countries, the Nigerian specification retained it nonetheless due to its theoretical importance in testing whether financial development can moderate climate impacts. Yet, the results indicate that aggregate financial depth does not yet cushion climate shocks for women. Conversely, the significant and positive temperature-urbanisation interaction in Nigeria indicates that rising temperatures, when combined with increasing urbanisation, are associated with higher women's agricultural participation, an effect consistent with gendered labour-reallocation dynamics, where climate stress accelerates male out-migration and shifts agriculture effects remain strongly negative and unmitigated by financial development or urbanisation. These associations align with theories of gendered institutions and structural transformation, while stopping short of causal claims.

Based on the findings, several policy measures are proposed to make structural transformation more gender-responsive:

(i) *Institutionalise GAPs*: Embed costed and time-bound GAPs in legal agreements and link disbursements to gender-specific performance.
(ii) *Strengthen devolved financing*: Expand simplified small-grant or EDA windows through capable national intermediaries to reach women's groups and agricultural micro, small, and medium-sized enterprises.
(iii) *Relax financial constraints*: Design instruments that relax binding constraints (guarantees/collateral substitutes, longer tenors, and tailored technical assistance through local financial institutions.
(iv) *Invest in climate adaptation infrastructure*: Prioritise adaptation in water/irrigation and climate-smart technologies to ease time burdens and bolster resilience.
(v) *Link education with enterprise development*: Pair education gains with rural enterprise and skills support so exits from agriculture translate into productive, secure livelihoods.

The study's main limitations include reliance on macrolevel time-series data, which may cause potential unobserved heterogeneity. Therefore, future research should combine subnational panels or mixed methods with programme-level data to test whether gender-responsive finance measurably improves adaptation and well-being, and extend the comparison to additional African economies.

References

Agarwal, B. (1997). "Bargaining" and gender relations: Within and beyond the household. *Feminist Economics*, *3*(1), 1–51. https://doi.org/10.1080/135457097338799

Angrist, J. D., & Pischke, J.-S. (2009). *Mostly harmless econometrics: An empiricist's companion*. Princeton University Press.

Angula, M. N., Mogotsi, I., Lendelvo, S., Aribeb, K. M., Iteta, A.-M., & Thorn, J. P. (2021). Strengthening gender responsiveness of the green climate fund ecosystem-based adaptation programme in Namibia. *Sustainability*, *13*(18), 10162.

Becker, G. S. (1965). A theory of the allocation of time. *The Economic Journal*, *75*(299), 493–517. https://doi.org/10.2307/2228949

Breusch, T. S., & Pagan, A. R. (1979). A simple test for heteroscedasticity and random coefficient variation. Econometrica: *Journal of the Econometric Society, 47*(5), 1287–1294. https://doi.org/10.2307/1911963

Bryan, E., Ringler, C., Okoba, B., Roncoli, C., Silvestri, S., & Herrero, M. (2013). Adapting agriculture to climate change in Kenya: Household strategies and determinants. *Journal of Environmental Management, 114*, 26–35. https://doi.org/10.1016/j.jenvman.2012.10.036

Buera, F. J., Kaboski, J. P., & Shin, Y. (2011). Finance and development: A tale of two sectors. *American Economic Review, 101*(5), 1964–2002.

Caldwell, M., & Larsen, G. (2021). *Improving access to the green climate fund: How the fund can better support developing country institutions* [Working Paper 1–28]. World Resources Institute (WRI). https://doi.org/10.46830/wriwp.19.00132

Caldwell, M., & Larsen, G. (2021). Improving access to the Green Climate Fund: How the fund can better support developing country institutions.

Demie, G., Bekele, M., & Seyoum, B. (2016). Water accessibility impact on girl and women's participation in education and other development activities: The case of Wuchale and Jidda Woreda, Ethiopia. *Environmental Systems Research, 5*(1), 11. https://doi.org/10.1186/s40068-016-0061-6

Earsom, J. (2024). Fit for purpose? Just energy transition partnerships and accountability in international climate governance. *Global Policy, 15*(1), 135–141.

Elwell, N., Shrestha, R., Martinez, A., Trivedi, A., & Ding, H. (2023). *Why gender-responsive agricultural adaptation is underfunded* [Working Paper, World Resources Institute, Washington, DC]. https://doi.org/10.46830/wriwp.21.00165

FAOSTAT. (2024). *FAO food security indicators*. https://www.fao.org/faostat/en/#data

Gerhard, M., Jones-Phillipson, E., & Ndeleni, X. (2023). Strategies for gender mainstreaming in climate finance mobilisation in southern Africa. *PLOS Climate, 2*(11), e0000254.

Gold, K. L. (2024). Food insecurity in West Africa: Is global warming the driver? *Research on World Agricultural Economy, 5*(4), 403–419. https://doi.org/10.36956/rwae.v5i4.1186

Gold, K. L., & Tregenna, F. (2025). Financial development, green innovation, green tax, industrialisation, and environmental performance in South Africa: The mediating role of institutions. *Journal of Environmental Management, 393*, 126942. https://doi.org/10.1016/j.jenvman.2025.126942

Graham, J. P., Hirai, M., & Kim, S. S. (2016). An analysis of water collection labor among women and children in 24 Sub-Saharan African Countries. *PLoS One, 11*(6), e0155981. https://doi.org/10.1371/journal.pone.0155981

Gray, C., & Thiede, B. C. (2024). Temperature anomalies undermine the health of reproductive-age women in low- and middle-income countries. *Proceedings of the National Academy of Sciences, 121*(11), e2311567121. https://doi.org/doi:10.1073/pnas.2311567121

Gujarati, D. N., & Porter, D. (2009). *Basic econometrics*. McGraw-Hill International Edition.

Herrendorf, B., Rogerson, R., & Valentinyi, A. (2014). Growth and structural transformation. *Handbook of Economic Growth, 2*, 855–941.

IPCC. (2021). *SBSTA: 4 November AR6 Climate Change 2021: Working Group 1: The physical science basis* (IPCC Sixth Assessment Report: Contribution of Working Group to the Sixth Assessment Report of the Intergovernmental Panel on Climate Change Issue). C.U. Press. https://www.ipcc.ch/report/ar6/wg1/

Kabeer, N. (1999). Resources, agency, achievements: Reflections on the measurement of women's empowerment. *Development and Change, 30*(3), 435–464.

Keyamo, F. (2024). *Keynote address at the public presentation of the 2024 Seasonal Climate Prediction (SCP)*, 20 February 2024, NAF Conference Centre, *Abuja, Nigeria*. NiMet https://scp.nimet.gov.ng/press/keynote_hma.htm

KMD. (2023). *State of climate Kenya – 2023*. https://meteo.go.ke/

KMD. (2024). *State of climate Kenya – 2024*. Kenya Meteorological Department. https://meteo.go.ke/

Konte, M., Kouamé, W. A., & Mensah, E. B. (2022). Structural reforms and labor productivity growth in developing countries: Intra or inter-reallocation channel? *The World Bank Economic Review*, *36*(3), 646–669. https://doi.org/10.1093/wber/lhac002

Manuamorn, O. P., & Biesbroek, R. (2020). Do direct-access and indirect-access adaptation projects differ in their focus on local communities? A systematic analysis of 63 Adaptation Fund projects. *Regional Environmental Change*, *20*(4), 139.

Nguyen, H., & Pienknagura, S. (2024). Rising temperature, heterogeneous effects: Evidence from seasonal and sectoral data. *IMF Working Papers*, *2024*(202), A001. https://doi.org/10.5089/9798400289248.001.A001

NiMet. (2024). *Seasonal climate prediction*. https://nimet.gov.ng/scp

Nussbaum, M. C. (2000). *Women and human development: The capabilities approach* (Vol. 3). Cambridge University Press.

Omukuti, J., Barrett, S., White, P. C., Marchant, R., & Averchenkova, A. (2022). The green climate fund and its shortcomings in local delivery of adaptation finance. *Climate Policy*, *22*(9–10), 1225–1240.

Price, R. (2021). *Access to climate finance by women and marginalised groups in the Global South* (K4D Helpdesk Report No 1004, Issue. I). o. D. S. (IDS).

Psacharopoulos, G., & Patrinos, H. A. (2018). Returns to investment in education: A decennial review of the global literature. *Education Economics*, *26*(5), 445–458.

Ranasinghe, R., Ruane, A. C., Vautard, R., Arnell, N., Coppola, E., Cruz, F. A., Dessai, S., Islam, A. S., Rahimi, M., Carrascal, D. R., Sillmann, J., Sylla, M. B., Tebaldi, C., Wang, W., & Zaaboul, R. (2021). Climate change information for regional impact and for risk assessment. In V. Masson-Delmotte, P. Zhai, A. Pirani, S. L. Connors, C. Péan, S. Berger, N. Caud, Y. Chen, L. Goldfarb, M. I. Gomis, M. Huang, K. Leitzell, E. Lonnoy, J. B. R. Matthews, T. K. Maycock, T. Waterfield, O. Yelekçi, R. Yu, & B. Zhou (Eds.). *In Climate Change 2021: The physical science basis. Contribution of Working Group I to the Sixth Assessment Report of the Intergovernmental Panel on Climate Change* (pp. 1767–1926). Cambridge University Press. https://doi.org/10.1017/9781009157896.014

Sen, A. (1987). Gender and cooperative conflicts. In I. I. Tinker (Ed.), *Persistent inequalities* (pp. 1–61). Oxford University Press.

Sen, A. (1999). *Development as freedom* (Business & Economics ed.). Oxford University Press. https://books.google.com.ng/books/about/Development_as_Freedom.html?id=NQs75PEa618C&redir_esc=y

Sesan, T., Clifford, M., Jewitt, S., & Ray, C. (2019). "We learnt that being together would give us a voice": Gender perspectives on the East African improved-cookstove value chain. *Feminist Economics*, *25*(4), 240–266.

Sonja, K. (2022, June 29). *Six insights from the 2021 World Bank Global Findex Data*. https://www.womensworldbanking.org/insights/global-findex-2021-womens-world-banking-response/

Stiglitz, J. E., & Weiss, A. (1981). Credit rationing in markets with imperfect information. *The American Economic Review*, *71*(3), 393–410.

Svirydzenka, K. (2016). *Introducing a new broad-based index of financial development*. International Monetary Fund.

Talib, M. N. A., Ahmed, M., Naseer, M. M., Slusarczyk, B., & Popp, J. (2021). The long-run impacts of temperature and rainfall on agricultural growth in Sub-Saharan Africa. *Sustainability*, *13*(2), 595. https://www.mdpi.com/2071-1050/13/2/595

TheGlobalEconomy.com. (2025). *Economic data*. https://www.theglobaleconomy.com/download-data.php

Trisos, C. H., Adelekan, I. O., Totin, E., Ayanlade, A., Efitre, J., Gemeda, A., Kalaba, K., Lennard, C., Masao, C., Mgaya, Y., Ngaruiya, G., Olago, D., Simpson, N., & Zakieldeen, S. (2022). Africa. Climate change 2022: Impacts, adaptation and vulnerability. In H.-O. Pörtner, D. C. Roberts, M. Tignor, E. S. Poloczanska, K. Mintenbeck, A. Alegría, M. Craig, S. Langsdorf, S. Löschke, V. Möller, A. Okem, & B. Rama (Eds.), *Contribution of Working Group II to the Sixth Assessment Report of the Intergovernmental Panel on Climate Change* (pp. 1285–1455). Cambridge University Press. https://doi.org/doi:10.1017/9781009325844.011

WDI. (2024). *World Bank World Development Indicators*. https://data.worldbank.org/indicator

White, H. (1980). A heteroskedasticity-consistent covariance matrix estimator and a direct test for heteroskedasticity. *Econometrica: Journal of the Econometric Society, 48*, 817–838.

World Bank. (2024a, April 17). *Financial inclusion in Sub-Saharan Africa—Overview* https://www.worldbank.org/en/publication/globalfindex/brief/financial-inclusion-in-sub-saharan-africa-overview

World Bank. (2024b). *The gendered burden of water collection in Sub-Saharan Africa*. https://www.worldbank.org/en/data/interactive/2024/03/13/gendered-burden-of-water-collection-in-afe-afw-sub-saharan-africa?utm_source=openai

Appendix. Diagnostic Tests for the Expanded Kenyan Model, Including Urbanisation and Water Stress

Diagnostic Test	Statistic/Value	Interpretation
Model Specification	FEA = TEMP + FINDEV + WSTRESS + URBAN + EDU_scaled	Full model initially estimated to test combined climate–finance–structural effects
No. of Observations	32	Annual data covering 1991–2022
R-squared/Adj. R^2	0.9967/0.9964	Inflated goodness-of-fit; likely over-fitting caused by collinear regressors
Root MSE	0.485	Extremely small residual variance, suggesting redundancy among predictors
Mean VIF	6.32	Above recommended ≤5 threshold → indicates moderate to severe multicollinearity overall
– URBAN VIF	15.41	Critical collinearity – URBAN explains almost the same variation as FEA
– WSTRESS VIF	8.49	High – strong linear dependence with URBAN and TEMP
Breusch–Pagan/Cook–Weisberg $\chi^2(1)$	12.45 (p = 0.0004)	Reject H_0 of homoskedasticity → heteroskedastic residuals present
Correlation Highlights	r(FEA, URBAN) = –0.9965; r(URBAN, WSTRESS) = 0.9376; r(WSTRESS, TEMP) = 0.7593	Severe linear overlap among structural and climate variables
Model Diagnostics Summary	—	Multicollinearity and heteroskedasticity render coefficients unreliable; the specification is therefore excluded from the main analysis

Source: Author's.

Note: Including urbanisation and water stress in the Kenyan model caused severe multicollinearity and heteroskedasticity, producing unstable estimates. The final model, therefore, retains only temperature, financial development, and education as explanatory variables for comparability with Nigeria.

Printed and bound by CPI Group (UK) Ltd, Croydon, CR0 4YY
15/09/2026
14962485-0002